Stepping Back

STEPPING BACK

Nuclear Arms Control and the
End of the Cold War

WILLIAM B. VOGELE

PRAEGER

Westport, Connecticut
London

Library of Congress Cataloging-in-Publication Data

Vogele, William B.
    Stepping back : nuclear arms control and the end of the cold war /
William B. Vogele.
        p.   cm.
    Includes bibliographical references and index.
    ISBN 0–275–94644–4 (alk. paper)
    1. Nuclear arms control.   2. Cold War.   I. Title.
JX1974.7.V55   1994
327.1'74—dc20   93–11861

British Library Cataloguing in Publication Data is available.

Library of Congress Catalog Card Number: 93–11861
ISBN: 0–275–94644–4

First published in 1994

Praeger Publishers, 88 Post Road West, Westport, CT 06881
An imprint of Greenwood Publishing Group, Inc.

Printed in the United States of America

The paper used in this book complies with the
Permanent Paper Standard issued by the National
Information Standards Organization (Z39.48–1984).

10 9 8 7 6 5 4 3 2 1

Copyright Acknowledgment

Major portions of "Tough Bargaining and Arms Control: Lessons from the INF Treaty," *Journal of Strategic Studies* 12 (September) 1989: 257–272, have been used courtesy of Frank Cass & Co., Ltd.

Dedicated to
Connie Parrish

and in the memory of
David A. Booth

Contents

Acknowledgments

Too many individuals and organizations have had a role in supporting the work that led to this book to really acknowledge properly. Several of the key concepts and the historical research were developed in my dissertation at Brandeis University under the guidance of Seyom Brown, Robert Art, and Robert Keohane. Without their individual and collective support, as well as their intellectual honesty, the project would have begun in much less favorable circumstances. In addition, David Larson offered patient advice on parts of the research as it evolved toward the present book. Their continuing support over the years has been greatly appreciated. They are all due credit for encouraging and promoting the good ideas that have grown into this work, and they bear no responsibility for whatever foolishness remains.

Several institutions have supported this work along the way. The Graduate School of Brandeis University made the bulk of the early work possible with fellowships and travel grants. In addition, I was fortunate to find other benefactors with faith in the project. My thanks to the Jewish Community Services of Cleveland, Ohio, which granted the Morris Abrams Award in International Relations, and to the Institute for the Study of World Politics in New York, which provided additional financial support. In more recent years, I have been fortunate to have the institutional support of the Program on Nonviolent Sanctions at Harvard University and the Albert Einstein Institution as I worked on what amounted to a new research project. Completing the present manuscript would not have been possible without the support of Doug Bond at the Program and Christopher Kruegler at Einstein. Their generous forebearance is greatly appreciated.

Colleagues, peers, mentors, and institutions all deserve credit in supporting any scholarly project. But in many ways their support cannot match the generosity, perseverance, and patience that one's family provides. Connie Parrish has lived with this project for a long time—every day after the colleagues have gone home for the night and every weekend when there were better things to do. Her love and encouragement have lasted through this and many other projects. I would be nowhere without it.

Abbreviations

ABM	Anti-ballistic missile
ACDA	Arms Control and Disarmament Agency
ALCM	Air-launched cruise missile
ASBM	Air-to-surface ballistic missiles
BMD	Ballistic missile defenses
CEP	Circular error probable
CFE	Treaty on Conventional Forces in Europe
CORRTEX	Continuous Reflectometry for Radius versus Time Experiments
CSCE	Conference on Security and Cooperation in Europe
CTB	Comprehensive Test Ban
CTBT	Comprehensive Test Ban Treaty
ENDC	Eighteen Nation Disarmament Conference
FBS	Forward based systems
GLCM	Ground-launched cruise missiles
GRIT	Graduated reciprocation in tension-reduction
ICBM	Intercontinental ballistic missiles
INF	Intermediate-range nuclear forces
IRBM	Intermediate-range ballistic missile
JVE	Joint Verification Experiments
LTBT	Limited Test Ban Treaty
MIRV	Multiple independently targetable reentry vehicles
MX	Missile Experimental
NATO	North Atlantic Treaty Organization

NCA	National command authority
NPT	Nuclear Nonproliferation Treaty
NRDC	Natural Resources Defense Council
NST	Nuclear and Space Talks
OSI	On-site inspections
PNE	Peaceful nuclear explosions
PNET	Peaceful Nuclear Explosions Treaty
SALT	Strategic Arms Limitations Talks
SDI	Strategic Defense Initiative
SLBM	Submarine-launched ballistic missile
SLCM	Sea-launched cruise missiles
SRINF	Shorter-range intermediate-range nuclear forces
START	Strategic Arms Reduction Treaty
TTB	Threshold Test Ban
TTBT	Threshold Test Ban Treaty
WTO	Warsaw Treaty Organization

Stepping Back

1

Security, Cooperation, and Arms Control

[The] process of attaining new accords may require extended and patient negotiations lasting for years. The tribulations of such negotiations, however, are more than justified if they help to avoid the outbreak of nuclear war. It is possible that arms control negotiations may be one of the roads or even the main road leading to significant future East-West accords. In that event, the negotiations would truly be a highway to peace and increased security. The West should remain in a position to travel speedily over that highway if and when its direction and destination become apparent.

Bernard Bechhoefer [1]

If arms control was a "highway to peace and increased security" during the thirty-five years following Bechhoefer's optimistic comment, then it was a rather bumpy ride. The United States and the Soviet Union engaged each other in arms control negotiations almost continuously. And they achieved a handful of agreements. Some treaties, like the 1972 Anti-ballistic Missile Treaty, placed significant restrictions on weapons development and deployment. Others, like the 1970 treaty on the Denuclearization of the Seabeds, banned weapons that neither side had any interests in developing.

Nevertheless, technological advances and the accumulation of new weapons often outstripped political efforts for arms limitations. In the most obvious example of this dynamic, the SALT agreement of 1972 limited the number of offensive nuclear delivery vehicles but did nothing to stop the multiplication of weapons through the development of multiple independently targetable reentry vehicles (MIRVs). Throughout the first three decades of arms control, moments of political détente and accord were often quickly dispelled by distrust and recrimination. By 1981 and the advent of the Reagan administration in the United

States, the whole framework of inherited arms control efforts was rejected in favor of "peace through strength."

Remarkably, the decade that began with an unapologetic return to the primacy of cold war competition and conflict concluded with official declarations of the cold war's end. In the security arena alone three landmark treaties were signed by the United States and the Soviet Union by 1991. The first, the treaty on intermediate-range nuclear missiles of 1987, established precedents for the elimination of entire classes of deployed modern weapons and for extensive and intrusive inspection processes. In 1990 a treaty for the reduction of conventional forces in Europe undid the Gordian knot of the immediate military confrontation across the divide of central Europe. By April 1991, that divide itself, along with the Warsaw Treaty Organization (WTO), was history. On 31 July, Presidents George Bush and Mikhail Gorbachev signed the START agreement, reducing by one-third the superpowers' strategic arsenals. At the end of the year, both Gorbachev and the Soviet Union were swept from the world stage. Arms control was central to all of these changes, both as a permissive factor and as a driving force. Precisely how arms control contributed to ending the cold war is one of the themes of this book.

Many factors contributed to this sea change in world politics. Popular explanations of the end of the cold war tend to focus on domestic change—in particular the compelling political and economic crises in the Soviet Union to which Gorbachev responded. There is much merit in the simple phrase, "The Cold War is over and the United States won it," but it overlooks the fact that the transformation of politics involved a strong reciprocal content.[2] Put another way, the Soviet Union could not have ended the cold war by itself. The end of the cold war is unthinkable in the absence of the remarkable arms control agreements achieved by mid-1991. In this sense, examining one of the key arenas of both competition and cooperation—nuclear arms control—permits us to understand better this important alteration in contemporary history.

This book examines most closely the nuclear bargaining of the 1980s. The core of the argument is simple. The arms control agreements achieved could only be reached through explicit bargaining and negotiation, and the transformation of the broader political relationship from intense rivalry to cooperation was only possible with these agreements. If arms control was part of the essential ground upon which the world began to step back from the brink of nuclear war, then it is vitally important to understand the bargaining processes that made such change possible.

This argument is not meant to overstate the case, let alone to argue that arms control bargaining was the only element of the U.S.-Soviet relationship that mattered. After all, bargaining positions only exist as products of highly specific political and institutional arrangements. Many layers of explanation will be required to fully understand this historic moment, including structural shifts in international power, the force of individual leaders, and the influences of domestic coalitions and economic forces.[3] However, my analysis focuses on the easily overlooked but arguably crucial process of the bargaining interaction itself.

Reflecting on the nuclear negotiations of the 1980s offers important lessons for how arms control might be continued. The treaties that emerged by the end of the decade set the legal and political framework for future reductions. In the meantime, these treaties remain unfinished business. Because the treaties also marked a dramatic departure from the previous decades of managing the arms race, understanding how the bargaining process contributed to the agreements that were reached (and those that were not) offers important insights into how future efforts may proceed. This is particularly true because that bargaining process ranged from extremes of hard-line posturing to broad concessions.

This book examines the nuclear arms control negotiations between the United States and the Soviet Union in the 1980s as a vehicle for "testing" theories of bargaining in security negotiations. The importance of bargaining strategies is evident from the public debate that routinely surrounds arms control policy. Scholars have devoted considerable effort to exploring various aspects of bargaining and negotiations. If it is possible to identify something like agreement among negotiation scholars, it is that bargaining strategies based on reciprocity—the commonsense notion of give and take—generally are the most effective means to achieve agreement. During the first thirty years of arms control negotiations, under widely varying political and military conditions, reciprocal strategies tended to promote agreement. The most obvious alternative, "hanging tough," on the other hand, was associated with negotiating failure.

Arms control in the 1980s appeared to challenge this position in two ways. First, the Reagan administration consciously adopted a tough strategy that by the decade's end seemed vindicated. Judging the extent to which this vindication is merited is one of the goals of this book. Second, the rapid transformation of Soviet domestic politics under Mikhail Gorbachev after 1986 produced changes on arms control issues through unilateral concessions. How did the new Soviet concessionary posture transform the bargaining process itself? In what ways did the U.S. bargaining strategy promote those changes on the part of the Soviet Union? The larger question upon which this special experience can shed light concerns the promotion of cooperation among adversaries. Certainly the end of the Cold War did not mean the end of rivalry among states; nor did it remove the dangers of conflict that make the search for cooperation compelling.

SECURITY, COOPERATION AND ARMS CONTROL

Security among states, although often viewed simply as a matter of conflict management, also can be provided through cooperation. The most obvious form of cooperation for security is alliance formation. Traditional analysis of international politics regards alliances as the natural consequence of international anarchy and the balance of power process.[4] Cooperation between adversaries, such as arms control, is less easily explained.

The difficulties of adversary cooperation are well known. Profound conflicts of interest between states exist that may prevent all but the slightest element of cooperation. In the international system of self-help, states often find themselves in a security dilemma that impedes cooperation. John H. Herz wrote in 1950: "In view of the security dilemma of competing powers, attempts to reduce power by mutual agreement, for instance through disarmament, were bound to fail, even if there had not been additional, economic factors driving them in the direction of imperialism."[5] Furthermore, misperceptions and distrust can set off spirals of arms racing, even when mutual restraint might be preferred.[6] Nevertheless, adversaries do engage in cooperative efforts to provide security. Arms control is one of the important arenas for those efforts.

In principle, arms control can encompass a wide range of behavior from unilateral self-restraint to the creation of explicit, formal treaties.[7] The process of formal negotiations and the agreements it produces deserve attention for several reasons. First, cooperation is a process of mutual policy adjustment involving acts of coordination between states.[8] Certainly, countries refrain from making military threats against many neighbors, but this is not usually regarded as cooperation. Rather than coordinating their behavior or policies, these countries are simply pursuing their self-interests. As Robert Jervis has argued, the absence of a nuclear war between the United States and the Soviet Union may simply have reflected national self-interests and should not be considered an antinuclear regime.[9] Formal negotiations are an important institutional forum that facilitates or creates cooperation.

Second, negotiations and agreements can provide benefits unavailable through informal bargaining. Downs and Rocke note that tacit bargaining's susceptibility to misinterpretation "is a function of its limited vocabulary. The extensive dialogue that surrounds the discussion of formal treaties is a rich and sensitive medium of communication."[10] Both the bargaining and the outcomes of a tacit exchange are less certain than those of negotiations and treaties. If one of the obstacles to cooperation is the difficulty of accurate perception, then formal processes provide one solution. Simulations by Downs and his colleagues, for example, show clearly how damaging to the prospects of cooperation even small degrees of misperception can be in tacit bargaining situations.[11]

Similarly, agreements reached in negotiation articulate specific bargains. All language and meaning potentially is subject to reinterpretation and dispute. But formal agreements reduce the range for this debate, providing avenues of action short of outright rejection and a return to direct competition. Agreements have the additional advantage of creating a cumulative framework of rules, norms, principles, and decision-making processes that can facilitate further negotiation and cooperation.[12] Institutionalizing cooperation between adversaries through explicit arms control agreements can be an important element in constructing future relationships.[13] The Conference on Security and Cooperation in Europe (CSCE), for example, provided the institutional framework for the "confidence-building" measures of the 1986 Stockholm Accord, which required notification of major troop exercises and the exchange of inspectors. Arguably, the existence of the CSCE (along with NATO and the European Community) was one of the factors facilitating German unification in 1990. One can easily contrast the German unification experience with the prospects for unification on the Korean peninsula, in a region where the networks of security and political cooperation are far less developed.[14]

Finally, arms control negotiations are a fact of political life. One of the remarkable aspects of forty-five years of cold war competition was the persistence of arms control negotiations. Through periods of intense competition, as well as times of relative détente, negotiations continued virtually without pause. Rarely were the superpowers not engaged in arms negotiations, however bright or dim were the momentary prospects for that effort. One of the important issues for the future of international security in the post–cold war world will be sustaining those forums for constructing and maintaining new avenues of coexistence.

The substantive analysis of this book is restricted to U.S.-Soviet efforts to control nuclear testing and to limit their respective offensive arsenals. These negotiations provide a continuous and direct background to current arms control efforts—the question of nuclear testing remains on the world's security agenda, as do efforts to implement the agreements to reduce strategic nuclear arsenals. From a comprehensive analysis of a special, highly related set of arms control negotiations it may be possible to learn lessons that are applicable to other arenas of security cooperation.

ARMS CONTROL NEGOTIATIONS

States enter arms control negotiations when their leaders perceive that some aspects of the nation's security may be enhanced by a degree of mutual restraint. Commonly, the desire to constrain the behavior or weapons of the adversary becomes bonded to the realization that this will only be possible through some kind of bargain. Mutual self-restraint thus becomes the vehicle for achieving greater security.

The motivations to begin (if not to conclude) these bargaining efforts are varied. One source of a "push" into arms control is a desire to mitigate the security dilemma. A security dilemma emerges when, acting under the self-help norms of international politics, a country's unilateral efforts to improve its own security degrade the security of its adversary. In such situations leaders on both sides are compelled to react in ways that promote arms racing and result in diminishing security for all. The situation is a dilemma when the leaders feel compelled to take actions they might otherwise prefer to avoid. Arms races may or may not lead to war.[15] But they do consume resources while producing questionable benefits. In addition, arms races aggravate hostilities between rivals, often impairing the creation of productive relationships in other issue areas.

So long as the states engaged in the dilemma act and react unilaterally, stopping the spiral is very difficult. Thus arms control efforts, especially negotiations, provide a forum for altering and managing their competition. Arms control permits creation of regimes of mutual restraint and accountability. Competition in some arenas may be restrained, knowledge and predictability can be enhanced, and individual national interests can be better achieved—whether those interests involve economic savings or the reduction of avoidable tensions. Arms control efforts, especially formal agreements, provide the essential forum for mutual adjustment that is otherwise difficult to achieve.

Other forces may "pull" political leaders into arms control efforts. These include the demands of allies, the obligations of other international agreements, and domestic political considerations. Allied governments, protecting their own interests, may see greater virtue in arms negotiations than their partner, reflecting differences in size, military vulnerability, or geographic situation.

Leaders within a country often differ in their personal perceptions of the benefits of arms control, and they will bring to power varying predilections for negotiated agreements. A chief executive predisposed to seeking compromise and negotiated settlements of conflicts may pull the state apparatus along with him in pursuing arms control goals. Indeed, this phenomenon is reflected in the conventional wisdom about arms control in the United States, that an arms control agreement is possible only if the president wants one. The key consideration about how domestic politics influences bargaining strategies is an administration's vision of the priorities for American foreign policy. This vision, or "grand strategy," which is ordinarily championed by the president, establishes the ways in which American position and security in the world will be maintained.[16] The search for security through negotiated arms control agreements is only one part of the set of possible policies.

An articulated grand strategy may not exist, although there may be an identifiable orientation and set of presumptions about the premises of power. In addition, this orientation may not necessarily be guided by the chief executive. It may emerge instead from influential advisors or from dominance among competing political interest groups. Thus, the differing institutional interests in arms control within the government will affect the choice to enter negotiations.

In the study of policy making, especially American foreign policy making, much attention has been paid to the role of the organization of the government.[17] The presumption is that "organization matters," not only the formal structures of policy making but also the informal networks that get things done. A fairly large academic subfield of bureaucratic politics has developed to study these issues. Of the two seminal works in this field, one deals with the Cuban missile crisis and the other analyzes ABM decisions.[18] Alexander George analyzed alternative organizational structures and the requirements of effective decision making in foreign policy that included attention to cognitive processes.[19] Similarly, Evangelista compared the differing organizational structures of the United States and the Soviet Union on policies of military innovation.[20] Snyder and Diesing also found that the explanations for actions taken in many of the crises they studied required them to modify their structural bargaining analysis with considerations of bureaucratic politics and decision making.[21] Bruce Russett has suggested that domestic factors were more influential than international conditions for explaining the causes of arms races.[22] Richard Ned Lebow and Janet Gross Stein have argued that the principal explanations for deterrence failures are found in domestic political and organizational imperatives.[23] Other domestic constituencies also can pull a government into negotiations, particularly in popular democracies. Shifts in popular opinion can exert pressure on political leaders if attention is sufficiently focused. The influence is never clear or direct, but it is unmistakable.[24]

These studies draw attention to questions of internal bargaining and other pressures of the political process, questions that can be extended to the study of arms control negotiations. What competing interests existed within the government? What actors and agencies participated? Were policy choices the product of formal consultation, collegial collaboration, or ad hoc decision making? Institutionally, one would expect military services to resist arms control efforts while the diplomatic corps would be more generous (although this is not always the case). Shifting institutional balances of power can alter a government's willingness to engage in arms negotiations and to take up different bargaining strategies.

Finally, perceptions of the international balance of power—especially the balance of military power—affect the choices to join negotiations. Traditional international relations study, based on "political realism," pays particular attention to the relative power of nations. Individual states derive their positions in the world political system by virtue of their capacity to wield power. Because the international system lacks a central authority to enforce order and provide security, all states are compelled to provide their own security. Thus the most relevant measurement of international power is military power.

National leaders assess the power of their adversaries and attempt to maintain a balance, or even a slight advantage as a "hedge." In this way, as Kenneth Waltz says, "balances of power recur."[25] A balance of power is often thought necessary to prevent war (by deterring aggression) and therefore is a prerequisite for national security. Thus, leaders acquire military capabilities to offset similar capabilities possessed by their real or potential adversaries. According to the perspective of political realism, the interaction of such policies among all states will be a stable system of counterbalancing power. Inis Claude wrote in 1962:

The basic assumption [of the balance of power system among states] is that states are not to be trusted in command of power which might be used to the detriment of other states; unrestrained power anywhere in the system is a threat to the security of all its units. It is further assumed that the effective antidote to power is power. Hence, stability in international relations requires equilibrium; when the power of every state or probable combination of states is counter-balanced by an approximately equal power elsewhere in the system. . . .[26]

Indeed, a central maxim of arms control efforts, common in both academic analyses and in policy debates, holds that a condition of "approximate equality" of military forces is necessary for the success of arms control negotiations. In other words, an arms control agreement will only be possible when a balance of military forces already exists. The presumed necessity of an existing "balance" or "parity" implies that an agreement will probably reflect, or even codify, that particular distribution of military forces.

How is the military balance to be estimated in relation to arms control negotiations? Harold Brown argued that arms control agreements are likely when there is a mutual sense of "approximate equality in the arms to be limited, before and after the negotiations."[27] But Brown did not specify what he meant by "equality"—equal numbers or equal capabilities are the two primary considerations. Joseph Kruzel suggested, for example, that the prenuclear limitations of the Washington and London Naval conferences were attainable because they embodied existing quantitative ratios of capital ships and because they excluded emerging naval technologies, particularly submarines. The numerical ratios embodied in those agreements reflected national determinations of military requirements (even though these numbers were not equal), while the allowance for new technologies permitted potential compensation with new capabilities.[28]

These observations suggest that both quantitative and qualitative measurements of the military balance are important for policy makers' decisions and should affect choices of negotiating strategies. Applied to U.S.-Soviet negotiations, this presumption poses several questions. What was the numerical balance of nuclear weapons during negotiations? Although Brown suggests that parity is necessary prior to a negotiation as well as in the agreement, a state with inferior capabilities may join negotiations in hopes of "leveling up" its own forces (either unilaterally during negotiations or jointly by agreement) or "leveling down" the adversary's capabilities.

Estimates of future capabilities and the qualitative military balance also may be related to the willingness to enter negotiations or to reach an agreement. In the unilateral pursuit of security, political leaders are likely to attempt to maintain each possible advantage; thus they may seek to exclude from negotiations a new technology that promises future superiority. An agreement may be difficult until the potentials of a new weapon are explored.[29]

A condition of dynamic parity—an expectation of stability in the military balance for the predictable future—will probably be most conducive to agreement. That is, the participants in a military competition will tend to seek a mutual solution to some of the problems and dangers of that competition when they recognize that a unilateral solution cannot be imposed.[30] Leaders of a state with demonstrably inferior military capabilities will not be inclined toward negotiation or agreement but will prefer to act unilaterally in an effort to narrow the difference. They will not want to give the impression that they desire agreement because of weakness. Similarly, leaders of an advantaged state will choose unilateral action so long as expected trends remain favorable.[31] Relative rates of change in the opposing forces, either numerically or in terms of capabilities, are likely to be important variables in an arms control negotiation. Simultaneous changes in force structures or capabilities are likely to facilitate agreement and therefore be approached through reciprocal behavior. Rapid changes that threaten either side's perception of an acceptable existing balance will make agreement more difficult and are more likely to produce tough bargaining.

What negotiating strategies would we expect under different distributions of power between the United States and the Soviet Union? Realist analysis suggests that no policy maker is likely to accept an arms control agreement that embodies significant inferiority for his or her state. In other words, if the state is "behind," then an outcome of failure (no agreement) is preferable to a treaty that codifies the status quo. Conversely, the state with superior capabilities is likely to want to preserve its advantages. Given a roughly equal distribution of military power, each side is likely to seek constraints on the other and thus maintain the balance.

Tough bargaining strategies, therefore, are likely when inferiority is feared. The political leadership has little to lose if the negotiations fail and much to gain if their position prevails. Softer strategies of initiative are the least probable in these circumstances. Only the state with important advantages can take the risk of initiative—presumably in the hope that this will make an agreement that does not entirely rectify the balance more palatable to the inferior side. Under the condition of relative balance a reciprocal bargaining strategy is likely to prevail.

Considerations of technical capabilities and the rate of change in a military competition are related to the creation of bargaining power—the acquisition of new capabilities and the demonstration of interests in the issues at stake.[32] The acquisition of bargaining power, as well as the expectations about trends noted above, will be evident in the negotiating strategies chosen. Because both inferiority and superiority will tend to produce unilateral action, the emergence of a mutual solution (and the stability of dynamic parity) is more likely when neither side pursues temporary advantage. This is similar to Robert Axelrod's tit-for-tat strategy, in which cooperation is always the initial move. Furthermore, there may be costs associated with attempts to maximize freedom of action by maximizing unilateral bargaining power—maintaining the flexibility to act unilaterally can create barriers to agreement by making a government an "undesirable partner for others."[33] A policy of restraint fits a bargaining strategy of initiative in its effort to demonstrate real preferences for an agreement—preferences that may be obscured by the accumulation of weapons for bargaining purposes.

Closely related to both assessments of the military balance and domestic political alignments are "ideational" forces. A common concept in foreign policy study is the idea of "grand strategy," an overarching vision of the place of one's country in the world and the kinds of objectives it seeks. More directly applied to military issues is the dominant strategic conception of the government, which relates technology to politics and often reflects changes in political leadership.[34]

COOPERATION THEORIES AND ARMS CONTROL NEGOTIATIONS

One of the most promising recent approaches to the investigation of international bargaining and cooperation derives from the work of Robert Axelrod.[35] Axelrod posed the central question as this: "Under what conditions will cooperation emerge among rational egoists?" In the competitive self-help environment of world politics cooperation is problematic. Yet it exists. Employing the game theory of the prisoner's dilemma, Axelrod explored the ways in which different strategies for behavior affect the ability of two players to realize their mutual interests. The results argue strongly in favor of reciprocal strategies such as "tit-for-tat."

Several scholars have employed Axelrod's framework to fruitfully explore the problems of cooperation in various areas of world politics.[36] Security issues have been the most resistant to explanation using this model.[37] My approach to arms control bargaining in this book, however, places Axelrod's theory at the center of the investigation. His model offers an elegant explanation of bargaining and cooperation that can be applied productively to arms control negotiations, if not to all security issues. Nevertheless, important criticisms of the theory have been offered, which in turn provide insights for modifications. As Chapter 2 elaborates, alternative negotiating strategies must be evaluated for better understanding of the process of interaction and the possibilities of obtaining cooperation.

Axelrod's cooperation theory emphasizes incentive structures and interests. This is a "third image" approach to explaining the outcomes in this political interaction.[38] Obviously, it is not the only approach, but the alternatives are less promising. For example, another third-image explanation focuses on the relative military power of the negotiating parties. As argued above, realist analysis predicts that only under conditions of rough equality will cooperation on arms control be likely. In an asymmetrical balance, the superior side has nothing to gain from an agreement, unless it formalizes its advantage. That outcome is precisely what the inferior side would seek to prevent. The inferior bargainer will be exerting itself to balance its adversary and therefore is unlikely to desire an agreement unless it will greatly reduce the difference in power. Only when both sides of the competition are roughly equal does an agreement become possible. Each then becomes interested in an agreement that might prevent the other from gaining an advantage in the future.

This powerful insight into the competitive nature of world politics, however, does not very well explain the outcomes of U.S.-Soviet arms negotiations. Agreements were reached when military capabilities were unequal (the Limited Test Ban Treaty of 1963) and when the military balance appeared headed toward parity (the Anti-ballistic Missile Treaty of 1972); the process failed when forces arguably were balanced (comprehensive testing limitation in the 1980s). Furthermore, this approach cannot explain the dramatic initiatives undertaken by the Soviet Union after 1985, which led to the Intermediate-Range Forces Treaty of 1987 and the Strategic Arms Reduction Treaty of 1991.

A second approach to explaining arms control agreements is to focus on the powerful impact of domestic politics. Domestic political explanations are second-image theories. Such approaches correctly recognize that the incentive structures employed by game-theoretic models of competition must be derived from a political system. It is only through the national political process that preferences are articulated and translated into foreign policy.[39]

Understanding the domestic sources of arms control policy and negotiation strategy is certainly necessary. Without this background it is impossible to comprehend how bargaining strategies have any effect. In addition, if the "game" is wrong, then a theory based on incentive structures is not very useful. If nothing else, the dramatic political upheaval in Soviet domestic politics compels some measure of second-image analysis. National level factors and changes profoundly affect the structure of the international security environment, as the dissolutions of the Soviet state and the Yugoslavian federation vividly show.

A purely domestic political approach to arms control negotiations, however, is as inadequate as the realist reliance on the military balance. One problem is that each negotiation becomes a separate entity without membership in a larger group of similar experiences. Thus it becomes difficult to understand common themes and patterns. For the process of building theoretical models of cooperation, losing sight of common patterns is undesirable. Furthermore, if the negotiation process itself is taken to have any meaning, then it must be given some importance in shaping preferences—effectively influencing the domestic process.

The bargaining analysis of this book is sensitive to these considerations. Indeed, while the bargaining theories employed are generally third-image perspectives, they are informed by the modified form of political realism suggested by Robert Keohane.[40] A modified realist theory of world politics rejects the image of international relations as a purely anarchic realm in favor of one rich in institutional connections. Adopting arms control negotiations as one arena for understanding the problems of international cooperation on security issues deliberately places the present inquiry in an area in which greater institutionalization is possible.

Bargaining strategies are difficult to examine directly. Identifying the causal links of action and response is also problematic. Rarely do officials offer an explicit statement outlining their approach to negotiations. Analysts, like opposing negotiators, must try to infer strategic behavior from actual negotiating exchanges. Even if no coherent bargaining strategy exists for one or both sides, determining what kinds of outcomes followed certain kinds of behavior is important. This is as much a part of official evaluations of an ongoing negotiation—where the question is "What did they do after our latest offer?"—as it is a piece of strategic analysis. Discovering particular patterns enables us to evaluate bargaining strategies that prescribe certain behavior. The empirical analysis of this book rests on an examination of negotiating exchanges—the offers, proposals, concessions, retractions, and disputes that are the substance of negotiators' work across the table—as a means to evaluate the effects of differing negotiating strategies.

To assume that bargainers always enter negotiations with explicit strategic conceptions of how to behave stretches the imagination. Anyone who has observed closely the behavior of a large organization knows that actions attributed to the organization commonly are the products of internal bargaining, bureaucratic routines, or ad hoc decisions. Although we tend to assume a basic rationality in human behavior, this does not necessarily mean that we should presume conscious strategic behavior, even in an explicit negotiating situation. Nevertheless, use of the concept of bargaining strategies as an analytical tool for examining negotiations has two justifications.

In the first place, bargaining interactions necessarily display the relationships that strategies either prescribe or predict. Therefore, careful evaluation of negotiating moves is essential to judging the utility of different strategies. In the second place, it is fair to assume that bargainers enter the arena of negotiations with some notion, perhaps unarticulated, of how to proceed. Similarly, a government's foreign policies can be illuminated by treating them "as if" they were driven by an explicit theory of international relations—although in reality this is rarely the case. Negotiating exchanges should be treated as if they embody a strategy in order to understand the bargaining process. The alternative is to assume that moves are inconsequential epiphenomena of other factors—a position that virtually excludes negotiations from serious analysis and flies in the face of the commonsense view that bargaining is what international relations is all about.

How is one to know what these moves and offers are? Obviously, as negotiations proceed, the interactions are private and secret. Even long after an individual round of talks has ended, the official negotiating record commonly remains classified. Without access to this official record a negotiating analysis must rely on data that are slightly removed. In practice, however, this is not a serious problem. Despite mutual agreement and desire for secrecy in arms control talks, each side has some interest in making its positions public. Sometimes these are presented in fairly detailed speeches by government officials and political leaders. Because too wide a disparity between what is described publicly as a position or offer and the actual proposals set on the negotiating table privately would impair negotiations, we can take these statements as reasonably authoritative sources. In addition, as negotiations are under way, a corps of journalists and scholars pays careful attention to the details and nuances of the interaction. Frequently, these accounts become outlets for unattributed "official" statements of positions offered or under consideration. Thus, the primary resources employed in this analysis are the documented positions exchanged in the negotiations as reported in official policy pronouncements and papers, testimony to Congress in the United States, and contemporary news coverage. These are supplemented with secondhand analyses, participants' memoirs, and a limited number of participant interviews. My analysis employs a loose form of bargaining analysis to judge whether the offers or moves at a particular point in time represent positions that are relatively closer or further away from the positions of the bargaining partner (including the possibility of no change). Unfortunately, the recent nature of the negotiations under study here prevents access to documents that would allow something like a rigorous, formal coding of verbatim transcripts, such as employed in studies by P. Terrence Hopmann and others.[41] Nevertheless, it is possible to reconstruct fairly accurately the pattern of exchanges from the documents and accounts available and then to make reasonable qualitative classifications.

The next chapter presents the theoretical framework of bargaining strategies and cooperation that is the core of the book. The discussion presents alternative models for bargaining strategies and compares their theoretical bases. The chapter also draws the linkages between bargaining strategies and the international and domestic negotiating environments.

Chapter 3 begins a series of analytical narratives of the negotiating efforts to control nuclear testing and to limit or reduce strategic forces. U.S.-Soviet negotiations to limit nuclear weapons testing and to control strategic nuclear arsenals from 1954 through 1980 are discussed in separate chapters within the framework of the three approaches to arms control bargaining. These negotiating histories provide narrative accounts of the bargaining and provide both the historical and political background for negotiations of the 1980s.

During the first thirty-five years of arms control negotiations, reciprocal bargaining behavior was most productive in moving negotiations to an agreement. Nevertheless, neither side employed a strict tit-for-tat approach—neither concessions nor retractions necessarily were matched right away. Successful bargaining, in other words, was "nicer" or more "forgiving" than the strategy promoted by cooperation theory. Although initiatives had some utility, their impacts were limited. Tough strategies, on the other hand, resulted in neither agreements nor the achievement of major advantages in the arms competition.

Turning to the arms control negotiations of the 1980s, individual chapters analyze efforts to reach a test ban agreement, the negotiations on intermediate-range nuclear forces, and the strategic arms reduction talks. The first set of efforts made little progress and failed to reach an agreement. The other two sets of talks, however, concluded with remarkable achievements. But the road to these achievements was anything but direct. And the bargaining experience differed as much from the past as did the agreements. Because the agreements of the 1980s were reached by such different bargaining strategies, these negotiations offer valuable insights into bargaining theories. The book concludes with a discussion of the role of bargaining in these nuclear negotiations and in the transformations of politics that marked the end of the cold war.

NOTES

1. Bernard Bechhoefer, *Postwar Negotiations for Arms Control* (Washington, DC: Brookings Institution, 1961), p. 598.

2. See Robert J. Art, "A Defensible Defense: America's Grand Strategy After the Cold War," *International Security* 15 (Spring 1991): 5.

3. For examples of these explanations see Jeff Checkel, "Ideas, Institutions, and the Gorbachev Foreign Policy Revolution," *World Politics* 45 (January 1993): 271–300.

4. See Stephen M. Walt, *The Origins of Alliances* (Ithaca: Cornell University Press, 1987) for an insightful analysis of alliances that focuses on the "balance of threat" as well as the "balance of power."

5. Reprinted as "Idealist Internationalism and the Security Dilemma," in John M. Herz, *The Nation-State and the Crisis in World Politics* (New York: David McKay, 1976), p. 90. See also Robert Jervis, "Cooperation Under the Security Dilemma," *World Politics* 30 (January 1978): 167–214.

6. See Robert Jervis, *Perception and Misperception in International Politics* (Princeton: Princeton University Press, 1976), pp. 58–113; George W. Downs, David M. Rocke, and Randolph Siverson, "Tacit Bargaining and Arms Control," *World Politics* 39 (April 1987): 297–325.

7. For analyses that emphasize alternatives to arms control negotiations see Kenneth Adelman, "Arms Control With and Without Agreements," *Foreign Affairs* 63 (Winter 1984/85): 240–263; Hedley Bull, *The Control of the Arms Race* (New York: Praeger, 1965); George W. Downs and David M. Rocke, *Tacit Bargaining, Arms Races and Arms Control* (Ann Arbor: University of Michigan Press, 1990); Thomas Schelling and Morton Halperin, *Strategy and Arms Control* (New York: Twentieth Century Fund, 1961).

8. See Robert O. Keohane, *After Hegemony: Cooperation and Discord in the World Political Economy* (Princeton: Princeton University Press, 1984), p. 12.

9. Robert Jervis, "Security Regimes," *International Organization* 36 (Spring 1982): 357–378.

10. Downs and Rocke, *Tacit Bargaining, Arms Races and Arms Control,* p. 16.

11. Downs et al., "Tacit Bargaining and Arms Control."

12. This is the now-accepted standard definition of international regimes from Stephen D. Krasner, "Structural Causes and International Consequences: Regimes as Intervening Variables," *International Organization* 36 (Spring 1982): 185–206.

13. See Keohane, *After Hegemony,* pp. 49–132, for a theoretical discussion of this issue.

14. See Roland Bleiker, Doug Bond, and Myung-Soo Lee, "Unification from Below? German Unity and Its Implications for Korean Unification Dynamics," Center for International Affairs, Working Paper no. 92–4 (Cambridge, MA: Harvard University Center for International Affairs, 1992).

15. The empirical evidence on this question is mixed. See Michael Wallace, "Arms Races and War," *Journal of Conflict Resolution* 23 (March 1979): 3–16; and Matthew Evangelista's discussion of Samuel Huntington's argument in *Innovation and the Arms Race: How the United States and the Soviet Union Develop New Military Technologies* (Ithaca: Cornell University Press, 1988).

16. Seyom Brown, *Faces of Power: Constancy and Change in United States Foreign Policy from Truman to Reagan* (New York: Columbia University Press, 1983), pp. 2–14.

17. Executive Office of the President, *Report of the Commission on the Organization of the Government for the Conduct of Foreign Policy* (Washington, DC: U.S. Government Printing Office, 1975).

18. Graham Allison, *Essence of Decision* (Boston: Little, Brown, 1971); Morton Halperin, "The Decision to Deploy ABM: Bureaucratic and Domestic Politics in the Johnson Administration," *World Politics* 25 (October 1972): 62–95.

19. Alexander George, *Presidential Decision Making in Foreign Policy: The Effective Use of Information and Advice* (Boulder: Westview, 1980).

20. Evangelista, *Innovation and the Arms Race.*

21. Glenn Snyder and Paul Diesing, *Conflict Among Nations* (Princeton: Princeton University Press, 1977), chap. 5.

22. Bruce Russett, *Prisoners of Insecurity* (New York: W. H. Freeman, 1983), pp. 91–95.

23. See Richard Ned Lebow and Janice Gross Stein, "Rational Deterrence Theory: I Think, Therefore I Deter," *World Politics* 41 (January 1989): 208–224; Janice Gross Stein, "Calculation, Miscalculation and Conventional Deterrence I: The View from Cairo," in *Psychology and Deterrence,* ed. Robert Jervis, Richard Ned Lebow, and Janice Gross Stein (Baltimore: Johns Hopkins University Press, 1985); Richard Ned Lebow, *Between Peace and War* (Baltimore: Johns Hopkins University Press, 1980).

24. On this topic generally see Thomas Risse-Kappen, "Public Opinion, Domestic Structure, and Foreign Policy in Liberal Democracies," *World Politics* 43 (July 1991): 479–512; Richard Eichenberg, *Public Opinion and National Security in Western Europe* (Ithaca: Cornell University Press, 1989); William Schneider, "Public Opinion," in *The Making of America's Soviet Policy,* ed. Joseph S. Nye, Jr. (New Haven: Yale University Press, 1984); Douglas C. Waller, *Congress and the Nuclear Freeze Movement* (Amherst: University of Massachusetts Press, 1987).

25. Kenneth Waltz, *Theory of International Politics* (Reading, MA: Addison-Wesley, 1979).

26. Quoted in Robert Art and Robert Jervis, eds., *Anarchy, Force and Order* (Boston: Little, Brown, 1973), p. 99.

27. Harold Brown, *Thinking About National Security* (Boulder: Westview Press, 1983), p. 187.

28. Joseph Kruzel, "The Preconditions and Consequences of Arms Control Agreements," Ph.D. diss., Harvard University, 1975, chap. 3.

29. Ibid., pp. 354–355.

30. Schelling, *The Strategy of Conflict* (Cambridge, MA: Harvard University Press, 1960), chap. 2.

31. Paul Pillar, *Negotiating Peace: War Termination as a Bargaining Process* (Princeton: Princeton University Press, 1983), chap. 2.

32. Snyder and Diesing, *Conflict Among Nations,* p. 525.

33. Robert Keohane, *After Hegemony: Discord and Cooperation in the World Political Economy* (Princeton: Princeton University Press, 1984), pp. 258–259.

34. See Michael McGwire, *Military Objectives in Soviet Foreign Policy* (Washington, DC: Brookings Institution, 1987), and *Perestroika and Soviet National Security* (Washington, DC: Brookings Institution, 1991); Matthew Evangelista, "Sources of Restraint in Soviet Security Policy," in *Behavior, Society and Nuclear War,* vol. 2, ed. Philip E. Tetlock, Jo L. Husbands, Robert Jervis, Paul C. Stern, and Charles Tilly (New York: Oxford University Press, 1991); and Checkel, "Ideas and Institutions."

35. Robert Axelrod, *The Evolution of Cooperation* (New York: Basic Books, 1984).

36. For example, see Kenneth Oye, ed., *Cooperation Under Anarchy* (Princeton: Princeton University Press, 1986).

37. For example, see Matthew Evangelista, "Cooperation Theory and Disarmament Negotiations in the 1950s," *World Politics* 42 (July 1990): 502–529; Deborah Welch Larson, "Crisis Prevention and the Austrian State Treaty," *International Organization* 41 (Winter 1987): 27–60; George W. Downs, David Rocke, and Randolph Siverson, "Arms Races and Cooperation," *World Politics* 38 (October 1985): 118–146. A recent extension of Axelrod's model is Steve Weber, *Cooperation and Discord in U.S.-Soviet Arms Control* (Princeton: Princeton University Press, 1991).

38. Joanne Gowa, "Anarchy, Egoism and Third Images: *The Evolution of Cooperation* and International Relations," *International Organization* 40 (Winter 1986): 167–186.

39. See Evangelista, *Innovation and the Arms Race*.

40. Robert O. Keohane, "Realism, Neorealism and the Study of World Politics," and "Theory of World Politics: Structural Realism and Beyond," in his *Neorealism and Its Critics* (New York: Columbia University Press, 1986).

41. See P. Terrence Hopmann and Charles Walcott, "Internal and External Influences on Bargaining in Arms Control Negotiations: The Partial Test Ban," in *Peace, War and Numbers,* ed. Bruce Russett (Beverly Hills: Sage, 1972); Charles Walcott and P. Terrence Hopmann, "Interaction Analysis and Bargaining Behavior," in *The Small Group in Political Science: The Last Two Decades of Development,* ed. Robert T. Golembiewski (Athens: University of Georgia Press, 1978).

2

Bargaining and Cooperation

Whatever their motivations, once states become engaged in arms control efforts, they are ostensibly pursuing some form of cooperation. Cooperation, however, should not be confused with "harmony" or the end of conflict (although either might be a long-term consequence). Rather, cooperation should be seen as a process of "mutual policy adjustment" on specific issues at specific times.[1] So long as the governments of the states involved perceive potential benefits that can only be obtained through joint action with others, we can consider the process as a problem of cooperation.

Negotiations are possible when a range of potentially acceptable solutions to a conflict exists.[2] Agreement on a mutual solution is not guaranteed because its achievement requires a degree of cooperation and therefore mutual accommodation. Negotiations are manifestations of the bargaining process that attempt to reach a formal agreement, often a treaty. "Explicit bargaining," notes Thomas Schelling, "requires, for an ultimate agreement, some coordination of the participants' expectations."[3] Similarly, the pursuit of agreement in an arms control negotiation should be considered a problem of cooperation and coordination—purposeful activity of states to improve their security through the process of mutual policy accommodation.

Explaining (and promoting) cooperation is one of the central dilemmas of world politics. On the one hand, traditional international relations theory (at least that rooted in the postwar realist school) finds competition and conflict easier to explain than cooperation. In realism's view the powerful logic of international anarchy makes competition the modal tendency for governments. Cooperation is not excluded from possibility, but cooperative policies will tend to be subordinated to self-help and the pursuit of national self-interest. Cooperation between adversaries is less interesting (it arguably lacks the drama of potential global conflict and violence) and is considered less likely.

Yet cooperative efforts, such as arms control in its various forms and forums, do exist and recur fairly frequently. Furthermore, increasing global interdependence on fundamental issues—including the preservation of the global environment, promoting economic wealth and development, and the avoidance of nuclear war—compel leaders to seek cooperative policies. Very few of the "global issues" of the late twentieth century can be addressed, let alone solved, through unilateral action. Almost all require some degree of coordination.

The puzzle of security cooperation is both analytical and normative. In the first place, the tools of analysis should be available to explain this persistent feature of world politics. In the second place, analysis should serve policy to the extent that improved understanding of cooperation facilitates the promotion of appropriate cooperative relations (or at least helps prevent missed opportunities).

In recent years scholarly interest in cooperation increased. Many of the efforts resulted from application of existing models of bargaining with new insights about the roles of institutions, choice, and rationality. Formal models, especially game theory, have strongly influenced academic analysis of conflict and cooperation—including arms races and arms control—for more than three decades. Thomas Schelling's classic work *The Strategy of Conflict* used game theory to illuminate the underlying logic of choice that leaders face in conflict situations. *Strategy and Arms Control,* written with Morton Halperin, applied the same logic to choices relevant to achieving arms control objectives.[4] Numerous studies have elaborated the notion of games to understand such problems as the obstacles to cooperation,[5] the dynamics of deterrence,[6] and the patterns of conflict initiation and escalation.[7]

This book examines bargaining interactions as the vehicle to explain cooperation in arms control negotiations. The next sections of this chapter discuss, in turn, the bargaining-based theory of cooperation developed by Robert Axelrod, an alternative model of bargaining related to Charles Osgood's concept of an initiative strategy, and the concept of "tough" bargaining strategies. The first two approaches received the most academic attention in the 1980s, but the third was much more prominent in arms control and security policy making in the United States. The strategic prescriptions of each ideal-type strategy are developed and used to examine the arms control negotiations of the 1980s.

BARGAINING THEORIES AND NEGOTIATING STRATEGIES

Negotiating strategies are adopted to define the government's objectives and to guide responses to the opponent's offers and actions. Fred Iklé suggested that at each moment negotiators and policy makers face a threefold choice. They may quit the talks and accept the status quo ante, determining that their state's security situation would be no worse without an agreement. Or they may choose to continue the negotiations and the search for a more attractive solution. Finally, negotiators may accept the positions established to that time as the basis for agreement—to decide, in other words, that the security interests of their state will be better served with the available agreement than without.[8] A bargaining strategy provides the larger framework within which negotiators evaluate these evolving choices.

A strategy is essentially a set of guidelines for behavior. In traditional military usage, a strategy provides a mechanism to "coordinate means and ends," where the objective to be gained and the environment to be confronted will determine choices for action.[9] In addition, as Schelling notes, decisions are often interdependent.[10] Bargaining situations are those "in which the ability of one participant to gain his ends is dependent to an important degree on the choices or decisions that the other participant will make."[11] The outcomes of an engagement (such as a conflict or a negotiation) result from the combined actions of the participants, taken either simultaneously or sequentially. Decision making, therefore, involves the calculation of interdependent moves in light of the identifiable interests of the actors.

In its simplest form a strategy prescribes which action to take in response to the opponent's move. For example, one strategy for negotiating might be to make a concession in response to every concession made by the opponent. Other strategies might involve a positive response only after a particular number of concessions, only after a concession is made on a particular issue, or even to make no concessions at all.

In a larger sense, a strategy also embodies general assumptions about how negotiations operate, how the particular opponent bargains, and the relative importance of the various issues at stake for oneself and for the opponent. Thus the tactical negotiating moves prescribed by a strategy reflect underlying values and priorities regarding the role of negotiations in security policy, the strategic importance of various weapons systems and the domestic political climate—many of the forces that brought the government into negotiations in the first place.

Policy makers, diplomats, and analysts offer varied advice for the conduct of negotiations, proposing strategies that range from "hard" to "soft." Similarly, a substantial theoretical literature on bargaining has evolved from the work of strategists, political scientists, psychologists, and sociologists. Many of these efforts explore the effectiveness of a variety of bargaining strategies under different types of conditions.

If an agreement is seen by the participants in a negotiation as having some value greater than maintaining the status quo (usually a condition of competition), how should a negotiator proceed? What strategy is likely to yield the best possible agreement from the range of potential outcomes? The answer is hardly obvious, as the intense and ongoing debates in both academia and the policy community reveal.

Three strategic approaches or models organize this inquiry. First, a strategy of conditional reciprocity seeks to promote agreement by engaging in a process of mutual compromise and concession making. By contrast, an initiative strategy seeks to accelerate the achievement of agreement by making unilateral concessions toward a presumed solution. Alternatively, a tough bargaining strategy attempts to extract the maximum concessions from the opponent by holding firmly to a position with little or no compromise. All three of these approaches have been used at some point in U.S.-Soviet nuclear negotiations. Policy arguments about which is best draw selectively upon some of this experience. It is useful, therefore, to explore the assumptions of each approach before examining the arms control record.

Reciprocal Strategies

Reciprocal strategies treat negotiations as a process of mutual exchange and compromise. A general definition of reciprocity combines the notions of contingency and equivalence: "exchanges of roughly equivalent values in which the actions of each party are contingent on the prior actions of others in such a way that good is returned for good, and bad for bad."[12] The give and take of bargaining exchanges, especially among competitors or adversaries, is conditioned by the desire to achieve the highest individual utility possible given that a solution will require some degree of mutual accommodation. As Keohane's definition suggests, a bargainer's choice for the "next move" is closely related to the previous behavior of the negotiating partner.

Many bargaining theories assume that reciprocity, specifically reciprocal concession making, is a necessary condition for agreement in a negotiation. Their underlying assumption is the existence of a mutual interest in agreement—that both participants in a dispute perceive the fulfillment of their own self-interest as requiring a negotiated settlement. Robert Axelrod argues that cooperation even between two adversaries is possible provided both adopt a reciprocal, or "tit-for-tat," strategy.[13] In the simplest terms, cooperation can develop over time if each party rewards continuing cooperation with similar cooperation.

Tit-for-tat also requires a willingness to punish noncooperation by the opponent. On the one hand, willingness to compromise is demonstrated by an initial "nice" opening move and subsequent reciprocation of cooperative policies. On the other hand, retaliation for noncooperation is used to demonstrate that cooperation must be mutual and exploitation will not be tolerated. Tit-for-tat is "forgiving" in that once the opponent returns to cooperation, so will the tit-for-tat bargainer.

Axelrod's reciprocal strategy, however, is similar to many studies of negotiation behavior that point to a pattern of "concession-convergence" and mutual compromise.[14] The concession pattern is one of incremental convergence between the opening positions.[15] Like Axelrod, these theories tend to see the convergence of positions in a negotiation as the "natural" outcome, although it may be obstructed by various factors. For example, some theories propose that although both sides seek agreement, they are deterred by their estimates of the risks of moving toward agreement. In this situation a concession by one side encourages reciprocation by the other by reducing the difference between the positions and thus reducing the risk of agreement that the second bargainer perceives.[16]

Convergence often implies the movement to some equitable "midpoint" between the two opening positions. Such a midpoint solution has several attractions in addition to the intuitive salience of mathematical symmetry. Its most important appeal is the general concept of fairness entailing a notion of equal or equitable division. Quantitative issues, especially those that are finely divisible (like money) are more likely to move toward agreement through a pattern of reciprocated concessions. Furthermore, when the implications of the settlement are unclear, the intuitive notion of fairness, or the salient midpoint, tends to prevail.[17]

Reciprocal concessions on an issue that involve convergent compromises may not always be possible, however. Not all negotiations involve matters where the substance at issue is easily divisible, like money, territory, or numbers of weapons. In addition, other values frequently intrude in a negotiation so that otherwise divisible issues become in effect indivisible. Ballistic missiles in the superpowers' arsenals, for example, are obviously countable. But each side attaches different values to different portions of their respective arsenal. The U.S. commitment to submarine-launched ballistic missiles (SLBMs) and the Soviet investment in heavy intercontinental ballistic missiles (ICBMs) create conditions that make the problem less easily divided. In these situations reciprocal compromises are still possible, but they require comparable trades on different issues.[18] Bargaining strategies that create interissue linkages within the negotiations may be employed to facilitate solutions.

Cooperation, however, is not the only possible outcome of tit-for-tat reciprocity. Arms racing also is a process of unilateral reciprocation of the opponent's behavior. Tit-for-tat, in other words, is just as likely to produce a spiral of competition as it is to facilitate sustained cooperation. The key difference lies in the existence of mutual interests in pursuing absolute rather than relative gains over the long term.[19]

Axelrod added three important conditions that are usefully applied to arms control negotiations. First, both sides must share a common interest that can only be obtained by cooperation. In the context of arms control, agreements are possible only if both sides prefer them to arms racing. In general, arms control between the United States and the Soviet Union resembled the incentive structure on the prisoner's dilemma game on which Axelrod's cooperation theory is based. That is, both sides often had a mutual preference for cooperation (through some control) over noncooperation (through continuing the arms race). But they also were powerfully disposed to avoid being exploited if they cooperated while the other did not.[20]

The incentive structures of the superpowers as they negotiated at any given time, or on any particular issue, however, did not always resemble the prisoner's dilemma,[21] and the differing sets of incentives were likely to be reflected in the bargaining strategy adopted. Insofar as preferences are somewhat malleable, we would expect bargaining behavior to have some effect on changing the incentive structures of the players. As we will see below, his assumption underlies other strategies more explicitly than it does Axelrod's theory.

Second, both negotiators must believe that they will continue to interact with each other for the foreseeable future. Axelrod argues that when the "shadow of the future" is long and both sides adopt the tit-for-tat strategy, cooperation can emerge and continue. If no expectations for the future exist, then tangible short-term gains, especially between adversaries, matter much more than potential long-term rewards. Between the superpowers this condition of continuing interaction was generally met. Neither side expected the other to suddenly withdraw from participation in world politics; their status as the competitive poles of the bipolar world precluded that option. Nor did either side seriously expect the other to suddenly "go out of business." American scholars and policy makers may have accepted George Kennan's prediction that a strategy of containment would eventually cause the Soviet Union to collapse, but the emphasis was on the indeterminate and unspecified future. As a rule, American policy grudgingly accepted the Soviet Union, and in some sense the cold war, as an unpleasant fact of life. Thus, it was a major shock when the Soviet Union and its authoritarian empire collapsed between 1989 and 1991.

The expectation of continuing interaction, however, was tempered by the regular process of political leadership change within the American system, and to some degree by the recognition of changes within the Soviet leadership. New individuals and their constellations of advisors often brought new ideas to the U.S.-Soviet relationship. New leaders had incentives to define their own unique contribution to policy, and they often arrived in power with alternative "grand strategies" for their country's role in the world.[22] This was certainly the case for American politics, but the uniformity of Soviet policy across leadership regimes should not be overstated either. Nevertheless, neither side tended to deviate too far from past precedent. Thus, as a general proposition, leaders on each side of the Soviet-American relationship could expect to face their counterparts for the foreseeable future and could expect some degree of consistency.

Third, the reciprocal strategy relies on punishing noncooperation as well as rewarding the preferred behavior. A learning context is created that should build the incentive to cooperate and discourage attempts at exploitation. Axelrod's model, however, implies little more than simple, or adaptive, learning.[23] He is quite explicit about this in using the concepts of evolution to frame his discussion of the ways in which cooperation can emerge among self-interested individuals. In evolutionary terms, the requirement for selection is simple: adapt or die. Thus, Axelrod argues that tit-for-tat is a simple and easily understood strategy for behavior. The willingness of the tit-for-tat bargainer to reciprocate both cooperation and defection permits the other side to recognize the optimal pattern of behavior to obtain the maximum gain. Axelrod does not presume that complex cognitive change in the opponent either does, or must, occur. Put another way, the underlying belief systems or "cognitive maps" of the participants do not change, and their fundamental interests remain the same. Tit-for-tat bargaining simply provides a mechanism to leverage existing interests in the service of mutual gain.

Other scholars of negotiations and bargaining suggest strategies that are essentially similar to Axelrod's theory, though they differ in emphasis. I. William Zartman and Maureen Berman, for example, suggest that negotiators should be "tough to demand and soft to reward."[24] Similarly, Paul Huth, in a study of extended deterrence that included a variable for bargaining behavior, argued for the utility of a "firm but flexible" diplomatic strategy.[25] Both approaches propose a willingness to compromise and engage in reciprocal concessions, but each advocates a harder initial strategy. Unlike Axelrod in his cooperation theory, however, neither Zartman and Berman or Huth provides a clear strategy. For example, exactly how long should one be "tough to demand"? Nor do either of these alternative reciprocal approaches suggest why these strategies should work. Because Axelrod offers both a clear strategic approach and a framework for explanation, his theory provides a better point of reference for analyzing arms control negotiating behavior.

Arms control negotiations differ from Axelrod's model of cooperation in two important ways, however. Most significantly, negotiations are goal oriented. They aim at the creation of a formal agreement that settles specific issues and creates a framework of mutual obligations. This is not the only manner in which arms control can be pursued, but, as was argued in Chapter 1, negotiations have several important political and security functions that tacit arms control efforts lack. In any case, the search for an explicit agreement is rather different than the development of ongoing condition of cooperation. A mutual desire to avoid nuclear war, for example, may require tacit cooperation, but it is not the same thing as the mutual willingness to accept detailed limitations on one's military capabilities.[26] Agreeing to the explicit rules of a treaty or agreement may be much more difficult than developing a cooperative pattern of behavior.

Axelrod suggested that the tit-for-tat strategy embodied in his theory of cooperation should be productive in U.S.-Soviet arms control efforts.[27] In arms control negotiations a strategy of reciprocity, or tit-for-tat, would work with one side making a concession that the negotiating partner in some way matches. If an offer or concession is retracted by one side, a similar hardening would be expected from the other. Similarly, a return to concession making would be rewarded with like behavior. The pattern of behavior should be discernible in negotiations that move both toward and away from agreement.

Initiative Strategies

Tit-for-tat is a nice but fundamentally neutral strategy. The bargainer's job is to copy the moves of the other side somewhat mechanically, whether this leads to cooperation or competition. In fact, unless the other party also chooses a tit-for-tat strategy, no alternative exists to mutual competition. Scholars also have noted that reciprocity in the world of human relations (as opposed to computer simulations) requires judgments about such things as the equivalence of moves. Judgments, in turn, are commonly filtered through motivated and unmotivated biases on the part of the individual and collective actors involved. In the simplest example, the leaders of a state may see their own behavior as an equivalent concession to the other party's last move, but the bargaining partner may regard it as insubstantial.[28]

The dilemma of how to begin the process of mutual cooperation, therefore, remains unresolved. An alternative approach embraces initiatives as the mechanism for moving negotiations forward. An initiative strategy is similar to a reciprocal approach in that both include the need for one bargainer to go first, and both see value in mutual accommodation. Axelrod's tit-for-tat strategy, for example, depends on an initial concession, a nice opener. A strategy based on initiatives, however, goes further. It asks: If small concessions tend to promote convergence, perhaps at a midpoint, then why not move directly to the presumed end? Similarly, if one obstacle to mutual agreement is distrust or fear of risk, why not take dramatic steps to reduce tensions and demonstrate good faith?

Proposals for initiative-oriented bargaining strategies have a fairly long history in the United States. In 1962 psychologist Charles Osgood proposed a strategy he called GRIT (for "graduated reciprocation in tension-reduction").[29] In Osgood's view the principal obstacle to mutual security arrangements with the Soviet Union (including some measures of disarmament) was a psychological climate of mistrust and fear that fostered misperception and reproduced itself. His core idea was that these psychological barriers should and could be broken: "if such unilateral initiatives are persistently applied, and reciprocation is obtained, then the margin for risk-taking is widened and somewhat larger steps can be taken. Both sides, in effect, begin edging down the escalation ladder."[30]

Osgood had little faith in formal negotiations as a means to reverse the arms race in the early 1960s, although he considered one of the aims of GRIT to be the creation of "an atmosphere of mutual trust within which negotiations on critical political and military issues will have a better chance of succeeding."[31] He wrote,

We have behind us a long and dismal history of unsuccessful negotiations with the Soviets. . . . The conclusion we seem driven to is this: *Negotiated agreements require commitments from both sides prior to any action by either, and under the conditions of cold war thinking commitments of any significance seem most unlikely; as long as both sides remain chained to the requirement of prior commitment from the other neither is able to take the initiative in moving toward a more peaceful world.*[32]

In place of relying extensively on negotiations Osgood proposed an alternative strategy with its own logic and set of rules, which he laid out in *An Alternative to War or Surrender*. His first set of principles for adopting unilateral initiatives emphasized the need to preserve, or at least to avoid undermining, existing levels of national security. This would be accomplished first by taking initiatives that retained fundamental military capabilities for defense and deterrence and second by diversifying the unilateral actions. Since the risk inherent in the initiatives was spread over several different substantive and geographical domains, the danger that any single action would significantly impair national security would be reduced.

(a) Unilateral initiatives must not reduce our capacity to inflict unacceptable nuclear retaliation on an opponent should we be attacked.

(b) Unilateral initiatives must not cripple our capacity to meet aggression by conventional weapons with appropriately graded conventional military responses.

(c) Unilateral initiatives must be graduated in risk according to the degree of reciprocation obtained by the opponents.

(d) Unilateral initiatives must be diversified in nature, both as to sphere of action and as to geographical locus of application.

(e) Prior to announcement, unilateral initiatives must be unpredictable by an opponent as to their sphere, locus, and time of execution.

Additional principles focused on the mechanisms for "inducing reciprocation" by the adversary. The purpose of the exercise was to provide a counterpoint to the psychological barriers that prevent cooperation. Thus, for GRIT to work, the initiatives had to contain some element of risk or cost as proof of the initiator's seriousness. In addition, the actions had to be as clear and understandable to the adversary as possible.

(f) Unilateral initiatives must present a sincere intent to reduce and control international tensions.

(g) Unilateral initiatives must be announced publicly at some reasonable interval prior to their execution and identified as part of a deliberate policy of reducing and controlling tensions.

(h) In their announcement, unilateral initiatives should include explicit invitation to reciprocation in some form.

(i) Unilateral initiatives that have been announced must be executed on schedule regardless of prior commitment by the opponent to reciprocate.

(j) Unilateral initiatives must be continued over a considerable period, regardless of immediate reciprocation or events of a tension-increasing nature elsewhere.

(k) Unilateral initiatives must, wherever possible, take advantage of mutual self-interests, mutual self-restraints, and opportunities for cooperative enterprise.

(l) Unilateral initiatives must be as unambiguous and as susceptible to verification as possible.[33]

Unlike Axelrod's tit-for-tat strategy and the tough bargaining approach discussed below, Osgood expected GRIT to facilitate a more complex learning process in which interests could change. In other words, Osgood saw the endemic competition between the superpowers as rooted in distorted perceptions of each other's interests and objectives. Because each saw the other as fundamentally hostile and threatening, they pursued policies that reinforced hostility. Interests became governed, in Osgood's view, by the desire to guard against this threat, despite the presence of mutual interests in coexistence and peace. By subverting the expected pattern of behavior, GRIT would pose a challenge to the reigning perception of hostility. The dissonance between observed behavior and expected behavior would eventually cause the adversary to adjust cognitive maps to create a "better fit." When this took place, the overall climate for making substantive policy adjustments would be greatly improved.[34] Policy changes, in both countries, that would follow from a GRIT strategy would be enduring, rather than reflecting instrumental adjustment to particular circumstances.

Psychologists and peace researchers remained interested in GRIT, even if the community of policy makers to which it was addressed did not. Experimental and empirical studies following Osgood examined and often supported some of the claims he made for the strategy.[35] For example, Deborah Larson argued that Soviet negotiators successfully employed a GRIT-like strategy during the Austrian state treaty negotiations in the 1950s. She suggested that GRIT is better suited than tit-for-tat to negotiations in which psychological factors (such as distrust or operational codes) are the main impediments to agreement.[36]

In the only book-length study of international politics to directly examine the utility of unilateral initiatives in U.S. arms control policy, William Rose argued that such strategies can work if certain conditions are met.[37] Rose found that the success of an American initiative effort was increased when, among other things, the American demands were signaled clearly, the Soviets interpreted the messages correctly, the proposed American agreement improved Soviet security, Soviet prestige was affirmed, and its alliance structures were strengthened. These empirical findings supported Osgood's principal arguments that initiatives must be clear and understandable and should always improve the security for the other side. Rose also found, however, that initiatives tended to succeed when they were in the "same currency" as the desired Soviet response, although this may have been because Rose focused on initiatives taken in the context of efforts to reach an arms control agreement.[38]

Although Osgood explicitly proposed GRIT as an alternative to formal negotiations, the strategic principles can be adopted to form an initiative strategy within negotiations themselves. The objective would be the same—to find a way to transform the "dismal" process by overcoming the adversary's perceptual barriers to cooperation. In arms control negotiations an initiative strategy would be pursued if one side takes deliberate steps to break a deadlock. Initiatives might involve the proposal of new concessions or a declaration and demonstration of restraint in a weapons acquisition decision. The initiative would be maintained even if reciprocal moves were not forthcoming, partly because the initial move should have been generally consistent with security objectives and partly to maintain the example of good faith and the goal of tension reduction.

Tough Strategies

A third negotiating strategy is a "tough bargaining" approach. This approach is not commonly associated with the question, How does cooperation develop?, but usually with the contrasting perspective on the prominence of conflict. Tough bargaining strategies are appropriate for a study of arms negotiations, however, for several reasons. First, they provide the logical completion to the set of approaches that could be employed in a negotiation. If the interactions of negotiations are taken to be important elements for understanding outcomes, then the full range of possible behavior should be considered.

Second, tough strategies correspond to the game theoretical construction of "deadlock." Thus there is continuity with the underlying analytical structure used to derive many cooperation theories. In Kenneth Oye's phrase, "When you observe conflict, think Deadlock—the absence of mutual interest—before puzzling over why mutual interests were not realized."[39] Finally, the problem of cooperation can be understood either as the process by which competitors arrive at the "Pareto frontier," where a mutual solution is possible, or the process by which they arrive at the solution point on that frontier. The distinction is important and corresponds to the debate over relative versus absolute gains in world politics.

The first process—moving onto the frontier—assumes that the dilemma involves finding the mechanism for realizing the long-term absolute gains available through mutual accommodation. This does not imply that the competitors are not self-interested, only that they are considering the long-term prospect for gains (the "shadow of the future"). As Axelrod's prisoner's dilemma tournament demonstrated, over time both parties gain the move from sustained cooperation.

The realist tradition of international relations, however, argues that relative gains matter most to actors in international politics, especially state adversaries. Some element of advantage, therefore, will always be the most desirable outcome for each of the parties individually. As Joanne Gowa points out, even in Axelrod's tournament of strategists well-versed in game theory and operating under explicit instructions to act only for gain maximization, the players almost invariably sought relative comparisons to measure their success.[40] Thus, even within the framework of seeking a solution of mutual accommodation, the imperative to prevail exists. In other words, each state has the rational incentive to achieve its own best deal. One approach, then, is to take a demanding, tough, strategy, akin to deadlock, in order to extract the greatest possible concessions from the adversary.

A strategy of toughness has several features. Opening proposals are often high, even extreme. Not only are initiating concessions avoided, but often reciprocation of the opponent's concessions is refused in order to maintain the pressure for further concessions. When concessions are offered, they are generally small. A tough strategy involves a willingness to retract existing offers and the linkage of difficult issues to ones that are easier to resolve.

Zartman cites experimental evidence suggesting the potential benefits, as well as costs, of a tough negotiating strategy: "One common pattern [among participants in a series of experiments] was to return toughness for toughness and softness for softness. . . . Another pattern saw a higher opener to produce a higher result, although not proportionally so. The 'outlandishly high' openers [in two experimental situations] produced a higher than expected outcome . . . but in addition yielded a higher incidence of breakdown."[41] In Axelrod's tournament of prisoner's dilemma, a tough strategy ("always defect") always yielded the highest relative score between the two players, although tit-for-tat resulted in much higher absolute gains for both over time.[42]

A tough strategy assumes that demonstrating greater resolve and determination in a negotiation will force the opponent to yield if he or she has any desire for agreement. To the extent that any learning is expected to occur, it would be simple and adaptive. The main goal of a tough strategy is to convey the willingness to use the superior power resources that the tough bargainer has available. It is neither necessary nor expected that any change in underlying interests would take place.

The choice of a tough bargaining strategy implies that the range of acceptable compromises is very limited and that mutual accommodation is valued only slightly more than unilateral efforts. More importantly, a tough strategy rejects an implicit similarity of interests between the United States and the Soviet Union in arms control negotiations. Roman Kolkowicz argued, for example, that "U.S. negotiators, bureaucrats, and analysts operate on the unquestioned assumptions of rough similarity of Soviet and U.S. interests and objectives in these negotiations, and the larger systemic, political and historical dissimilarities between the two protagonists are rarely considered."[43]

If indeed the superpowers have little in common, then arms control agreements ought to serve the purpose of maximizing one's own advantage. Furthermore, if Soviet nuclear strategy and policy are seen as rooted in preparation to prevail in an armed conflict, even through preemption, then it makes sense for American negotiators to demand the most from them in any negotiation.[44] Of course, maximum demands are also perfectly rational for Soviet negotiators to employ.[45]

Advice and Advisors

Former American participants in arms control negotiations have offered advice that echoes all of these negotiation approaches. Gerard Smith and Raymond Garthoff, both participants in the first strategic arms limitation talks (SALT I), Smith as the chief negotiator argued, for example, that even if Soviet negotiators were hard bargainers, they generally were serious and interested in reaching agreements. U.S. negotiators were advised to be patient in their pursuit of arms control objectives.

Garthoff argued that U.S. negotiators "should not shy away from taking the initiative" with their Soviet counterparts. This was productive, he suggested, because the Soviet political system was inherently less flexible than the U.S. system, in part because it lacked a mechanism for coordinating intragovernmental policy preferences below the Politburo. U.S. initiatives, therefore, could push the Soviet system into action. At the same time, these initiatives should not embody "demands that may obscure the possibilities for real negotiation."[46] In Garthoff's view, U.S.-Soviet negotiations function more like the "concession-convergence" models in which a concession encourages a reciprocal response. Similarly, Smith advised other U.S. negotiators to avoid "obviously inequitable propositions" and "uncertain positions," both of which are time-consuming and unproductive.[47]

Other American arms control participants and analysts favored tougher U.S. bargaining strategies, in part because they viewed concession behavior as an indicator of bargaining resolve. For example, Fred Iklé, former head of the U.S. Arms Control and Disarmament Agency (ACDA), and Ambassadors U. Alexis Johnson and Abraham Beam suggested that the apparent sluggishness of Soviet diplomatic behavior was designed to encourage "self-negotiation" within the United States. The pluralistic nature of U.S. politics, they argued, created greater pressures on policy makers to be more forthcoming and to make concessions in negotiations.[48] The Soviet practice of withholding concessions in the early stages of bargaining and reciprocating U.S. concessions only reluctantly was seen as a conscious effort to exploit the presumed U.S. propensity to concede in favor of Soviet maximum demands.

Proponents of a tough strategy advised American negotiators, therefore, to resist the temptation to take the initiative (because it was viewed as counterproductive), to encourage Soviet concessions by firmly holding original U.S. positions, and even to engage in strategic deception about "true" U.S. interests. In 1961 Henry Kissinger offered an explicit plea for the use of high opening bids:

If agreement is usually found between two starting points, there is no point in making moderate offers. Good bargaining techniques would suggest a point of departure far more extreme than what one is willing to accept. The more outrageous the initial proposition, the better is the prospect that what one "really" wants will be considered a compromise.[49]

Few policy makers argued explicitly for an American arms control initiative strategy, even though, as Rose showed, the actual use of initiatives as tactics was not trivial. Nevertheless, two policy makers made the case for initiatives. In the mid-1960s, Amitai Etzioni, a former advisor to President John F. Kennedy, argued that Kennedy's unilateral testing moratorium, announced on the eve of negotiations to complete a test ban treaty, was a practical model to follow.[50] Twenty years later, Herbert Scoville, a nuclear scientist and former negotiator, made a stronger case, arguing that Charles Osgood's perception of the incapacity for negotiations to seriously constrain the nuclear arms competition had become a prediction fulfilled many times over. He stated,

An effective policy of reciprocal national restraint does not necessarily lead to a formal arms control agreement. Our objective is not to have arms control agreements; it is to make nuclear war less likely. Nevertheless, reciprocal national restraint should not mean that more formal commitments should be foregone. In fact, such restraint can be seen as a valuable first step in facilitating the eventual achievement and ratification of arms control treaties. No longer will arms programs be barreling ahead while negotiators are securing all the details that must be sought in a formal treaty.[51]

Scoville suggested some specific steps as illustrations for his argument, including a ban on flight tests of missiles with multiple warheads, a halt to nuclear testing, and restraint of activities that undermine the 1972 ABM treaty.[52]

NEGOTIATIONS AND STRATEGIES

In the narrative accounts of U.S.-Soviet nuclear arms control efforts that follow, the patterns of exchanges within the negotiations provide the primary means of "testing" the prescriptions and predictions of bargaining strategies. The interest is to determine empirically whether the process of bargaining that led to success or failure supports any of the presumed strategies. Because this method of analysis relies on establishing correlations between strategies and outcomes, any claims of causality must be cautious. Nevertheless, the enterprise serves two important purposes. First, the strategies do predict patterns of behavior—follow strategy X and behavior Y will happen. The causal logic of the strategies themselves is not always strong, but each suggests a distinctive bargaining relationship. Second, few analyses of arms control efforts attempt to provide a comparative empirical account of several negotiations. This effort is much more valuable for assessing the relative strengths of negotiating strategies because it illustrates the variety of experiences with negotiations.

The narrative chapters on the negotiations of the 1980s are preceded by a historical summary of the relevant negotiations that had already taken place. These chapters are provided as background, although each necessarily offers only an abbreviated picture. However, each also reveals the background patterns of bargaining and negotiation that set the stage for the more recent efforts.

NOTES

1. This discussion follows closely on Robert O. Keohane, *After Hegemony: Cooperation and Discord in the World Political Economy* (Princeton: Princeton University Press, 1984).

2. For a recent study of the process of beginning negotiations see Janice Gross Stein, *Getting to the Table* (Baltimore: Johns Hopkins University Press, 1990).

3. Thomas Schelling, *The Strategy of Conflict* (Cambridge, MA: Harvard University Press, 1960), p. 70.

4. Thomas Schelling and Morton Halperin, *Strategy and Arms Control* (New York: Twentieth Century Fund, 1962); reprinted in 1985 by Pergamon-Brassey's, McLean, VA.

5. See Robert Jervis, "Cooperation Under the Security Dilemma," *World Politics* 30 (January 1978): 167–214.

6. See, for example, Schelling, *Strategy of Conflict*; Steven Brams, *Superpower Games* (New Haven: Yale University Press, 1985); Robert Powell, *Deterrence* (New York: Oxford University Press, 1990).

7. See Glenn Snyder and Paul Diesing, *Conflict Among Nations* (Princeton: Princeton University Press, 1977).

8. Fred Iklé, *How Nations Negotiate* (New York: Praeger, 1964), pp. 59–61.

9. B. H. Liddell Hart, *Strategy*, 2nd ed., rev. (New York: Meridian, 1991), p. 320.

10. Schelling, *Strategy of Conflict*, p. 3, n. 1.

11. Schelling, *Strategy of Conflict*, p. 5.

12. Keohane, *After Hegemony*, p. 8.

13. Robert Axelrod, *The Evolution of Cooperation* (New York: Basic Books, 1984).

14. See Otomar Bartos, "A Simple Model of Negotiation: A Sociological Point of View," in *The Negotiation Process*, ed. I. William Zartman (Beverly Hills: Sage, 1978); John G. Cross, "Negotiation as a Learning Process," in *The Negotiation Process*, ed. Zartman; Paul R. Pillar, *Negotiating Peace: War Termination as a Bargaining Process* (Princeton: Princeton University Press, 1983); Oran Young, ed., *Bargaining: Formal Theories of Negotiation* (Urbana: University of Illinois Press, 1975).

15. Bartos, "A Simple Model of Negotiation."

16. Pillar, Negotiating Peace, pp. 92–94.

17. Ibid., pp. 130–132.

18. Ibid., pp. 137–140, 224–226.

19. Absolute gains refer to the maximization of individual interest (or "utility") regardless of how well (or poorly) the other side fares. Relative gains, on the other hand, are strictly comparative between the players—short of extinction, the only thing that matters is doing better than one's opponent. Political scientists, especially traditional realists, tend to assume that relative gains, usually stated as "power," are the principal motivations for states and leaders. Both extreme positions oversimplify real behavior, and leaders tend to be motivated by shifting mixtures of both ways to value gains.

20. The game is depicted as a two-by-two matrix giving preference ordering for two players. The choices are commonly labeled as "cooperate" (C) and "defect" (D). The players' preference rankings are symmetrical. Each prefers to exploit the other's cooperation by defecting (D, C = 1). Mutual cooperation is preferred over continuing mutual defection (C, C = 2; D, D = 3). Being exploited by the other is least preferred (C, D = 4). See Axelrod, *Evolution of Cooperation*, pp. 12–13.

21. See George Downs, David Rocke, and Randolph Siverson, "Arms Races and Cooperation," *World Politics* 38 (October 1985): 118–146.

22. Seyom Brown traces the patterns of alternating grand strategies in American foreign policies: *Faces of Power: Constancy and Change in United States Foreign Policy from Truman to Reagan* (New York: Columbia University Press, 1983). See also John

Gaddis, *Strategies of Containment: A Critical Appraisal of Postwar American National Security Policy* (New York: Oxford University Press, 1982).

23. See Joseph S. Nye, Jr., "Nuclear Learning," *International Organization* 41 (Summer 1987): 378–379; Philip E. Tetlock, "Learning in U.S. and Soviet Foreign Policy: In Search of an Elusive Concept," in *Learning in U.S. and Soviet Foreign Policy*, ed. George Breslauer and Philip E. Tetlock (Boulder: Westview, 1990); and Steven Weber, "Interactive Learning in U.S.-Soviet Arms Control," in *Learning in U.S. and Soviet Foreign Policy*, ed. Breslauer and Tetlock.

24. I. William Zartman and Maureen Berman, *The Practical Negotiator* (New Haven: Yale University Press, 1983), p. 171.

25. Paul K. Huth, "Extended Deterrence and the Outbreak of War," *American Political Science Review* 82 (June 1988): pp. 435–436.

26. See Robert Jervis, "Security Regimes," *International Organization* 36 (Spring 1982): 357–378.

27. Axelrod, *Evolution of Cooperation*, p. 181.

28. Some of the important works in political science on this topic include Robert Jervis, *Perception and Misperception in International Politics* (Princeton: Princeton University Press, 1976); Robert Jervis, Richard Ned Lebow, Janice Gross Stein, eds., *Psychology and Deterrence* (Baltimore: Johns Hopkins University Press, 1985); Richard Ned Lebow, *Between Peace and War* (Baltimore: Johns Hopkins University Press, 1980); Philip E. Tetlock, Jo L. Husbands, Robert Jervis, Paul C. Stern, and Charles Tilly, eds., *Behavior, Society and Nuclear War*, vol. 2 (New York: Oxford University Press, 1991); Deborah Welch Larson, *The Origins of Containment: A Psychological Explanation* (Princeton: Princeton University Press, 1985).

29. Charles Osgood, *An Alternative to War or Surrender* (Urbana: University of Illinois Press, 1962), p. 86.

30. Charles Osgood, "GRIT for MBFR: A Proposal for Unfreezing Force-level Postures in Europe," *Peace Research Reviews* 8:2 (1979): 521.

31. Osgood, *Alternative to War or Surrender*, p. 88.

32. Ibid., p. 84; original emphasis.

33. Ibid., pp. 88–108.

34. See Jervis, *Perception and Misperception*; and Breslauer and Tetlock, eds., *Learning in U.S. and Soviet Foreign Policy*. These concepts of learning are applied to a different conflict situation in William B. Vogele, "Learning and Nonviolent Struggle in the Intifadah," *Peace and Change* 17 (July 1992): 312–340.

35. For example, Svenn Lindskold, Pamela S. Walters, and Helen Koutsouais, "Cooperators, Competitors and Response to GRIT," *Journal of Conflict Resolution* 27 (September 1983): 521–532; also George W. Downs and David M. Rocke, *Tacit Bargaining, Arms Race and Arms Control* (Ann Arbor: University of Michigan Press, 1990), pp. 49–51.

36. Deborah Welch Larson, "Crisis Prevention and the Austrian State Treaty," *International Organization* 41 (Winter 1987): 27–60. See also her "Game Theory and the Psychology of Reciprocity" (Paper presented at the 1986 Annual Meetings of the American Political Science Association, Washington, DC).

37. William Rose, *U.S. Unilateral Arms Control Initiatives: When Do They Work?* (New York: Greenwood, 1988), pp. 123–142.

38. Rose, *U.S. Unilateral Initiatives*, p. 125.

39. Kenneth Oye, "Explaining Cooperation under Anarchy: Hypotheses and Strategies," *World Politics* 38 (October 1985): 7.

40. Joanne Gowa, "Anarchy, Egoism, and Third Images: The *Evolution of Cooperation and International Relations," International Organization* 40 (Winter) 1986, p. 177.

41. I. William Zartman, "Negotiation as a Joint Decision-making Process," in his *Negotiation Process*, pp. 82–83.

42. Axelrod, *Evolution of Cooperation*, pp. 33, 61–62, 63.

43. Roman Kolkowicz, "The Soviet Union, the Elusive Adversary," in *The Soviet Calculus of Nuclear War*, ed. Roman Kolkowicz and Ellen Propper Mickiewicz (Lexington, MA: Lexington Books, 1986), p. 17.

44. See Douglas Seay, "What Are the Soviets' Objectives in Their Foreign, Military and Arms Control Policies?" in *Nuclear Arguments: Understanding the Strategic Nuclear Arms and Arms Control Debates*, ed. Lynn Eden and Steven E. Miller (Ithaca: Cornell University Press, 1989) for a comparison of alternative perspectives on Soviet behavior.

45. Raymond L. Garthoff notes that in SALT the United States tried to constrain Soviet programs while leaving American programs unimpaired, and the Soviets did the same: "Objectives and Negotiating Strategy," in *A Game for High Stakes: Lessons Learned in Negotiating with the Soviet Union*, ed. Leon Sloss and M. Scott Davis (Cambridge, MA: Ballinger, 1986), p. 75.

46. Quoted in Joseph Whelan, *Soviet Diplomacy and Negotiating Behavior* (Washington, DC: U.S. Government Printing Office, 1979), p. 503.

47. Quoted in ibid., p. 497.

48. Quoted in ibid., pp. 493–494.

49. Quoted in Bennett Ramberg, *The Seabed Arms Control Negotiations: A Study of Multilateral Arms Control Conference Diplomacy* (Beverly Hills: Sage, 1978), p. 46.

50. Amitai Etzioni, *The Hard Way to Peace* (New York: Collier, 1962); and his "The Kennedy Experiment: Unilateral Initiatives," *Western Political Quarterly* 20 (June 1967): 361–380.

51. Herbert Scoville, "Reciprocal National Restraint: An Alternative Path," *Arms Control Today* 15 (June 1985): 7.

52. Ibid., p. 8.

3

Controlling Nuclear Testing: 1954–1980

Early on in the nuclear age, policy makers and arms control negotiators recognized the critical link between nuclear weapons testing and the nascent arms race. Constraining the ability of the adversary to test new weapons was seen by both sides as a potential means to slow, if not halt, their ability to compete. For the Soviet Union, striving to catch up, a test ban would at worst freeze the military balance before it deteriorated further. At best, an agreement to end testing would allow the Soviet military to improve its position over time, perhaps through clandestine violations of the ban. For the United States, as the leader in the arms race, a test ban could potentially preserve the margin of superiority enjoyed and dampen the need to sustain an expanding nuclear weapons program.

Thus, suggestions for a ban on nuclear weapons testing were part of disarmament proposals as early as 1952, in which they were linked to general disarmament measures by both East and West.[1] Tentative proposals for a separate test ban agreement were first presented by the Soviet Union in the comprehensive disarmament negotiations in 1956.

In August 1957 American proposals for comprehensive disarmament contained a ten-month testing moratorium to precede a full test ban agreement. They also allowed that a test ban could precede a cut-off of the production of fissionable materials (one of the other measures on the table at the time). U.S. policy, however, demanded the establishment of a reliable verification and monitoring system in advance of all disarmament actions. Although Soviet negotiators generally sought a test ban agreement that did not depend on the creation of an international control system, in 1957 they agreed in principle to some kind of monitoring mechanism on Soviet territory.

In January 1958 President Dwight Eisenhower suggested a technical study of various test ban proposals, "without commitment to the ultimate acceptance" of the study's results. Shortly thereafter the Soviet Union proposed a testing mora-torium, which would begin at the end of its current series of tests. Predictably, the United States rejected the Soviet moratorium proposal because it contained no provisions for verification or enforcement.

Leaders of Great Britain and the Soviet Union, however, accepted the Amer-ican suggestion for a technical conference. Comprehensive test ban negotiations in the 1950s began in July 1958 as the Conference of Experts convened. The re-port they submitted in August was accepted by all three parties as the basis for negotiation of a verifiable test ban treaty.

The Experts Conference reported that nuclear weapons tests could be ade-quately monitored in the earth's atmosphere, undersea, and in outer space. In addition, they argued that underground explosions as small as five kilotons could be monitored with a probable accuracy of 90 percent. Verification would require establishment of 170 to 180 seismic monitoring stations ("control posts") world-wide and a limited number of on-site inspections. Soviet acceptance of the Ex-perts' report indicated both acceptance of the principle of inspection for verification and the willingness to submit to a specified monitoring system, op-erated by an independent international agency, on Soviet territory.

When Eisenhower accepted the conference report on 27 August, he pro-posed tripartite negotiations, to begin on 31 October 1958. He also pledged that the United States would suspend testing for one year from the beginning of the conference, provided that the Soviet Union reciprocated. The suspension would be renewed annually if an inspection network were established and as efforts to-ward disarmament progressed. Within two days, Soviet leaders accepted the U.S. proposal for negotiations and the Tripartite Conference on the Discontin-uance of Nuclear Weapons Tests began in November 1958.

An early deadlock on the agenda—in which the Soviet Union insisted on an immediate treaty and the United States demanded the establishment of an in-spection system—was resolved quickly in favor of the United States. But the conference remained stuck on defining the specific powers of the on-site con-trol team, which would carry out the on-site inspections, and determining the mix of the nationalities for the groups operating the 180 control posts. On both issues Soviet negotiators sought to maximize their control—to be able to veto proposed on-site inspections and to dominate the personnel of the control posts.

In January 1959 the United States formally separated a test ban treaty from comprehensive disarmament. This move was promising because it allowed the test ban discussions to proceed without the requirement of prior resolution of all the complex issues involved in a global disarmament scheme. Similarly, the po-litical elements of the test ban treaty stood a better chance of resolution if the technical aspects of the program, as reflected in the Experts' report, remained relatively uncontroversial. At the same meeting, however, the U.S. delegation also introduced new data derived from tests made in 1958 and from continuing theoretical studies. The U.S. data from underground tests suggested that a greater number of earthquakes occurred in the Soviet Union than the Experts had estimated. Distinguishing the seismic signal of an earthquake from that of a nuclear explosion, therefore, would be more difficult. The implication was that more control posts on Soviet territory would be required to provide adequate verification.

In addition, high-altitude tests in 1958 raised questions about the verification of testing in the upper atmosphere and outer space. American negotiators therefore suggested additional technical studies. Finally, investigations in U.S. weapons laboratories of techniques for cheating on a treaty produced theoretical speculation that the seismic signal of an explosion could be decoupled from the earth's bedrock by using a large underground cavity. The resulting signal reaching outside seismic control posts would be significantly lower than the explosive yield would otherwise produce. Such technical uncertainties would dog the political process of comprehensive test ban negotiations for over thirty years.

Soviet negotiators initially protested the U.S. introductions as a retreat from acceptance of the Experts' report as the basis for negotiations and rejected the U.S. data. However, they relented somewhat and consented to a technical working group to deal with the issues of verifying tests in space. The working group satisfactorily resolved these technical problems by summer 1959.

The Conference nevertheless remained at an impasse over the system to monitor underground tests. In an effort to stimulate action by the Soviets, the United States offered a short-term treaty banning only atmospheric tests. The American proposal also suggested that annual inspections could be limited to a specified quota, a departure from the original position that a treaty must preserve each party's right to inspection on demand.

American proposals initiated a series of exchanges in which the two sides spoke favorably of the other's suggestions about inspection quotas while simultaneously employing different criteria for determining the proper number. In November 1959 the Soviet Union agreed to a second technical conference to discuss the new data of the United States.

Negotiations in Geneva, however, were stalled. In February 1960 the United States presented another new proposal, calling for a ban on all tests in the atmosphere and in outer space, the environments in which inspection capabilities were not in dispute. The new American proposal also suggested a ban on all underground tests that registered above 4.75 on the Richter scale of seismic events—the equivalent of a nuclear explosion of about twenty kilotons. Finally, the United States stated it was prepared to accept a fixed number of on-site inspections, rather than an unlimited right of inspection on demand.

Soviet negotiators quickly accepted the quota element of the U.S. proposal and conceded that these should be determined by seismic criteria rather than by purely political compromise. In mid-March 1960 Soviet negotiators accepted the 4.75 threshold on the condition that the West accept a moratorium on tests below that limit. Despite initial hostility, the United States accepted the Soviet proposal, allowing that the duration of the moratorium be decided at the May 1960 Paris summit meeting of the United States, the Soviet Union, France, and

Great Britain. None of the three major parties to the negotiations had conducted any nuclear tests since the end of 1958.

Two weeks before the Paris summit an American U-2 reconnaissance plane was shot down over the Soviet Union. On 16 May, Premier Nikita Khrushchev denounced the United States and stormed out of the sessions. The Tripartite Conference continued to meet in Geneva, but negotiations were effectively stalled through the end of Eisenhower's administration.[2]

Serious negotiation on nuclear testing seemed to resume in 1961 as the United States accepted some Soviet positions remaining from the Eisenhower administration's efforts.[3] In April the Kennedy administration offered a draft treaty that included a relatively low seismic threshold, accepted some of the Soviet positions on safeguards for research tests, and reduced the number of proposed inspections. In so doing, the new administration demonstrated its interest in serious negotiations and its willingness to take a stand among the conflicting pressures of scientific judgments and military interests.[4]

Soviet negotiators rejected the new offer. The United States and Great Britain took the initiative again in August 1961 to present two draft treaties—one for a comprehensive ban and the other for a treaty excluding limits on underground testing.[5] This offer made explicit the Western willingness to consider an agreement that provided for less than comprehensive prohibitions. The Soviet response again was negative. Throughout 1961 Soviet negotiators backtracked from compromises they previously had made toward testing limitations. Their positions again demanded that a test ban treaty required neither inspection nor the elaboration of other verification measures. In addition, they declared the need for comprehensive disarmament instead of "partial measures." At the end of August the Soviet Union resumed testing with the detonation of an extremely large nuclear device, ending more than two and a half years of tacit cooperation on the testing moratorium. Between September and December 1961 the Soviet Union conducted over fifty nuclear tests, almost twice the number it had conducted in the whole year before the moratorium. The United States also resumed testing and detonated ten devices by the end of the year. Testing by Great Britain, which had numbered no more than a half dozen tests in the seven years before the moratorium, resumed in 1962.[6]

For the next year, negotiations remained in this deadlock, and the superpowers' political relationship deteriorated. Creation of the Eighteen Nation Disarmament Committee (ENDC) by the United Nations in 1961 emphasized the growing international consciousness of test ban efforts. Demands by many nonaligned states for seats at the table produced the enlarged international forum. Nevertheless, the loci of decision remained within the governments of the nuclear weapons states, which then consisted of only the United States, Great Britain, and the Soviet Union. The international arena was maintained, as the ENDC enlarged and became the Conference of the Committee on Disarmament, but the substantive negotiations took place in trilateral or bilateral subgroups. Rarely, if ever, could the larger international effort move one of the main parties to the test ban efforts until the latter was ready to move. This point was highlighted in the events of 1962 and 1963 that led to the first test ban treaty and in all subsequent negotiations.

The Cuban missile crisis in October 1962 marked a turning point in U.S.-Soviet relations in many ways. Both sides were chastened by their brush with a major war in the nuclear age. During the crisis Khrushchev indicated renewed Soviet interest in a testing agreement. Almost immediately following the crisis, the Soviet negotiator at the ENDC suggested taking advantage of the moment to make progress on the test ban talks. In December 1962, in private correspondence with Kennedy, Khrushchev reasserted Soviet interest in a testing agreement, suggesting that the resolution of the Cuban crisis demonstrated the potential ability of the superpowers to "solve the far simpler problem of the cessation of test explosions of nuclear weapons in time of peace."[7] Soviet negotiating positions dropped the linkages of a test ban to general disarmament, or to the cessation of French nuclear testing, which had begun in 1960 but was far more independent from the American efforts than was the British test program.

At the same time Soviet leaders made several concessions to U.S. positions on verification. In the ENDC, Semyon K. Tsarapkin proposed automated seismic stations to complement existing national control posts. The objection to the principle of inspection also fell away. During an interview with publisher Norman Cousins, Khrushchev repeated the Soviet position that inspection was unnecessary. But if this was the only obstacle to an agreement, Khrushchev said, then the Soviet Union would accept a few inspections annually. At the ENDC, Soviet negotiators proposed that the number be two or three. The United States previously had reduced its demands to between eight and ten inspections per year.

Between April and June 1963 the United States, the Soviet Union, and Great Britain planned for a series of top-level discussions to take place in July. In the ENDC, however, the differences on inspection issues could not be resolved. In early June, President Kennedy declared the intention of the United States to seek a test ban. He also promised a halt to U.S. testing in order to facilitate the negotiations.

On 15 July, as negotiations began in Moscow, the United States initially pressed for a comprehensive ban. But the Americans quickly abandoned this effort in the absence of Soviet concessions on the number of inspections. Khrushchev briefly attempted to link a test ban agreement to a nonaggression pact, a concern generated largely by the serious deterioration of Sino-Soviet relations. American negotiator Averill Harriman, however, refused to link the test ban to other agreements, although he allowed the implication that the two states would take up such discussions in the future.[8]

A partial ban, excluding prohibitions on tests underground, was initialed on 5 August 1963 and ratified by the U.S. Congress on 10 October. The duration of the Limited Test Ban Treaty (LTBT) was unlimited, although it permitted a party to withdraw from its provisions on three months' notice if "extraordinary events, related to the subject matter of [the] treaty, have jeopardized the supreme interests of the country." The treaty provided for no inspection system to monitor compliance but relied on national technical means of intelligence and information gathering.

Little progress occurred for a decade after the LTBT, although testing issues remained on the agenda of the UN disarmament conference, and the technical questions related to verification through seismic techniques continued to interest scientists. In 1974, on the Soviets' initiative, bilateral test ban talks resumed.[9]

In February 1974 Soviet Ambassador to the United States, Anatoly Dobrynin and Foreign Minister Andrei Gromyko proposed to Secretary of State Henry Kissinger that the superpowers agree to a comprehensive test ban (CTB) treaty at the upcoming July summit. The Soviet proposal stipulated, however, that all other nuclear powers must also accept such a ban. Although the United States rejected this Soviet overture, in March meetings with Kissinger in Moscow, Leonid Brezhnev proposed an alternative threshold treaty—prohibiting explosions above a specified level—that did not require French or Chinese approval. (These latter two states were outsiders to nuclear test ban efforts. Neither government had signed the LTBT or the Nuclear Nonproliferation Treaty of 1968. And each maintained independent security policies that reflected their political disagreements with at least one of the superpowers. Soviet leaders frequently had used the requirement for French and Chinese participation as a convenient technique to stall progress.)

Meetings on a threshold treaty between the United States and the Soviet Union began in Geneva in April 1974. Negotiators reached a tentative agreement on a 150-kiloton limit by the end of May. As they had in the past, Soviet negotiators initially called for a very low threshold, contending that discrimination between nuclear explosions and natural seismic events was possible to a fairly low level. Data from seismic evaluations in the United States tended to support this position.[10] American negotiators argued that even at very low levels too much uncertainty remained, thus increasing the possibilities for clandestine testing, but they recognized that within a wide range of possible threshold limits, the technical verification problems remained the same.[11] The delegations also agreed that monitoring by national technical means would be adequate only if supplemented by the exchange of technical data on geological formations and seismic activity at specified testing sites.

The actual threshold limit was left for negotiation at the July summit. At the summit Brezhnev and Prime Minister Alexei Kosygin at first renewed their call for a comprehensive ban. President Richard Nixon interpreted this as a determination to be tough. Nixon responded that Congress would accept only a threshold treaty, although he indicated that he saw such an agreement as "reaching the same goal [a comprehensive ban] by a different route."[12]

Nixon and Kissinger's actual negotiating was confused, however. Raymond Garthoff recounts the following process of exchanges between the two leaders, based on interviews with American participants.

The evening before the meeting Kissinger discovered that a TTB [Threshold Test Ban] briefing book or talking points did not exist. Someone recalled that a 100-kiloton limit would be a good round number and so it was agreed. The next day, after evading a head-on rejection of a CTB [Comprehensive Test Ban], Nixon proposed a 100-kiloton TTB. Before the Soviets could respond Kissinger corrected him to a 150-kiloton limit (having overnight called Washington to check and having learned that Secretary of Defense James Schlesinger insisted on not going below a 150-kiloton level). The Soviets, bemused once again by the American negotiating acrobatics, agreed on the 150-kiloton-level TTB.[13]

New negotiations were scheduled to address the problems raised by peaceful nuclear explosions (PNEs), which could not be overcome by the July summit. The Threshold Test Ban Treaty (TTBT) signed at the 1974 summit was not to become effective until 31 March 1976, the expected date for completion of negotiations on PNEs.

Negotiations for the Peaceful Nuclear Explosions Treaty (PNET) began in October 1974 and concluded in April 1976. The result was a highly detailed agreement providing constraints on nuclear explosions for peaceful purposes, under the threshold of the TTBT, and including detailed verification procedures using on-site inspections.

American policy makers reasoned that there was no difference in principle between military and civil-engineering explosions of nuclear devices. Thus without controls on PNEs, a significant loophole would remain in any treaty system. This argument was demonstrated dramatically by the Indian explosion in 1974, which the New Delhi government asserted was the test of a device for peaceful purposes.

Negotiations evolved from a process of initial exploration and probing to actual textual negotiations over the course of four sessions. The bargaining process illustrated both the convergence of the positions through mutual concessions and the application of a "fair standard" to resolve other issues. The major issues at stake were the principle of inspections and the details of inspection procedures and equipment.

In 1974 the Soviet Union was much more interested than the United States in the use of groups of nuclear explosions for large-scale excavations and therefore was reluctant to give up this ability. The United States initially argued that the individual explosions in a group could not be verified as being within the 150-kiloton limit of the TTBT. They argued, therefore, that the total yield of the group should be limited to 150 kilotons. The U.S. negotiators, however, consented to the position that if individual explosions within a group could be adequately verified, then the total yield for the group could exceed the TTBT limit.

Once U.S. negotiators consented to this principle, Soviet negotiators proposed a system of on-site inspections to monitor explosions and verify compliance. This was a major Soviet concession, marking the first time since 1963 that Soviet negotiators accepted the legitimacy of more than a very small number of

inspections for treaty verification. Warren Heckrotte, a participant in the negotiations, commented:

In describing the Soviet's negotiating tactics some have claimed that they seek agreements "in principle" that they then bend or distort to avoid dealing with the hard issues.
In fact, however, most negotiations must proceed on the basis of some agreements in
principle, either explicit or implicit, for otherwise no progress can be made. If the hard
issues can not be resolved to the satisfaction of both parties, the agreement in principle
should be rejected. Had no satisfactory verification scheme for groups of explosions
emerged [in the PNET talks], the U.S. would have returned to its initial position of banning them altogether.[14]

Subsequent bargaining over the details of the physical equipment to monitor
explosions was more detailed and difficult. Both sides changed positions in various concessions and retractions. The final agreement was based on the intro-
duction by the United States of the acknowledged fair standard of chance.

The Soviet Union wanted access to U.S. monitoring equipment. The Soviets
felt that inspection of the equipment was necessary to detect and prevent what
they termed "espionage," or the collection of data in excess of that necessary for
verification. American negotiators at first accepted the need for inspection of
the equipment but insisted on the presence of U.S. personnel to prevent tampering. Alteration of the equipment might distort data and effectively conceal a
clandestine military test or an explosion that exceeded the TTBT limit. Soviet
negotiators rejected the U.S. position.

The next Soviet proposal, however, was essentially a concession to the U.S.
position. The negotiators proposed the use of two sets of equipment, one to be
inspected before the event and the other to be used to monitor the explosions.
Both sets would be retained by the Soviet authorities after the event and then
returned to the United States. The U.S. negotiators rejected this plan and retracted their earlier acquiescence to the principle of equipment inspection. The
motivating concerns of the United States continued to be data validity, and the
negotiators felt that too much room for Soviet manipulation remained.

Nevertheless, the United States submitted another proposal embodying the
inspection principle, but introducing an element of chance into the process. Two
sets of equipment, with identical recorders, were to be used for each event. Soviet personnel could choose either recorder for inspection before the explosion.
Following the event, one of the machines would be chosen by the flip of a coin
for Soviet inspection and retention. The U.S. negotiators argued that the resulting uncertainty about which set of equipment would be inspected and then
which recorder would be retained by the United States would prevent any prohibited tampering with either set. Similarly, the retention by the United States
of data recorded on an untouched machine would ensure data validity.

Neither test ban treaty from the 1970s ever progressed beyond preliminary
hearings in the U.S. Senate in 1977. When international negotiations for a full

comprehensive test ban began later that year, American attention shifted away from the threshold treaties. President Jimmy Carter proposed tripartite negotiations for a Comprehensive Test Ban Treaty (CTBT) in March 1977 as part of a new set of arms control talks to supplement SALT II efforts. The new negotiations lasted from June 1977 through November 1980, although no progress was made after 1979.[15] Negotiating failure in the talks during the Carter administration was significant, partly because, during the first year of negotiations, the Soviet Union made significant compromises and thus appeared to move a treaty into the realm of the politically achievable. However, in a pattern that paralleled the negotiations of the late 1950s, American negotiators retreated from their own positions and ended the forward momentum.

Initially, the United States sought a treaty of unlimited duration (like the LTBT and ABM treaties), subject to periodic review conferences (like the Nuclear Nonproliferation Treaty) and open to all states. All nuclear explosions would be prohibited by the treaty, including explosions for peaceful purposes. American reassessment of the relationship between PNEs and weapons development had concluded that all nuclear explosions provided some military benefit. Therefore, the dual U.S. goals of increasing the difficulty of clandestine testing (especially by the USSR) and strengthening the nuclear nonproliferation regime were best served by a complete test ban. Finally, the United States stated that adequate verification required some form of independent, reliable on-site inspection (OSI). As in the PNET, the operational details were negotiable, but the principle was not.

The Soviet Union had offered a comprehensive treaty in the United Nations in 1976 that included "voluntary" on-site inspections. Soviet negotiators reiterated their acceptance of voluntary OSIs at the beginning of the tripartite talks in 1977. Under a voluntary inspection scheme a state could raise a challenge to an ambiguous seismic event. The challenged state would then either permit the requested inspection or provide a documentary explanation of the reasons for their refusal. "On demand" inspections, which the United States initially required, provided within agreed implementation procedures, for the right to inspect any ambiguous event.

The United States reassessed its own inspection position, however, and concluded that either voluntary or guaranteed inspections would provide an equal deterrent to cheating, since refusal to permit inspection, or the provision of inadequate explanation, would amount to refusal to accept the treaty's central provisions—virtually an admission of guilt between adversaries. The early concession by the Soviet Union to the principle of inspection removed a major obstacle that had plagued negotiations since the early 1960s. The difficult details of an effective inspection system remained, however, and these were not to be resolved by the end of negotiations in 1980.[16]

A second major issue of principle was resolved in November 1977 when Soviet leader Brezhnev announced that the Soviet Union would accept a moratorium on peaceful nuclear explosions for the duration of a comprehensive test ban treaty. To American negotiators this indicated "serious commitment on the Soviet side" to the conclusion of a treaty.[17] The Soviets also accepted the placement of so-called black boxes for remote seismic monitoring and agreed to establish an international commission to facilitate the exchange of seismic information.

In June 1978, U.S. negotiators began a retreat from their earlier positions on two important aspects of the proposed treaty.[18] First, they sought a treaty of three to five year duration, instead of unlimited length. They also sought allowance for some nuclear testing at very low yields to maintain the reliability of the weapons stockpile. Although both Soviet and British negotiators accepted these changes, the U.S. retractions jeopardized the chances for a far more comprehensive treaty, which had seemed possible as recently as March 1978.[19]

From June 1978 forward, little progress was made in the negotiations, although none of the parties retreated any further. In July 1980 the U.S. Arms Control and Disarmament Agency submitted a report to the UN Committee on Disarmament in Geneva. Drafted jointly by the U.S., Soviet, and British negotiators, the report stated without elaboration the general agreements that had been reached on verification, data exchange, and the inclusion of peaceful nuclear explosions—essentially the positions established in June 1978. The report also noted that the question of the duration of the treaty was unresolved.

CONCLUSIONS

By the beginning of the Reagan administration in 1981 three testing agreements had been made, but only the first was in effect. The treaties of the 1970s, at first overtaken by the promise of a more comprehensive agreement, were withdrawn from debate in the U.S. Congress and not resubmitted. A great deal of progress had been made on the details of a treaty, in many ways overcoming the obstacles that had plagued the original negotiations of the 1950s. How and whether that progress would continue was left to the new U.S. administration.

The history of test ban negotiations reveals that while initiative strategies were not uncommon, the success of those strategies was rare. The Soviets took major initiatives on three occasions. During the comprehensive test ban talks in 1958, Soviet negotiators initiated a unilateral testing moratorium (which subsequently was joined by the United States and Britain) and made significant concessions on the principle of inspection for verification. In the 1970s, Soviet negotiators made two similar moves to unlock the verification issues that were impeding progress. Soviet initiatives on inspection for the PNET contributed substantially to the success of those negotiations. Similarly, in the comprehensive test ban talks under the Carter administration, Soviet concessions on inspection and duration brought an agreement seemingly within reach.

The United States took several initiatives during the negotiations between 1961 and 1963. By proposing alternative testing limitations, in which the inspection issues were largely unproblematic, the United States created the conditions for the LTBT. By the same token, Kennedy's June 1963 announcement of a unilateral American test moratorium is widely credited with improving the political conditions of the LTBT endgame. Initiatives, however, were more frequently used by the Soviet side.

On the two occasions when the prospects for a comprehensive treaty brightened, the late 1950s and the late 1970s, progress in the negotiations was halted or reversed when American negotiators retracted standing offers, substantially revised their positions, or presented new and more demanding proposals. From the point of view of moving negotiations toward agreement, the U.S. use of tough strategy tactics was counterproductive. Notably, in the second instance, Soviet negotiators did not reciprocate the American behavior. Instead, they maintained the positions they had presented by 1978 on inspection and duration. Thus, if initiatives did not always succeed, they at least promoted progress, while tough strategies consistently obstructed agreement.

Finally, within those negotiations that led to agreement, the role of reciprocal behavior is clear. Both U.S. and Soviet negotiators responded in something similar to tit-for-tat in the bargaining for the LTBT, TTBT, and PNET agreements.

NOTES

1. See Bernard Bechhoefer, *Postwar Negotiations for Arms Control* (Washington, DC: Brookings Institution, 1961); John Barton and Lawrence Weiler, eds., *International Arms Control* (Stanford: Stanford University Press, 1976); Seyom Brown, *The Faces of Power: Constancy and Change in United States Foreign Policy from Truman to Reagan* (New York: Columbia University Press, 1983); Robert Divine, *Blowing on the Wind* (New York: Oxford University Press, 1978).

2. See Michael Bechloss, *MayDay: Eisenhower, Khrushchev, and the U-2 Affair* (New York: Harper and Row, 1986).

3. For discussions of these negotiations generally, see Ivo H. Daalder, "The Limited Test Ban Treaty," in *Superpower Arms Control: Setting the Record Straight*, ed. Albert Carnesale and Richard Haass (Cambridge, MA: Ballinger, 1987); P. Terrence Hopmann, "Internal and External Influences on Bargaining in Arms Control Negotiations," in *Peace, War and Numbers*, ed. Bruce Russett (Beverly Hills: Sage, 1972); Harold Jacobson and Eric Stein, *Diplomats Scientists and Politicians* (Ann Arbor: University of Michigan Press, 1966); Christer Jönsson, *Soviet Bargaining Behavior* (New York: Columbia University Press, 1979); Alan Neidle, "Nuclear Test Bans: History, Future and Prospects," in *U.S.-Soviet Security Cooperation: Achievements, Failures, Lessons,* ed. Alexander George, Philip J. Farley, and Alexander Dallin (New York: Oxford University Press, 1988); Arthur Schlesinger, *A Thousand Days: John F. Kennedy in the White House* (Boston: Houghton Mifflin, 1965); and Glenn Seaborg, *Kennedy, Khrushchev and the Test Ban* (Berkeley: University of California Press, 1981).

4. Jacobson and Stein, *Diplomats. Scientists and Politicians*, pp. 277–278.

5. Ibid., p. 381–389.

6. See Herbert F. York, "The Great Test Ban Debate," in *Arms Control: Readings from "Scientific American"* (New York: W. H. Freeman, 1980).

7. Quoted in Christer Jönsson, *Soviet Bargaining Behavior,* p. 35.

8. Seyom Brown, *Faces of Power,* pp. 250–251.

9. For accounts of these negotiations, as well as those around the Peaceful Nuclear Explosions Treaty, see Barton and Weiler, eds., *International Arms Control;* Duncan Clarke, *The Politics of Arms Control* (New York: Free Press, 1979); Raymond Garthoff, *Detente and Confrontation: American-Soviet Relations from Nixon to Reagan* (Washington, DC: Brookings Institution, 1985); Warren Heckrotte, "Negotiating with the Soviets," *Energy and Technology Review,* ed. William C. Potter, May 1983; Heckrotte, "Verification of Test Ban Treaties," in *Verification and Arms Control,* ed. William C. Potter (Lexington, MA: Lexington Books, 1985); Henry Kissinger, *Years of Upheaval* (Boston: Little, Brown, 1982); Senate Committee on Foreign Relations, *Hearings: Threshold Test Ban and Peaceful Nuclear Explosions Treaties,* 95th Cong., 1st sess., 1977.

10. For example, see Senate Committee on Foreign Relations, Subcommittee on Arms Control, International Law and Negotiations, *Hearing: Prospects for a Comprehensive Nuclear Test Ban,* 92nd Cong., 1st sess., 1971; *Hearings: Toward a Comprehensive Test Ban,* 92nd Cong., 2d sess., 1972; *Hearings: To Promote Negotiations for a Comprehensive Test Ban,* 93rd Cong., 1st sess., 1973.

11. Interview with Warren Heckrotte (December 1985), member of the 1974 delegation and policy-making staff.

12. Quoted in Garthoff, *Detente and Confrontation,* p. 427.

13. Ibid., p. 427.

14. Heckrotte, "Negotiating with the Soviets," p. 19n.

15. See Heckrotte's "Negotiating with the Soviets" and "Verification of Test Ban Treaties"; and William Kincade, "A Comprehensive Test Ban," *Bulletin of the Atomic Scientists* (November 1978). Also, House Committee on Armed Services, Subcommittee on Intelligence and Military Applications of Nuclear Energy, *Hearings: Department of Energy Authorization. National Security Programs FY 1979,* 95th Cong., 2d sess., 1978; *Hearings: Current Negotiations on the Comprehensive Test Ban,* 96th Cong., 1st sess., 1979; *Hearings: Effects of a Comprehensive Test Ban on U.S. National Security Interests,* 96th Cong., 1st sess., 1979; Subcommittee Panel on Strategic Arms Limitation Talks and Comprehensive Test Ban, *Report: Effects of a Comprehensive Test Ban on U.S. National Security,* 96th Cong., 1st sess., 1979.

16. Heckrotte, "Verification of Test Ban Treaties," p. 73.

17. Heckrotte, "Negotiating with the Soviets," p. 17.

18. See Herbert F. York, "Negotiating and the U.S. Bureaucracy," in *A Game for High Stakes: Lessons Learned in Negotiating with the Soviet Union,* ed. Leon Sloss and M. Scott Davis (Cambridge, MA: Ballinger, 1986).

19. Kincade, "Comprehensive Test Ban."

4

Negotiating Limits on Nuclear Testing: 1981–1992

At the beginning of his presidency, Ronald Reagan rejected the continuation of bilateral or multilateral negotiations to limit nuclear testing. The administration stepped back even further from accepting restrictions on the U.S. test program than had the Carter administration at the end of its tenure. Policy toward test ban negotiations under Carter operated under the assumption that some security benefits for the United States could be derived from a treaty. The two treaties of the mid-1970s—the Threshold Test Ban Treaty and the Peaceful Nuclear Explosions Treaty—although set aside and overshadowed by negotiations for a comprehensive agreement, were not rejected by Carter.

Policy in the Reagan administration, however, not only rejected the TTBT and the PNET agreements but questioned the strategic wisdom of limiting nuclear testing at all. In June 1981, during a speech to the cadets at West Point, Reagan pledged to restore American military strength through a military buildup and to oppose any arms control measures that would impede that policy. Eugene Rostow, the new director of the U.S. Arms Control and Disarmament Agency, stated at the United Nations in October that the United States was committed to a comprehensive test ban as a "long-term goal" but claimed that the international situation at the time was "not propitious." Almost a year later, in July 1982, President Reagan formally withdrew the United States from the standing tripartite negotiations on nuclear testing. Through the end of the Bush administration in 1993, U.S. policy maintained the position that a comprehensive cessation of nuclear testing was counter to American security interests.

Unlike negotiations to limit and reduce offensive strategic arms and intermediate-range nuclear forces, test ban talks did not move from impasse to dramatic agreement. Additional protocols specifying new verification procedures for the

TTBT and PNET were signed in June 1990 after two years of bilateral negotiations, and the aging treaties were ratified by the U.S. Senate and the Supreme Soviet in September and October, respectively. In many ways the testing protocols elaborated and strengthened verification measures already achieved, but they did not break new ground. In fact, even after the existing treaties were ratified, American policy sought a substantial delay before resuming negotiations for a comprehensive agreement so as to provide for "experience" with the new techniques.

By the end of the Reagan-Bush era, as new offensive arms agreements specified the elimination of MIRVed intercontinental ballistic missiles and unprecedented cuts in warheads, efforts to reach a comprehensive test ban languished. In an equally stark contrast to the offensive arms negotiations, the series of dramatic unilateral gestures and concessions made by the Soviet Union under Gorbachev failed to transform the bargaining process.

REVISING THE CARTER POLICIES

Negotiations on testing did not resume until August 1986, when the United States and the Soviet Union entered bilateral discussions to draft new verification protocols for the TTBT and PNET and to work toward a comprehensive agreement. For nearly six years following Reagan's inauguration, the test ban dialogue between the United States and the Soviet Union took place largely at the level of public pronouncements and gestures. Formal bargaining, in which alternative positions on an issue are exchanged, did not exist. Rejecting arms control as a legitimate element of national security policy was one way in which the new administration dramatically revised the inherited policies of the Carter presidency.

During 1981, the new American administration committed itself to a buildup of both nuclear and conventional armed forces to redress what it saw as the new Soviet superiority. Reagan and his advisors on military and arms control issues were convinced that only a muscular military position of the United States could hold off what they saw as relentless attacks by the Soviet Union and its allies. The motto of the new cold warriors was Peace Through Strength. As Reagan said in his 1981 address at West Point, arms control was no substitute for military strength. Limiting or banning nuclear weapons testing was inconsistent with the peace through strength approach and the military buildup it implied.

Similarly, many of the weapons in the new buildup required testing. In particular, the administration promoted deployment of the MX ICBM (named the Peacekeeper by President Reagan) and the D-5 submarine-launched ballistic missile for the new Trident ballistic missile submarines. Both of these weapons systems involved launchers designed to carry far more warheads than existing missiles and to deliver them with greater accuracy. Consequently, both systems required newly designed warheads and components, for which testing was essential.

Equally important was the strong presidential support for new space-based strategic defenses that emerged in mid-1983. Although by the end of the decade research on components for the Strategic Defense Initiative (SDI) emphasized nonnuclear weapons, some of the first elements to be proposed (such as the X-ray pumped laser) relied on nuclear explosions. Their development, therefore, depended on a continuing testing program.

Nor were nuclear test limitations high on the agenda of the Soviet leadership. Brezhnev maintained the Soviet position favoring arms control negotiations generally and testing limits in particular. Soviet positions did not retreat from the commitments made in the Carter CTBT rounds. But neither were any new positions offered; nor was the matter of testing pushed very strongly in bilateral or multilateral forums.

THE GORBACHEV INITIATIVES

Leonid Brezhnev's death in 1982 began a three-year process of political transition and uncertainty that brought many new Soviet leaders into power. Testing limits were not a first priority for the Soviet government, either internally or internationally. Shifting factions and the collective process of choice for a new leader brought Yuri Andropov to the position of general secretary of the Communist party. Andropov was the former head of the KGB and not a noted reformer. His immediate external situation involved the apparent determination by the United States and NATO to deploy new intermediate-range missiles in Europe. The end of 1983 became a crucial time as the two tracks of arms control negotiations and missile deployments converged. At the end of the year, NATO deployed its new missiles, and the Soviet Union refused to set dates for the resumption of any arms control talks.[1]

Andropov was succeeded on his death in February 1984 by Konstantin Chernenko, a member of the Politburo closer to Brezhnev's philosophical legacy. During 1984, U.S.-Soviet negotiations on test limitations were at a virtual standstill, along with talks on all other issues. Chernenko's period in power, however, lasted only a year. Following his death in March 1985, the Politburo elevated Mikhail Gorbachev, its youngest member, to the post of general secretary. Gorbachev's selection was significant as a generational change from the leadership that had been formed in the Second World War and the last years of Stalin's rule. Gorbachev's policy inclinations also appeared to lie more with the reformist character of Khrushchev's policies than with the subsequent Brezhnev doctrines. Perhaps most importantly, Gorbachev was keenly aware of the economic decline of the final Brezhnev years and of the increasing isolation of the Soviet Union in the face of revived anticommunism in the U.S. and parts of Western Europe.

Using the arena of nuclear testing limits, Gorbachev quickly began what became a series of dramatic gestures and initiatives. In mid-April, Soviet Ambassador to the United States Anatoly Dobrynin, joined former Presidents Jimmy

Carter and Gerald Ford in declaring the need for a comprehensive test ban.[2] On 18 April 1985, Gorbachev announced a unilateral moratorium on nuclear testing which the Soviet Union would begin on 6 August and maintain at least through the end of the year. He called on the United States to follow the Soviet example.[3] The initiative did not require reciprocity on the part of the other nuclear powers, although Gorbachev stated that the Soviet decision on continuing the self-imposed restrictions was contingent upon cooperation by the other states.

The American response immediately dismissed Gorbachev's action, reiterating the U.S. position on the need for testing and questioning Soviet compliance with existing arms control treaties, especially the unratified TTBT and PNET agreements. At the end of July, the United States and the Soviet Union staked out these positions at the UN Conference on Disarmament talks in Geneva. Reagan invited Soviet scientists to observe a test at the Nevada test range, as part of the American effort to demonstrate the virtues of on-site inspections and direct measurements. Soviet leaders rejected the American invitation.[4]

Nor did any other state possessing nuclear weapons follow the Soviet lead. Between August 1985 and January 1986, for example, the United States conducted at least three nuclear tests. Overall, the United States conducted seventeen nuclear tests during 1985, compared to the nine tests undertaken by the Soviet Union before 6 August. Of the other nuclear weapons states, Great Britain conducted a single test, France held eight, and China did not test a nuclear device.[5]

In November 1985, Reagan and Gorbachev met in Geneva for the first superpower summit of the decade. Gorbachev hinted at a change toward accommodating U.S. verification concerns in his closing statements: "If the U.S. authorities call a halt to any nuclear testing, and if we can arrive at agreement on that, there will be absolutely no problems on our side with regard to verification."[6]

Gorbachev's statement, however, was still quite ambiguous and could be interpreted as consistent with existing Soviet positions. In one sense, previous Soviet governments had already committed themselves to various forms of intrusive inspection techniques, both in the protocols of the TTBT and PNET ban agreements and in the positions they took during the Carter test ban talks. Gorbachev had renounced neither of these prior commitments. In a broader sense, the traditional Soviet argument was that independent national seismic monitoring provided satisfactory verification. Thus, Gorbachev could be seen as saying simply, "Join us in a moratorium and you will see that national technical means and the provisions of the existing treaties are sufficient." In a letter to President Reagan on 5 December, Gorbachev reiterated the standing Soviet position to accept on-site inspections as part of any comprehensive testing treaty that would be signed, although he linked the treaty and the inspections to U.S. participation in a testing moratorium. On this basis, Reagan rejected the offer. At the end of the year, however, U.S. officials indicated a willingness to return to testing negotiations, but they suggested that the American position would not likely please the Soviets.[7]

On 15 January 1986, in a major speech outlining a dramatic plan for general disarmament by the year 2000, Gorbachev extended the Soviet moratorium until 31 March, despite the absence of American reciprocation. Once again he called upon others to begin similar restrictions, but the only element of contingency was the decision on whether the moratorium would again be extended. He suggested again that on-site inspections could supplement national technical means for verification. Six leaders of nonaligned countries called for both sides to halt nuclear tests, at least until the next U.S.-Soviet summit.[8] On 13 March Gorbachev used their request as an opportunity to extend the moratorium for the second time. He said, "In response to your appeal we state that the Soviet Union will not conduct nuclear explosions after March 31, until the United States carries out its first nuclear explosion."[9] The call for reciprocity remained, but now the initiative contained a specific contingent threat that had been absent, or only implicit, before.

Following the Soviet announcement, the United States called for bilateral talks on improving the verification measures for the TTBT and PNET agreements. The United States reiterated its invitation to Soviet scientists to observe an American test and provided technical information on its preferred monitoring technique, known as CORRTEX. The Soviet Union rejected the invitation as "propaganda." Less than a week later President Reagan stated that the Soviet Union was beginning preparations to resume nuclear testing.[10] Furthermore, Marshall Sergei Akhromeyev confirmed Soviet plans to renew testing. On 22 March and on 10 April, the United States conducted nuclear tests, despite domestic protests and international appeals.[11] Citing the failure of the United States to reciprocate its initiative and the erosion of its own security, Moscow declared an end to its moratorium on 11 April.[12]

Soviet testing did not resume in 1986, however. On 26 April, one of the reactors in the power plant at Chernobyl, near Kiev in the Soviet Republic of the Ukraine, experienced a catastrophic accident in which the reactor core melted down. Some opponents of the test ban pointed to this as evidence that the American concern with nuclear safety and reliability (for which they asserted testing was required) was prudent and a contrast to Soviet attitudes.[13] Gorbachev, however, used the opportunity of the disaster to begin demonstrating new policies of *glasnost* (openness). Rather than hide the disaster, Gorbachev admitted the extent of the accident and pledged cooperation with the countries of Western Europe that might be affected by airborne radiation. In a speech about Chernobyl, on 14 May, he also renewed the Soviet test moratorium until 6 August 1986. On 18 August, Moscow extended the moratorium for the final time, until the beginning of the new year.

By mid-December, Soviet statements about the continuation of their moratorium became more clearly couched as reciprocal threats. On 18 December 1986, Moscow stated that nuclear testing would resume following the first U.S.

nuclear test of 1987. The door to a continued halt remained open in an offer to
refrain from testing if the United States did likewise, but the tone of Soviet
statements indicated that they had little hope for this course of events. The nine-
teen-month moratorium finally ended on 23 February, a week after the second
American test of the year.

The continuing series of renewals of the Soviet moratorium had varying effects. Liberal members of Congress, who had favored speedy ratification of the
TTBT and PNET agreements, as well as expeditious movement toward a CTBT,
increased their pressure on the administration to resume test ban negotiations
and to submit the existing agreements for ratification as they stood. In response
to administration statements that the treaties were unverifiable and to charges
of Soviet noncompliance with the TTBT (among other treaties), liberal politicians and interest groups (such as the Federation of American Scientists and the
Arms Control Association) pointed to the Soviet moratorium as evidence of the
validity of national technical means for verification. During a hearing of the Senate Foreign Relations Committee in January 1987, for example, Senator John
Kerry pressed administration officials to concede that throughout the continuing unilateral moratorium, neither the United States nor any other country had
charged that the Soviets had conducted a nuclear test. H. Allen Holmes, assistant secretary of state for politico-military affairs, stated that no such charges
had been made. Robert B. Barker, assistant to the secretary of defense, however,
equivocated, stating that "under the current circumstances it is certainly possible for the Soviets to have tested without our detection because no verification
mechanism is in place to verify a comprehensive test ban."[14] American public
opinion at the time appeared to be on the side of test ban advocates. In June
1986 the *Los Angeles Times* reported on a Gallup poll with a majority favoring a
ban on U.S. tests if the Soviet moratorium continued.[15]

Executive officers in the Reagan administration and conservative politicians
were much less sanguine about the presumed virtues of either the Soviet moratorium or the unratified treaties. They deviated very little from Eugene Rostow's
1981 comment that the time was not "propitious." In May 1986 hearings before
the Senate Armed Services Committee, for example, Kenneth Adelman, director of the U.S. Arms Control and Disarmament Agency argued:

The Comprehensive Test Ban is not in our national interests right now under the conditions prevailing in the world today. This is simply because nuclear testing is required for
the reliability and safety of nuclear weapons on which our security and our deterrent posture ultimately depends. . . . [W]e have found that there are likely Soviet violations over
the years [of the Threshold Test Ban Treaty and the Peaceful Nuclear Explosions
Treaty].[16]

At the same hearing Adelman and Assistant Secretary of Defense Richard Perle affirmed that the administration opposed reopening negotiations on a comprehensive test ban treaty, even if it was satisfied that such a treaty would be verifiable.[17]

Soviet initiatives certainly had a degree of public relations or propaganda value. Within the attentive developing world, in states such as India, Egypt, and Mexico, where support for a comprehensive test ban traditionally had been high, the Soviet image was polished.

In addition, as the moratorium continued, its impact on Soviet planning and weapons development became more significant. Between 1975 and 1985 the United States averaged a dozen nuclear tests per year, and the Soviet Union conducted about twenty tests annually.[18] Between August 1985 and the end of 1986 the United States conducted about two dozen nuclear tests,[19] and some experts predicted a significant increase in the number of tests needed to develop new weapons.[20] Even opponents of testing moratoria in the United States did not claim that the Soviet Union's tests of the previous year were of no military value or that they accomplished so much that a sustained pause was already planned or that such self-restraint would not have military costs.[21] Thus, in the arena of nuclear testing the Soviet Union made a public commitment to a course that would significantly affect future weapons developments.

EVOLVING VERIFICATION AGREEMENTS

Beginning in 1986, each side increasingly argued for its preferred means of verification. The U.S. government asserted that only direct measurement of nuclear tests could provide sufficient confidence in compliance with any treaty's provisions. Soviet officials maintained that seismic measurements and other national technical means of verification (such as satellite observation) were adequate. Two developments began to bring the sides together.

Gorbachev hinted at a change in the Soviet position in his 5 December letter to President Reagan, in which he suggested that inspections might be acceptable. Soviet officials, however, continued to resist American verification demands without broader commitments and rejected specific American offers to exchange expert observations of tests. In May 1986, as the Soviet test moratorium continued, the Soviet Academy of Science entered an agreement with the private American environmental group, the Natural Resources Defense Council (NRDC) to establish seismic monitoring stations near each other's test sites. The move seemed designed to have great propaganda value at relatively little cost to the Soviets—no Soviet tests were going to occur so long as the moratorium continued, and the Soviets retained ultimate control over the NRDC installation. Politically, the Soviets could also accomplish a "visit" to the Nevada testing range without having to accept the invitation of the U.S. government. In addition, the agreement with the NRDC could be portrayed as another element of the emerging policies of glasnost and the redirection of Soviet security policies.

By the end of the year private American scientists had visited the Soviet Union and members of the Soviet Academy had come to the United States. Together they identified sites in Kazakhstan, Nevada, and California in which to install monitoring equipment. In July, American scientists installed their sensing devices near the Soviet test site in Kazakhstan. A year later, in the fall of 1987, American scientists established a monitoring site for Soviet data collection in Nevada.[22]

Perhaps goaded by the private diplomacy of the NRDC, the U.S. government ended its boycott of negotiations. On 16 July 1986 Soviet Foreign Minister Eduard Shevardnadze announced that the United States had agreed to resume talks.[23] In one sense, the American move was a concession to the Soviet position, stated repeatedly since 1981, calling for the resumption of talks. But the announcement also signaled a concession by Moscow. Soviet leaders agreed that the substance of the talks would be improvements in the verification methods for the existing TTBT and PNET agreements. Standing Soviet policy had been that the treaties were adequately verifiable in their original form, and negotiations should focus on a new comprehensive agreement. Any other measures were denounced as American attempts to "legalize," rather than halt, nuclear testing.[24] Thus, the Kremlin acquiesced to the American agenda for the negotiations. Furthermore, the Soviet side called on the United States to join the moratorium but did not make this a requirement for the talks.

At the end of July, bilateral negotiations resumed in Geneva. At the end of August, in another effort to win the United States over to the moratorium, Soviet negotiators offered to permit inspection of their test sites.[25] The United States continued to reject the unilateral ban, however. Nevertheless, in September, the Soviet government took foreign journalists on a tour of the Soviet test site in Kazakhstan, in a surprising example of the emerging military glasnost.[26]

The resumption of talks did not produce much progress. At the end of August, Oleg M. Sokolov, an official at the Soviet Embassy in Washington, echoed the public policy of his government, stating that the Soviet Union had no interest in improving verification because that might suggest that "it was all right to continue testing." American officials privately suggested, however, that within the negotiations the Soviets had inquired about the details of American verification proposals in a way that suggested serious interest.[27] In September, the United States offered a new set of proposals that included a stated willingness to seek further partial limits on testing. Future limits, however, were conditioned upon Soviet agreement to new verification measures for the existing treaties and the agreement by both governments to a program of offensive force reductions.[28] Testing limits, in other words, were dependent on success in the START negotiations. In October an American official described the two sides as "miles apart."[29]

At the same time, however, President Reagan was under pressure from members of Congress. In an effort to defuse criticism in advance of his summit in Reykjavik, Iceland, with President Gorbachev the following month, Reagan sent a letter to the Senate Foreign Relations Committee stating his commitment to seek the Senate's advice and consent to the existing testing agreements. Reagan stated in his letter, "I will make ratification of these treaties [the Threshold Test Ban Treaty and the Peaceful Nuclear Explosions Treaty] a first order of business for the Congress, with an appropriate reservation to the treaties that would ensure they would not take effect until they are effectively verifiable. I will work with the Senate in drafting this reservation."[30] Administration officials argued that congressional support for the treaties with the president's reservation was a proper legal procedure. Furthermore, it was argued that legislative support would benefit ongoing negotiating efforts to create new verification measures.[31] In the end, these arguments did not hold up in the Senate. Democratic critics of the administration's arms control policies refused to go along with the president's request. Senator Paul Sarbanes, for example, accused the administration of engaging the Senate in a "meaningless exercise."

[Y]ou are coming up here and urging us to ratify these treaties, as I understand it, but attaching a condition to them that in effect makes their ratification meaningless, since they would only become applicable if we subsequently ratify another agreement relating to verification. There will be nothing of substance that will take effect until the subsequent agreement on which you are conditioning this is in effect reached, advised and consented to, and finally ratified by the President.[32]

For Sarbanes, and others protective of the institutional rights and roles of the Senate, ratification was not ratification until the agreements under question were final. Anything else was simply an exercise in politics, lending support for the administration's bargaining positions. The Senate was not going to give up its right in advance to approve (or disapprove) of final treaty documents.

In March 1987, Soviet negotiators signaled another shift toward the American position. Andronik M. Petrosyants, chief of the Soviet delegation at the testing talks in Geneva, expressed Moscow's willingness to put off the issue of a total ban on tests. He suggested that the sides should concentrate on ratifying the existing treaties and seek to create additional partial limits on the number and size of tests.[33] Three days later, Reagan rejected this proposal, saying that no talks on further limitations were possible until the Soviet Union agreed to new verification measures.[34] Soviet negotiators persisted, however, and modified their position again in June. Petrosyants stated that American experts could be allowed to make direct measurements of some Soviet tests if the United States agreed to start negotiations for further limitations.[35] Also in June, at the UN Conference on Disarmament in Geneva, the Soviet Union proposed an international organization for monitoring a test ban and suggested that test sites could be open for mandatory inspections.[36]

In mid-September the United States agreed to this formulation, and the two sides pledged to begin "stage-by-stage" negotiations before December to address drafting verification protocols, pursuing additional partial limitations, and determining the path to a comprehensive ban. Although formal discussion among nuclear testing experts had occurred since mid-1986, the new talks would be the first bilateral political negotiations on testing treaties since 1980. Negotiations began in November and quickly focused on drafting new protocols, however, as the United States had proposed consistently. On 20 November Robert Barker, chief U.S. testing negotiator, announced agreement to conduct joint observations of explosions at each other's test sites (which would become known formally as the Joint Verification Experiments, or JVE). The purpose of the experiments was to demonstrate and test the monitoring techniques of each side, in order to facilitate completion of new verification protocols. Barker stated that the parties plan to "proceed to negotiating further intermediate limitations on nuclear testing, leading to the ultimate objective of the complete cessation of nuclear testing as part of an effective disarmament process."[37] This agreement was affirmed at the December summit meeting in Washington.

In terms of the bargaining process, the Soviet Union had accepted the U.S. positions on the need to directly monitor explosions for the purposes of verification, as well as Washington's procedural suggestion to develop the monitoring systems through a process of direct experience. Attention and energy given to the JVE would overshadow the other issues on the test ban negotiating table.

Between January and August 1988, scientists and negotiators from each side visited the nuclear test sites of the other, in preparation for the joint experiments. Troy Wade, acting assistant secretary for defense programs at the Department of Energy, contrasted the Soviet and American agendas in the experiments in an interview in May:

The purpose of the JVEs, from the U.S. perspective, is to demonstrate to the Soviets our method for verification of the yield of Soviet tests. . . . The Soviet wish to come with an acceptable means of verifying a TTBT, such that they can move on, they believe, into talks on further testing limitations. So we're moving in a much slower, deliberate way than they are.[38]

In August 1988, American and Soviet scientists conducted the first test under the JVE in Nevada. Americans witnessed a Soviet test in Semipalatinsk in September.[39]

The JVE process was an important departure from the cold war legacy of secrecy, although it was a departure in keeping with the new willingness of both sides to accept verification schemes that were both intrusive and required cooperation, which the 1987 Intermediate-Range Nuclear Forces Treaty (INF) represented. Technically, however, the results of the experiments did not move the negotiators closer together. Press reports immediately after both the American and Soviet test experiments suggested that seismic measurements produced more accurate estimates of the explosions' yields than did CORRTEX. The first reports even suggested that by CORRTEX, the American test exceeded the 150-kiloton threshold, although seismic estimates put the yield at about 145 kilotons.[40] Although scientists, both within and outside the U.S. government, agreed that generalizations about overall accuracy of the methods could not be drawn from only two tests, at best, the results of the experiments suggested that neither method had a substantial technical advantage.

As a result of the inconclusive experiments, negotiators had difficulty making progress. A White House official was quoted as saying, "The experiments essentially convinced each side that their own approach is best. We seem to be stuck."[41] Soviet negotiators accepted the American position that new verification protocols should include some form of on-site measurement. However, they resisted the American demand for direct observation of all tests over fifty kilotons, arguing instead that only a limited number was necessary and thus creating an impasse on the issues of how many and how often the observations should be. Furthermore, they insisted that CORRTEX could not be the only permissible measurement method. Seismic observations, long the preferred Soviet approach to monitoring, had done well in the JVE. Soviet negotiators insisted that the option for their use be included in the new agreements.

In a sense, the United States had achieved several of its long-standing objectives. Verification problems with the existing treaties were the main issues addressed in the negotiations. On-site monitoring was accepted in principle as a necessary element of new verification measures. And Soviet officials had accepted the invitation to witness U.S. nuclear tests, thus further enabling the United States to set the test ban agenda. Still, progress on the issues was not easy. The third round of talks ended on 15 December 1988, and the fourth round did not begin until 26 June 1989. By the time the fourth round adjourned, on 7 August, negotiators had made only modest gains. The Soviet Union formally accepted the use of intrusive measurements (like CORRTEX), conditioned upon American acceptance that other methods be included in a list of acceptable techniques. In addition, negotiators had not resolved the problem of deciding how large an expected explosion had to be to engage the right to use direct observations.[42]

The Soviet proposal at the end of the test negotiations in August caused a split within the Bush administration. Secretary of State James Baker and Foreign Minister Eduard Shevardnadze met in Jackson Hole, Wyoming, in September to plan a summit meeting for later in the year. Their discussions resolved several arms control issues, including some of the outstanding testing problems. Baker and Shevardnadze announced that all tests above an expected yield of thirty-five kilotons would be subject to on-site inspections. For tests above fifty kilotons, the monitoring party could choose between direct hydrodynamic and seismic measurements. Finally, each side would be allowed up to two hydrodynamic measurements annually during the first five years of the treaties, and one annually thereafter, even if no tests above fifty kilotons were planned.[43]

Resolution of the matter of measurement technique in favor of the Soviet position required overcoming opposition within U.S. government from the military. Some Defense officials resisted permitting seismic methods, because this would undermine their general opposition to further test limits, including a comprehensive test ban.[44] As C. Paul Robinson noted in 1990, after the new protocols were signed, use of CORRTEX requires an invitation by the testing party. Under a comprehensive test ban agreement, the side intending to violate the treaty would not be likely to invite an inspection of a test it was not allowed to conduct. "And so you are clearly going to need seismic [monitoring] because it is the only thing that, without being invited, you can always use to monitor 365 days a year, 24 hours a day."[45]

Nevertheless, even with these resolutions of problems at both the international and domestic levels, the prospects for an accord beyond the new protocols for the existing treaties was unclear. On 29 September, President Reagan told Congress that the United States might need to expand its testing program, even if offensive arms reductions were agreed. He also was skeptical of the prospects and value of negotiating future testing limits.[46]

STUCK AT THE BEGINNING

By the end of 1989, negotiations had settled into the process of defining new verification protocols. The series of experiments under the JVE had at least demonstrated the technology of hydrodynamic measurements, even if they had failed to resolve the technical debates on relative accuracy and virtues. Politically, Soviet negotiators acquiesced to the American desire to use CORRTEX in new verification protocols. The Americans had accepted the use of seismic measurements, satisfying Soviet desires for "technological equity." And agreement was reached at the ministerial level on the size and frequency of tests subject to inspections. It seemed that new protocols would emerge in the fairly near future. The presumption among arms control advocates in the United States may have been that negotiations for future limits would then proceed. This had been a staple element of Soviet policy since mid-1987 and was embodied in the agreement to begin negotiations in late 1987.

In the first part of 1990, however, negotiations on the details of new verification protocols moved forward, but the politics of the enterprise became more uncertain. The U.S. administration lost whatever enthusiasm it had for more extensive testing limitations, even while the achievement of two years of negotiations and nine years of policy pronouncements was within reach. For the Soviet government, glasnost and *perestroika* (restructuring) were reconstructing the nature of power and legitimacy within the alliance and within the Soviet Union.

Early in January President Bush approved a policy statement on nuclear testing to the effect that the administration would not pursue any limitations beyond the implementation of protocols for the TTBT and PNET. Furthermore, the administration backed away from President Reagan's 1986 pledge to Congress to undertake negotiations for a comprehensive agreement once the verification issues of the existing treaties were resolved.[47] The policy statement, echoing Eugene Rostow of 1981 and Kenneth Adelman of 1986, was that a CTBT remained a "long-term goal" of the United States, but that so long as American security relied on nuclear deterrence, some level of testing would be necessary. The American position remained somewhat confused. At ministerial meetings in Moscow in February, Baker and Shevardnadze summarized progress on testing issues in a joint statement:

The sides agreed on the right to simultaneous use of hydrodynamic and in-country seismic sensing yield measurements. The sides also resolved several long-standing problems regarding the implementation of the hydrodynamic yield measurement method. The sides identified the three seismic sites in each country to be used for in-country seismic yield measurements. The sides reaffirmed their adherence to the agreement reached in September 1987 with regard to the negotiations on nuclear testing.[48]

In February, Secretary of Energy James Watkins argued that it would take another decade to determine whether the U.S. national security could withstand additional limitations on nuclear testing.[49] Interviewed in June 1990, however, Ambassador Robinson stated flatly, "I am not aware that DOE ever made such a statement. That is certainly not the administration's position."[50]

Nevertheless, new limitations on testing, in the American view, remained linked to the larger process of offensive force reductions. Ronald F. Lehman, Director of ACDA, testified to the Senate Armed Services Committee in September that "so long as the U.S. must rely upon nuclear weapons for deterrence, we must also have a sensible test program."[51] Senator Timothy Wirth argued that the practical meaning of this policy was that the only way to get a comprehensive testing treaty was to first get rid of all nuclear weapons.[52]

The Soviet government faced greater uncertainties than the criticism of a few senators. Unilateral Soviet troop reductions announced in 1989 had undermined the military coherence of the Warsaw Treaty Organization. Communist governments in Eastern Europe increasingly faced disaffection and various crises of legitimacy as their populations expressed dissent through both exit and voice. Nowhere was the problem so acute as in the German Democratic Republic. First, thousands of German citizens began to emigrate by means of travel to Hungary, which provided proximity to Austria. In a break with alliance discipline, Hungary finally decided it could not cope with the mounting East German population and allowed them to cross to Austria. The first waves of inter-German movement had begun and would rapidly have profound consequences. In November 1989 the Berlin Wall collapsed, figuratively, and was dismantled physically. This opened the gates on political reform that had been tightly locked through the combined coercion of the East German and Soviet military states. By the end of 1990 East Germany dissolved in what amounted to an *anschlüss* with West Germany.

Regional and national discontent also appeared in the Soviet Union, itself a multinational empire. Responding to the new policies of glasnost and the new voices of a critical and independent media, people of various regions and interests engaged more openly in collective action and protest. In February 1989, for example, an antitesting movement grew in Kazakhstan, near the Semipalatinsk test site. By April 1989 the protests had forced Communist party leaders to reassess the continued use of the country's main testing grounds.[53] By March 1990, in a move apparently responding to popular pressure, the Ministry of Defense recommended to the Supreme Soviet that nuclear tests at Semipalatinsk be discontinued within three years and that a smaller test program operate at the Arctic site of Novaya Zemlya.[54] As the Soviet crisis of legitimacy deepened through 1990 and 1991, Soviet officials found themselves suspending their nuclear test program, not because of bargaining or security policy decisions, but in response to continuing protests and the increasingly independent actions of the governments of the various republics.[55]

The New Verification Protocols

In Washington on 1 June 1990, Presidents Bush and Gorbachev finally signed the new verification protocols for the TTBT and PNET agreements. The new documents established several important provisions specifying new rights and obligations in more detail than the existing provisions of the treaties. Because the Threshold Treaty had the less developed verification measures of the two, it received the greater attention. All tests above thirty-five kilotons of expected yield would be subject to on-site inspections. Each side would be permitted three seismic monitoring stations within the territory of the other party for information obtained on all tests above fifty kilotons. Finally, each side had the right to use hydrodynamic yield measurement techniques or seismic measurements.[56]

CONCLUSIONS

Of all the nuclear arms control issues in the 1980s, nuclear testing was the most dramatic example of a deliberate and sustained strategy of unilateral initiatives. Yet, by the end of the Bush administration, negotiations to limit nuclear testing showed very modest progress. The Gorbachev initiative strategy did not have much to show for itself within the issue area. The outcomes of the bargaining process tended to reward the hard-line strategy maintained by the Reagan and Bush administrations.

In many ways the Gorbachev initiatives followed closely Osgood's prescriptions for GRIT. The test moratorium was clearly announced well in advance. The stated objectives of the initiatives were clear, as were the calls for reciprocation. The stated actions were carried out as planned and, often in the face of opposition, extended.

Furthermore, the moratorium imposed identifiable costs on the Soviet military. In August 1985, as the moratorium was beginning, Gorbachev denied that the Soviet Union had accelerated its testing program and proclaimed the moratorium simply because the test series had ended. Instead, he asserted, Moscow had decided to interrupt an ongoing series of tests. "It was not an easy matter at all to take such a step," he said.[57] A year later military chief of staff, Marshall

Sergei F. Akhromeyev asserted, "We had to accept a certain damage to us [in undertaking the moratorium], although for the time being we consider the damage acceptable."[58] Whatever the particular veracity of these claims, even skeptical observers of Soviet behavior did not suggest that the eighteen-month halt in testing had no effect on Soviet military programs.

The long Soviet initiative, however, had little effect on American negotiating positions. American leaders consistently rejected Soviet calls to join the moratorium. They frequently derided it as mere propaganda and frivolous positions. On several occasions U.S. officials suggested that the moratorium was little more than a massive ruse, given their view that the Soviet Union was fundamentally untrustworthy.

Initiatives failed to transform this bargaining situation. Arguably, one purpose of the initiatives was to induce in Americans a degree of "complex learning." In other words, to achieve the Soviet goals of reaching a comprehensive nuclear test ban, U.S. policy makers had to be persuaded that this was both practical (that it could be verified) and, more importantly, that the Soviet Union could be trusted to comply with the treaty. Substantial and costly unilateral initiatives could challenge long-standing images of the Soviet Union, force adjustments in the underlying cognitive conceptions of the Soviet-American relationship, and promote an environment more conducive to cooperation.

But it is not clear that any of these changes in American perception took place among the key executive personnel of either the Reagan or Bush administrations. Instead, the pattern of negotiating exchanges on the test ban issues revealed continuing American resistance to change and an unwillingness to reciprocate Soviet behavior. Twice, when faced with specific threats that the moratorium would end, the United States tested a nuclear device. After ending its moratorium and resuming testing, the Soviet Union could only resume negotiations by giving in to the American positions. First, the leaders conceded on the principle of addressing verification concerns, but in the context of negotiations for further limits. Later Moscow simply accepted the American agenda to fix the verification problems with the existing treaties, with no promises for anything else. In the end, the new protocols were signed at a time when the explicit American position was to wait, rather than proceed with ongoing negotiations.

The continuing reluctance of American policy makers to abandon their commitment to nuclear testing was illustrated again in 1992. In January, Boris Yeltsin, Russia's first postcommunist president, declared a moratorium on nuclear testing. In April, in a reversal of long-standing French policy, Prime Minister Pierre Beregovoy announced that his government would discontinue testing for the remainder of the year.[59] However, the United States neither joined the moratorium nor supported calls for a formal treaty. American Secretary of Defense Dick Cheney, for example, restated the position that a test ban would adversely affect the reliability of the nuclear weapon stockpile.[60] Nevertheless, congressional pressure on the Bush administration for more positive policy action increased. As President Bush assured Congress that the United States would conduct no more than six tests a year for the next five years, the Senate imposed a nine-month moratorium and called for an end to all testing by 1996. Testing opponents cleverly added the measure as an amendment to a bill containing funding for unrelated issues, including a major new science project in Texas. Reluctantly, Bush signed the legislation.[61] The following July, President Bill Clinton extended the American moratorium through September 1994, so long as other countries also refrained from testing, and promised efforts to reach a multilateral comprehensive test ban treaty.[62]

Initiatives did not work well for the test ban negotiations. Tough bargaining by the United States had a much greater effect, at least in terms of achieving a measure of cooperation on the terms desired by Washington. The degree of cooperation achieved, however, was very modest, compared either to the potential achievement on testing limits that the 1970s negotiations promised or to the dramatic successes in offensive weapons reductions of the 1980s. Arguably, the hard line worked for the United States on testing because these issues were of secondary importance for both parties and because Gorbachev and the Soviet Union were not strong enough to reciprocate with their own tough strategy.

NOTES

1. See Chapter 6 for discussion of the INF treaty.

2. Rudy Abramson, "Carter, Ford Support A-Test Ban Treaty," *Los Angeles Times*, 13 April 1985: I17.

3. Norman Kempster, "Soviets Ready for a Moratorium on Atomic Tests," *Los Angeles Times*, 18 April 1985: I4.

4. Gerald M. Boyd, "U.S. and Russians Make New Offers on Nuclear Tests," *New York Times*, 30 July 1985: A1; "News and Negotiations," *Arms Control Today* 15 (July/August 1985): 7.

5. See the table "Forty-five Years of Nuclear Testing" in *Arms Control Today* 20 (November 1990): 6–7. Their data are derived from Natural Resources Defense Council and the Stockholm International Peace Research Institute.

6. Initially quoted in "Factfile: Chronology of the Comprehensive Test Ban," *Arms Control Today* 20 (November 1990): 34.

7. Michael R. Gordon, "U.S. Aides Find Hope as Soviets Urge Test Ban," *New York Times*, 23 December 1985: A1.

8. "U.S.-Soviet Arms Test Halt Is Urged," *New York Times*, 11 March 1986: A5.

9. "Moscow Again Extends A-Test Halt," *New York Times*, 14 March 1986: A3.

10. Michael R. Gordon, "Soviet Reported Acting to Begin New Atom Tests," *New York Times*, 18 March 1986: A1.

11. "U.S. Tests Device Despite Opposition," *New York Times*, 23 March 1986: A8; Michael R. Gordon, "U.S. Carries Out a Disputed A-Test," *New York Times*, 11 April 1986: A1.

12. Philip Taubman, "Moscow Ends Ban on Nuclear Tests, Citing Its Security," *New York Times*, 12 April 1986: A1.

13. See remarks of Senator Byrd in Senate Committee on Armed Services, *Nuclear Testing Issues,* 99th Cong., 2nd sess., 1986.

14. Senate Committee on Foreign Relations, *Threshold Test Ban Treaty and Peaceful Nuclear Explosions Treaty,* 101st Cong., 1st sess., 1987, p. 31.

15. *Los Angeles Times,* 8 June 1986: I2.

16. Senate Committee on Armed Service, *Nuclear Testing Issues,* 99th Cong., 2d sess., 1987, pp. 8–9.

17. Ibid., p. 29.

18. Brad Pokorny, "Testing Bombs Without the Blast," *Boston Globe,* 16 December 1985: 49.

19. Peter Applebome, "Hundreds at Nevada Site Ask End to Nuclear Tests, " *New York Times,* 1 October 1986: A18.

20. William J. Broad, "U.S. Researchers Foresee Big Rise in Nuclear Tests, " *New York Times,* 21 April 1986: A1.

21. Philip Taubman, "Moscow Ends Ban on Nuclear Tests, Citing Its Security," *New York Times,* 12 April 1986: A1; Philip Taubman, "Soviet Says Its Nuclear Ban Is Militarily Beneficial to U.S.," *New York Times,* 26 August 1986: A4.

22. William J. Broad, "U.S. Group Checks Soviet Atom Site," *New York Times,* 14 July 1986: A1; Janny Scott, "Gear Put in Desert to Supply Data to Soviets," *Los Angeles Times,* 20 October 1987: I3.

23. Michael R. Gordon, "2 Powers Agree to Discuss Ways to Verify A-Tests," *New York Times,* 10 July 1986: A1.

24. Gerald M. Boyd, "U.S. and Russians Make New Offers on Nuclear Tests," *New York Times,* 30 July 1985: A1.

25. "USSR Offers to Allow Monitoring of Nuclear Test Sites by U.S.," *Boston Globe,* 30 August 1986: 8.

26. "Soviet Govt Allows Foreigners Unprecedented Inspection of Nuclear Test Site," *Los Angeles Times,* 29 September 1986: I9.

27. Michael R. Gordon, "U.S. Aides Looking to Gains at A-Test Talks Resuming Today," *New York Times,* 4 September 1986: A10.

28. Michael R Gordon, "Atomic Test Plan Has New Elements," *New York Times,* 23 September 1986: A1.

29. *Atlanta Journal,* 24 October 1986: A2.

30. Excerpt read by Senator Claiborne Pell in Senate Committee on Foreign Relations *Threshold Test Ban,* p. 2.

31. See testimony of Robert B. Barker, Assistant to the Secretary of Defense for Atomic Energy, Senate, Hearings, *Threshold Test Ban,* p. 22.

32. Senate Committee on Foreign Relations, *Threshold Test Ban,* p. 23.

33. Michael R. Gordon, "Moscow Offering to Put Off a Ban on Atom Testing, " *New York Times,* 7 April 1987: A1.

34. Michael R. Gordon, "Reagan Rejects Soviet Proposal to Curb A-Tests," *New York Times,* 10 April 1987: A1.

35. Michael R. Gordon, "Soviet Offers to Allow Some On-Site Test Monitoring," *New York Times,* 4 June 1987: A3.

36. "Chronology of the Comprehensive Test Ban," *Arms Control Today* 20 (November 1990): 34.

37. Quoted in Jesse James, "U.S., Soviet Union Agree on Joint Nuclear Tests," *Arms*

Control Today 17 (December 1987): 26.

38. Interview with Robert Travis Scott, "Testing the Waves for a New Agreement," *Arms Control Today* 18 (June 1988): 21–22.

39. "U.S. and Soviets Conduct Joint A-Test in Nevada," *Christian Science Monitor,* 18 August 1988: p. 2; "Chronology of the Comprehensive Test Ban," p. 35.

40. Robert T. Scott, "Joint Nuclear Tests Raise Questions About Administration Policy," *Arms Control Today* 18 (October 1988): 26; Jesse James, "Joint Nuclear Test Casts More Doubt on U.S. Verification Stand," *Arms Control Today* 18 (December 1988): 31.

41. Jesse James, "No Agreement on Testing Verification," *Arms Control Today* 19 (January/February 1989): 25.

42. R. Jeffrey Smith, "Monitoring of High-Yield Blasts Offered," *Washington Post,* 12 August 1989: A13; Thomas E. Halverson, "Limited Movement in Nuclear Testing Talks," *Arms Control Today* 19 (September 1989): 30.

43. James P. Rubin, "Baker, Shevardnadze Generate Arms Control Progress," *Arms Control Today* 19 (October 1989): 27.

44. Rubin, "Baker, Shevardnadze," p. 27; R. Jeffrey Smith, "Nuclear Test Proposal Splits U.S. Officials," *Washington Post,* 14 September 1989: A6.

45. Jack Mendelsohn and Dunbar Lockwood, "Ambassador C. Paul Robinson: Verifying Testing Treaties—Old and New," *Arms Control Today* 20 (July/August 1990): 7.

46. Michael R. Gordon, "Reagan Links Fewer Nuclear Arms to More Tests," *New York Times,* 30 September 1988: A1.

47. R. Jeffrey Smith, "Breaking Pledge, U.S. to Defer Underground Nuclear Test Talks," *Washington Post,* 24 January 1990: A24; Gregory P. Webb, "U.S. Repudiates Testing Pledge," *Arms Control Today* 20 (February 1990): 33.

48. Excerpts printed as "Arms Control Documents from Moscow," *Arms Control Today* 20 (March 1990): 28.

49. R. Jeffrey Smith, "DOE Says Decade Is Needed to Weigh More A-Test Curbs," *Washington Post,* 10 April 1990: A10; Dunbar Lockwood, "Continued Testing 'Essential' DOE Tells Congress," *Arms Control Today* 20 (May 1990): 29.

50. Mendelsohn and Lockwood, "Ambassador C. Paul Robinson," p. 7.

51. Senate Committee on Armed Services, *National Security Implications of Nuclear Testing Agreements,* 101st Cong., 2d sess., Hearings, 17 September 1990, p. 5.

52. Ibid., pp. 26–27.

53. Paul Quinn-Judge, "Activists Mute Soviet Nuclear Tests," *Christian Science Monitor,* 12 April 1989: 1.

54. R. Jeffrey Smith, "Soviets to Close Major Site of Underground Atomic Tests," *Washington Post,* 10 March 1990: A1.

55. "Soviets Suspend Nuclear Tests for 4 Months," *Washington Post,* 13 January 1991: A11; "Kazakhstan Orders Closing of Nuclear Test Range," *New York Times,* 30 August 1991: A13.

56. See Senate Committee on Foreign Relations, *Nuclear Test Ban Treaties, Advice and Consent,* 101st Cong., 2d session., Executive Report 101-31, 1990.

57. Seth Mydans, "Gorbachev Denies Soviet Completed Nuclear Tests," *New York Times,* 14 August 1985: A10.

58. Philip Taubman, "Soviet Says Its Nuclear Ban Is Militarily Beneficial to U.S.," *New York Times,* 26 August 1986: A4.

59. Ronald Koven, "French to Suspend Atom Tests, Premier Says," *Boston Globe*, 29 April 1992: 29.

60. Donna Cassata, "Cheney Opposes Nuclear Test Ban," *Boston Globe*, 27 June 1992: 3.

61. Michael Gordon, "U.S. Tightens Limit on Nuclear Tests," *New York Times*, 15 July 1992: A5; Michael Gordon, "Senate, in Defiance of Bush, Votes to End all Nuclear Tests in '96," *New York Times*, 4 August 1992: A7; H. Josef Hebert, "Bush OK's Test Ban to Get Supercollider," *Boston Globe*, 3 October 1992: 49.

62. "Clinton Extends Ban on U.S. Nuclear Tests," *New York Times*, 3 July 1993: A4.

5

Negotiating Limits on Strategic Nuclear Forces: 1954–1980

Over the course of three decades, while negotiators exchanged broad plans and minute details of various schemes to limit strategic forces, the nuclear arsenals of the United States and the Soviet Union grew dramatically. In the mid-1950s the United States had a nuclear arsenal of perhaps four dozen long-range bombers (although not yet with full intercontinental capabilities) and two to three thousand nuclear weapons, mostly bombs. The Soviet Union had tested a nuclear device in 1949, but the creation of usable and deliverable nuclear weapons still lagged about four years and several thousand bombs behind that of the United States. By 1980 the United States maintained a strategic weapons arsenal of over 8,500 nuclear weapons deployed on over 2,000 land- and sea-based intercontinental missiles and intercontinental bombers. The Soviet arsenal had about 6,300 nuclear weapons deployed on over 3,000 missiles and bombers. The total number of nuclear weapons possessed by each side was between 25,000 and 30,000, after counting the battlefield, short-range, and intermediate-range systems.[1]

Nevertheless, by 1980 leaders of the United States and the Soviet Union also had signed two treaties designed to limit strategic forces—the 1972 treaty on anti-ballistic missiles and the 1979 Strategic Arms Limitation Treaty—although only the first was in force. The ABM Treaty placed fairly strict and specific limitations on deployments of ballistic missile defenses. Under the 1972 agreement, each party was limited to two ABM facilities, which were reduced to one each under a 1974 protocol. The treaty did not constrain development or deployment of offensive strategic weapons. These were limited under the 1972 Interim Agreement on offensive forces and subsequently by SALT II. But by effectively prohibiting both hard-point countrywide defense against ballistic missiles, the ABM Treaty removed an important propellant for offensive force expansion.[2]

The SALT II treaty imposed limitations on offensive forces by specifying permitted numbers of strategic nuclear delivery vehicles (missiles and bombers) and defining counting rules that placed ceilings on the number of weapons each launcher carried. None of SALT II's essential restrictions were very restrictive. The treaty demanded little change from the existing arsenals at the time and permitted the weapons programs each side had planned. Nevertheless, while it was very permissive of existing programs, SALT II contributed to regulating the Soviet-American competition by establishing limitations at then current arsenals and adding a degree of transparency and predictability to the relationship. If implemented and observed, SALT II would have slowed the strategic arms race from the headlong accumulation of new weapons, especially multiple warheads, that characterized the 1970s.

The road to this modest instrument of "security and peace" wound through a series of negotiating efforts aimed at ending or regulating the emerging and then accelerating arms race. Early attempts at control included plans for comprehensive disarmament of all military forces. By the end of the 1950s the comprehensive approach to strategic nuclear arms control gave way to partial measures and efforts at regulation. Despite this partial, and often plodding approach, the domain of military behavior and the portions of the arsenals to be regulated or limited gradually expanded. Each new achievement also applied restrictions and requirements, so that by the 1980s the next steps in arms control would almost certainly involve some kinds of reductions. In this sense, the relative paucity of agreements and the burgeoning arsenals did not mean that arms control efforts had no influence on policy.

COMPREHENSIVE DISARMAMENT

Between 1954 and 1957, the United States, the Soviet Union, Great Britain, France, and Canada conducted negotiations in the Five Power Subcommittee of the United Nations Disarmament Commission.[3] These negotiations, which attempted to control or eliminate both conventional and nuclear military forces, failed to reach agreement. They also were the last serious attempt to discuss comprehensive arms control measures. By the end of the decade arms control negotiations had been divided into partial topics—test ban, environmental prohibitions, and strategic nuclear forces. The efforts to negotiate comprehensive controls in the 1950s, however, are an important backdrop to the later strategic arms control talks.

Prior to the formation of the subcommittee in April 1954, U.S. and Soviet positions on disarmament issues were firmly opposed. The U.S. working paper emphasized the priority role of verification and international control. It called for "methods of implementing and enforcing disarmament programs," including the establishment of "international control organs with appropriate rights, powers and functions." Conversely, Soviet negotiators argued for "basic provisions of a draft international convention for the prohibition of atomic, hydrogen and other weapons of mass destruction, substantial reduction in armaments and armed forces, and for the establishment of international control over the observance of the convention."[4]

In June 1954 the British and French delegations offered a compromise proposal envisioning a three-part process of disarmament. The first stage was a freeze on conventional force levels and military spending at December 1953 levels. The second part called for a one-half reduction of military forces to agreed levels. The third stage involved a prohibition of nuclear weapons and a complete reduction of conventional military forces. Initiation of each stage, including the first, depended on the development of suitable monitoring capabilities by an international organization.

The United States accepted this draft, although it did not cosponsor it. In late 1954, Soviet negotiators accepted the Anglo-French paper as the basis for negotiation. In May 1955, the Soviets presented a new proposal that largely reversed Soviet policy and accepted the Western document, including the definitions of military force ratios and the principle of an international inspection and control agency.

American policy makers did not act on this shift in Soviet policy, however. Instead, at the Geneva summit President Eisenhower presented a new proposal for "Open Skies"—an international aerial inspection program involving the exchange of blueprints of military facilities and ostensibly aimed at reducing the risk of surprise attack. Soviet leaders at the summit apparently were surprised by the president's plan and did not want to appear opposed to peace proposals. The fact that they did not reject the proposal outright led to the impression of a new "spirit of Geneva" that promised disarmament and peace.[5]

When the subcommittee reconvened in August 1955, however, Soviet negotiators rejected Open Skies as a thin veil for espionage. They also reiterated their proposals of the previous May. But American negotiators "reserved" the U.S. position on all proposals presented before the Geneva summit, in effect withdrawing U.S. support for the comprehensive plan.

Throughout 1956, U.S. and Soviet exchanges on disarmament measures moved further apart. On inspection issues, for example, the United States held to the universal geographical scope of the Open Skies, while the Soviets argued for very limited observance in central Europe. The beginnings of stronger interest in partial measures were evident in the subcommittee negotiations, but no new presentation stirred serious negotiating effort.

By the spring of 1957, U.S. negotiators were again prepared to deal seriously with comprehensive proposals. In March, U.S. negotiator Harold Stassen was authorized by the president to make new offers and concessions, including a definition of aerial inspection that split the geographical difference. Stassen revealed the internal U.S. memorandum containing these new provisions to Soviet negotiators, who quickly responded with their own concessions that further narrowed the gaps.[6]

Stassen's negotiating approach was unauthorized, however, and policy makers in Washington publicly disavowed the memo's contents. Stassen was recalled.

When negotiators returned to Geneva in August 1957, the U.S. positions had been modified significantly. Whereas the March presentation had compromised the geographical scope of inspection areas and had not made progress on disarmament contingent upon resolution of European political issues (especially German unification), the August paper presented the reverse. The gap between U.S. and Soviet negotiators remained as large as it had been in 1955. Soviet negotiators declined to set a date for resumption of the subcommittee's meetings when the session ended in September 1957.

Efforts to limit strategic nuclear arms did not resume until the mid-1960s. In January 1964 President Lyndon Johnson proposed a freeze of strategic delivery vehicles in an address to the UN Eighteen Nation Disarmament Committee.[7] The plan included long-range bombers as well as ground- and sea-launched ballistic missiles and covered defensive as well as offensive weapons systems. Johnson and U.S. negotiators argued that the first step toward disarmament should be taken by stopping the growth of existing arsenals.

William Foster, director of ACDA and chief negotiator at the ENDC, added details to Johnson's plan at the end of January. The freeze would include long-range missiles and aircraft (defined by range and weight) as well as anti-ballistic missile systems. A specified annual number of test firings of missiles without warheads would be permitted to maintain reliability. Replacements would be on a one-for-one basis, and replacement with a new type of missile or plane would be prohibited. Verification would be by inspection of existing production and testing facilities. The creation of undeclared facilities would be deterred by periodic spot checks.

By August 1964 the United States had spelled out its freeze proposal in some detail. Negotiators had suggested the types of major subassemblies, as well as complete weapons systems that would be controlled. They also had clearly stated the broad scope of the proposed verification system. However, U.S. representative Clare H. Timberlake noted on 27 August 1964, "The United States does not feel that either declarations or inspections of existing inventories of armaments or of the number and deployment of existing launchers would be required as part of a strategic nuclear vehicle freeze agreement."[8]

The Soviet response to the U.S. proposal in January, as well as to subsequent elaborations, was condemnation of the plan as "control without disarmament." In its place Soviet negotiators argued for the 1963 Soviet plan for general and complete disarmament, in which nuclear weapons would be destroyed in the first stage. They also submitted a number of partial (although still sweeping) measures, including the withdrawal of all troops from foreign territories, reductions of the total numbers of armed forces, reductions of military budgets by 10 to 15 percent, a nonaggression pact between NATO and WTO, and the elimination of bomber aircraft.

The ENDC negotiations did develop some support from nonaligned nations and U.S. allies for the freeze proposal. Some of the nonaligned states' suggestions attempted to bridge the gap between the U.S. and Soviet positions, but ultimately this effort to control strategic weapons failed. Both sides presented far more extreme proposals than the other was ready to accept.

STRATEGIC ARMS LIMITATION TALKS

The SALT I negotiations were more complex than the freeze proposals.[9] The bargaining involved a variety of concessions, retractions, and issue linkages by both sides, but reciprocal compromises were key to the agreements that resulted.

In 1967 the Soviets indicated mild interest in strategic arms limitation talks. One of the primary American concerns at the time was the potential development of ballistic missile defenses (BMDs) by the Soviet Union. Both countries had initiated missile defense programs earlier in the decade. But while the United States had not begun construction on a substantial dedicated BMD project (it had deployed air defense missiles with limited missile defense capabilities), a Soviet system was under construction around Moscow, and a second site was suspected near Leningrad. Congressional opinion in the United States strongly supported work on an ABM system, although Secretary of Defense Robert McNamara resisted the pressure on the grounds of high cost and limited effectiveness.[10] At a June summit in Glassboro, New Jersey, between Soviet General Secretary Alexei Kosygin and President Johnson, Secretary McNamara argued that ballistic missile defenses would destabilize the military balance that was emerging because each side would be less certain about its ability to retaliate after a surprise attack. At Glassboro, however, the Soviets rejected the connection between missile defense and the arms race, asserting that defense was morally superior to offense and therefore should not be constrained. In addition, they were not prepared to enter bilateral talks on strategic arms until the Nuclear Nonproliferation Treaty (NPT) was completed. In September 1967, responding to congressional pressure and the Soviet reluctance, McNamara announced that the United States would proceed with a limited, "anti-Chinese" missile defense system.[11]

In mid-1968 Soviet attitudes toward bilateral negotiations changed. One of their conditions for strategic arms talks with the United States had been completion of the Nuclear Nonproliferation Treaty through which both West Germany and Japan would formally pledge not to acquire nuclear weapons. Thus, on 1 July both superpowers signed the NPT, and President Johnson announced their agreement to begin strategic arms negotiations "in the nearest future."[12] The first session was scheduled to begin with a Johnson-Kosygin summit on 30 September. The summit and the arms talks, however, were canceled by the United States following the Soviet-Warsaw Pact invasion of Czechoslovakia on 21 August.

The new American administration of Richard Nixon chose to review security and arms control issues during its first few months in office, so that SALT negotiations did not begin until November 1969. The first session was a preliminary exploration of each other's interests and commitment to serious negotiations. The U.S. negotiators presented a list of items that might be included in a limitation agreement—including missile launchers, radar systems, MIRVs, and warhead penetration aids, such as chaff and decoys. But neither side offered a formal set of proposals at that time. Over the next two years the negotiations would revolve around three fundamental questions—limiting ballistic missile defenses, defining which offensive weapons were to be controlled by an agreement, and setting numerical restrictions for those weapons.

Ballistic Missile Defense Limitations

In April 1970 the United States offered a proposal for one ABM site deployed at the national command authority (NCA) of each country, which essentially were the national capitals. Soviet negotiators quickly accepted the NCA offer, which allowed them to continue their ABM deployment under construction around Moscow. The American offer, however, was inconsistent with U.S. plans to deploy its missile defense around ICBM installations, rather than as a population or area defense. Rapid acceptance of the NCA-only plan by the Soviets, therefore, created a dilemma for Nixon, who favored construction of some ABM system. He recognized that the American public would likely reject defenses around Washington, and the end result would be no American ballistic missile defenses.

In August 1970 American negotiators presented a new plan for zero-ABM, which was said to have equal status with the NCA-only proposal. Henry Kissinger, who was Nixon's national security advisor in 1970, later admitted that the second plan was deliberately designed to be rejected by the Soviets.[13] American policy makers believed that the Soviet leadership would be unwilling to give up their existing ABM system. Thus the United States would find it easier to retreat from the NCA-only plan.

Soviet negotiators continued to press for an agreement that permitted only an NCA defense site. In December 1970 they sought to remove the linkage of a defensive agreement to offensive limitations (the talks for which were stalled at the time). They proposed a separate ABM treaty, which they in turn attempted to link to another U.S.-Soviet agreement concerning the superpowers' response to a "provocative nuclear attack" by a third state. Soviet intentions were clearly aimed at frustrating the nascent rapprochement of the United States and China. American negotiators rejected both the separation of offensive and defensive strategic issues and the provocative attack agreement.

In March 1971 the Soviet delegation tabled a draft ABM treaty. This draft included the NCA-only limitation but did not offer specific details on radar related to ballistic missile defense, which was another American concern. The U.S. negotiators continued to reject the separate ABM treaty and now offered a third ABM proposal that more accurately reflected U.S. ballistic missile defense activities. The new plan permitted the United States to construct four ABM sites at ICBM installations, as it was planning, and allowed the Soviet Union to keep its system around Moscow. In practical terms, the United States would be permitted roughly 400 ABM missiles in four separate locations, while the Soviet Union would have only 100 in a single site.

During the fifth session of the talks, between July and September 1971, both sides presented new ABM positions. The United States began by revising its latest proposal to permit each side a choice of either three sites at ICBM installations or one site at the national command authority. This plan was shortly revised to allow only two ICBM defensive installations or an NCA deployment. Soviet negotiators rejected each of these plans on the grounds that only equal limits were acceptable. They countered with a proposal for "one-plus-one." Each side could retain one of its existing defensive sites plus have the option to build one more. If they chose, the Soviet Union could build ABMs at an ICBM location, and the United States could defend Washington. Although the final agreement in 1972 approximated this plan, the United States rejected it in the fall of 1971 until an offensive agreement was reached.

At this point American negotiators again raised the zero-ABM option. Informal explorations revealed continuing Soviet interest. American military leaders, however, opposed the zero option, partly because they did not believe the Soviets would give up the Moscow site. So despite indications of Soviet interest, the United States backed away from further explorations of the issue. In August of 1971 Nixon decided finally that zero-ABMs was not an acceptable position for the United States.

By the end of 1971 the negotiating exchanges had returned to the symmetrical position in which each state would be permitted two defensive sites, one at an ICBM location and one around the national command authority. In addition, Soviet leaders had accepted the American position on technical limitations of radar systems, which defined permissible types and locations. They also had accepted the U.S. prohibition of future ABM systems based on "exotic technologies," such as laser beams. Finally, the second ABM site was required to be no closer than 1,300 kilometers from the first, effectively placing a second Soviet site on the eastern side of the Ural Mountains.[14]

Final agreement on the terms of the ABM treaty in 1972 reflected these late 1971 agreements. As noted above, however, one of the continuing American concerns was to obtain limits on both offensive and defensive weapons systems. Not until the final bargaining over numerical limitations of offensive weapons at the Moscow summit, therefore, did the ABM treaty come into existence.

Strategic Definitions

American definitions of strategic offensive weapons differed fundamentally from Soviet concerns. Soviet negotiators argued that U.S. forward-based nuclear forces, primarily located in Europe but also in the northern Pacific, should be included in the limitations. At the same time, Soviet medium-range forces, which could not strike U.S. targets, should be excluded. The U.S. negotiators and policy makers found this position unacceptable; they could not take these steps, which would have serious impact on the Western alliance, in bilateral negotiations. In August 1970, U.S. proposals presented simply a freeze of offensive missiles at 1,710, removing many of the previous impediments, but not compromising on the question of definitions. A stalemate resulted in the offensive limitation parts of the talks that would remain until May 1971. This, in turn, produced delays in the ABM agreements.

Definitional disagreements also impeded decisions about which offensive weapons other than forward-based forces to include, especially whether or not to control multiple warheads on missiles. American proposals for offensive weapons limits began with the presentation of alternative packages. The first package included a freeze on offensive missiles at 1,710 (the combined total of U.S. ICBMs and SLBMs), a ban on MIRVs (which included stipulations for on-site inspections) and the NCA-only ABM position. The alternative American package retained the NCA-only ABM limit, placed no restrictions on MIRVs, and froze ballistic missiles at 1,710, but with reductions to 1,000 over seven years. Both packages sought special sublimits for the Soviet SS-9 ICBMs (very large missiles) and included limits on Soviet intermediate- and medium-range missiles targeted on Europe.

Soviet negotiators rejected both packages. The first included unacceptable inspection provisions in its MIRV limitations, and the second package proposed deep cuts in the very heart of Soviet strategic missile strength, large land-based missiles. Even though the second set of proposals placed no restriction on multiple warhead deployments, Soviet programs would be dramatically constrained by the limits on its largest missiles.

The position adopted by the United States for its MIRV ban proposal during the first SALT talks, especially the provision for inspection, probably contributed to the failure of that element of the SALT negotiations.[15] During the first SALT meetings in Helsinki in late 1969, each side probed the other for indications of interest in MIRV limitation. Gerard Smith, head of the U.S. delegation, recounted that "if the Soviets [raised the issue of a MIRV moratorium] we were to respond that the United States believed that the general scope of SALT should be explored [first]."[16] Because of the relative advantage of the United States in developing MIRV technology at the time, American delegates expected the Soviets to raise this issue. However, Soviet negotiators indicated that they expected the United States to take the initiative. One American supporter of MIRV limits in 1969 later characterized this Soviet inaction as "amazing."[17]

The American delegation first mentioned MIRVs in December 1969 in the context of a "component list" of items that might be included in a SALT agreement, along with such items as missiles, radar, and penetration aids. Soviet negotiators specifically rejected each item on the list, except for MIRVs. Smith reported that during informal discussions the Soviet delegates indicated that this selective exclusion was deliberate. However, they declined to raise the issue themselves, perhaps to avoid displaying what could be perceived as a weakness in the bargaining.

In April 1970, the United States formally offered a MIRV limitation proposal that would ban deployments and prohibit flight tests of missiles with multiple warheads but permit production and stockpiling. The American proposal required on-site inspections of ballistic missiles to supplement national technical means of surveillance. Soviet delegates rejected these proposals, as many American officials, including Smith, expected. They countered with a ban of production and deployment that nevertheless permitted testing. Informal discussion in June 1970 indicated a Soviet interest in reaching a SALT agreement that did not include a MIRV ban. In July, President Nixon chose to pursue this more narrow treaty, largely as a result of the American military's preference to maintain the technical advantage and the ambiguous Soviet attitude toward limitations. Both the U.S. Air Force and Navy, for example, strongly supported MIRV programs. Development of multiple warheads had been part of an internal political bargain between Secretary McNamara and the services in the mid-1960s to hold down the number of ballistic missiles in the U.S. arsenal. By 1970, the ICBM and SLBM missile programs had both been designed to exploit multiple warhead technology.[18] Furthermore, even though Henry Kissinger had been briefed on the potential negative consequences of mutual MIRV deployment in 1969, he did not press the limitation case in the face of military opposition.[19]

American negotiators later stated that stronger U.S. efforts in the early negotiations would have revealed the true Soviet position. They did not claim that an agreement on MIRV was inevitable, and Smith clearly conveyed the ambiguity of Soviet interests. But the potential to control a technology that would become a major issue in the strategic balance and negotiations may have been missed.[20]

Offensive Force Limitations

In May 1971 Nixon announced a breakthrough in the negotiations. From the beginning of the year, Kissinger had been negotiating directly and secretly with the Soviet leadership through Soviet Ambassador Anatoly Dobrynin. Kissinger had achieved Soviet commitment to limitations on ICBMs in conjunction with an ABM agreement. In effect, Soviet leaders had agreed to the offensive-defensive linkage. This agreement was obtained, however, at the exclusion of SLBMs from the May 1971 agreements and at the retreat of the United States from a single comprehensive treaty. Instead, the superpowers agreed to seek an ABM treaty and an interim measure on offensive arms, pending further negotiations. In addition, the May agreement removed forward based (nuclear) systems (FBS) from the agenda—tacit admission by the United States that an offensive treaty was not possible without either a change in the Soviet FBS position or inclusion of these forces in the treaty.

Gerard Smith later argued that the May agreement was not really a breakthrough because it simply repeated offers and discussions already made by the delegations. Soviet negotiators had hinted of willingness to reach a less formal agreement on offensive forces that excluded FBS when they offered a separate ABM treaty in December 1970. Because of Kissinger's intervention, the Soviet negotiators stalled the talks from December 1970 until May 1971—to the mystification of the U.S. delegation. Furthermore, Smith felt the language of the breakthrough agreement appeared to favor Soviet interests. The wording about "agreeing to agree" was indefinite and resembled the recurring Soviet call for "agreement in principle," which many American negotiators took to mean agreement without details. In addition, the agreement failed to include SLBMs in the offensive limitations, which was a concern for U.S. policy makers because this was the area of most rapid Soviet force growth at the time.[21]

The final negotiations by Nixon and Kissinger in Moscow also produced some questionable compromises on offensive forces, in part because of the manner in which the talks were conducted. The U.S. leaders relied heavily on frequent telephone communication with the delegation in Helsinki and misinterpretations of the meanings of Soviet proposals were narrowly avoided. For example, Nixon and Kissinger almost agreed to a limitation on the size of modernized ICBMs that would have prohibited the continuation of the Minuteman III MIRV program.[22]

A more important agreement, which remained, was the acceptance by the U.S. leaders of the Soviet position on the number of submarines they possessed or were building, as well as the types of subs that would be considered for counting and deactivation.[23] The effect of this agreement was to establish a large numerical imbalance in SLBMs formally frozen by the Interim Agreement, even though the United States had an advantage of 200 SLBMs deployed. In 1972 the Soviet Union had deployed 459 SLBMs, compared to 656 in the United States. The ceilings under the Interim Agreement, however, allowed for 950 Soviet SLBM launchers versus 710; ICBM trade-ins would begin at 740 and 656 SLBMs, respectively. Secretary of Defense Melvin Laird apparently was willing to accept the imbalance in return for administration support for the Trident submarine and missile system. The Joint Chiefs of Staff, however, were not consulted on the acceptability of the numbers.[24]

The 1972 Agreements

Of the two agreements signed on 26 May 1972 in Moscow, only the one restricting strategic defenses was a completed treaty. Offensive strategic weapons were subject to restrictions in the Interim Agreement on Strategic Offensive Arms, which was considered the basis for a future formal treaty. In practice, the Interim Agreement was generally observed by both parties until the SALT II negotiations produced a final treaty.

The ABM Treaty substantially restricted ballistic missile defenses by both sides. Under this Treaty each side could maintain only two missile defense sites. One site was permitted around the respective capitals, and the other could protect offensive ballistic missiles if they were deployed no closer than 1,300 kilometers from the capital. No more than 100 defensive missiles and launches could be deployed at either site. The treaty also specified the permissible types and locations of missile radar installations. Finally, the ABM Treaty constrained future missile defense developments by prohibiting the testing and development of new ABM systems based on then exotic technologies.

The Interim Agreement more or less froze the levels of strategic ballistic missile launchers for a period of five years, in which time completion of a formal treaty was expected. Each party was prohibited from constructing new fixed ICBM launchers and held to the number then in place—1,054 for the United States and 1,618 for the Soviet Union. The agreement prohibited the conversion of "light" to "heavy" ICBMs, which effectively restricted Soviet large ballistic missiles to 313. In addition, submarine-based launchers and modern ballistic missile submarines were limited, although as noted above, in a way that favored Soviet building programs—710 launchers and 44 submarines for the United States, and 950 launchers on 62 submarines for the Soviet Union.

Left unrestricted by the agreement were any limitations on strategic bombers (in which the United States held a significant advantage) or on the modernization of existing systems, except for the heavy missile prohibition. As discussed above, no constraints were placed on the development and deployment of multiple warhead missiles. These omissions had two consequences for future arms control negotiations. First, each party devoted considerable energy to modernizing its strategic missile forces, principally by improving the accuracy of the delivery systems and by deploying multiple warheads. As a result each side's strategic arsenal became increasingly threatening to the other. The second consequence for arms negotiations followed from the first. Constraining the most threatening weapons systems of the other side became a more urgent concern in the negotiations. For the United States, controlling or eliminating heavy ICBMs in the Soviet arsenal was a primary objective. Soviet negotiators, on the other hand, sought to maintain the degree of overall parity, plus some of the marginal advantages that they had acquired under SALT.

SALT II

After 1972, negotiations focused on transforming the Interim Agreement into a formal treaty. Efforts in the next two years did not produce a new treaty, but by November 1974 negotiators had reached an agreement on a new framework for offensive limitations. The Vladivostok Accord marked agreement on how to count the weapons, and as well resolved some questions of what to count. Based on the accord, Henry Kissinger claimed in early 1975 that SALT II was "90 percent complete."

No new proposals were submitted during 1973, and negotiations did not really resume until early 1974. In February U.S. negotiators presented a proposal for equal launcher aggregates and equal ICBM-MIRV throw-weight. The permissible launcher total would be 2,350, including ICBMs, SLBMs, and long-range bombers. Equal MIRV throw-weights on ICBMs, however, would have greatly constrained Soviet MIRV programs, which was the U.S. desire. Because Soviet ICBMs were generally larger than U.S. missiles, the kinds of Soviet missiles that could be MIRVed effectively was limited, and so too was the potential number of Soviet multiple warheads. Soviet negotiators rejected the plan.

American support for unequal launcher aggregates surfaced briefly in top-level negotiations in early 1974. On a trip to Moscow in March, Kissinger (at the time both secretary of state and Nixon's national security advisor) proposed compensating the Soviet numerical advantage in launchers with a U.S. advantage in warheads. The Soviet counterproposal suggested unequal aggregates (as in the Interim Agreement), but equal MIRV limits. Kissinger found this unacceptable. In an April meeting with Foreign Minister Gromyko in Geneva, Kissinger proposed retaining the Interim Agreement limits until 1980 and adding unequal MIRV limits—850 for the Soviet Union, and 1,000 for the United States. The Soviets rejected this plan.[25]

The U.S. and Soviet delegations resumed meetings in Geneva from mid-September until early November 1974, but neither side exchanged concrete proposals. Kissinger, however, offered a new American plan through his back channel with Dobrynin and also in a personal visit to Moscow in October. The October plan set equal total numbers at 2,200, with a MIRV subceiling of 1,320. Heavy systems (which meant the very large Soviet ICBMs and heavy bombers) would be limited to 250, with no multiple warheads permitted on the missiles. Air-to-surface missiles with ranges exceeding 3,000 kilometers would be banned. Finally, the pace of modernization would be set to 175 systems per year.

Kissinger discovered in Moscow that Brezhnev would accept an agreement in either of two forms. First was "equal numbers," which permitted either a total number of systems of 2,400 with a MIRV subceiling of 1,320, or an aggregate of 2,200 with a MIRV sublimit of 1,200. The second option consisted of "offsetting asymmetries," which set Soviet totals at 2,400 with 1,100 to 1,200 MIRVed systems and U.S. totals at 2,200 with 1,300 MIRVed systems. Brezhnev was unwilling to accept reductions in Soviet large ballistic missiles (then at 308), but he was willing to defer the issue of U.S. forward-based nuclear forces in Europe.[26]

At the Vladivostok summit the Secretary General originally offered equal aggregates at 2,500, which was close to the actual level of Soviet forces. President Ford countered with 2,100, which was about the level of deployed U.S. forces. They quickly settled on 2,400 total launchers and a MIRV subceiling of 1,320 systems.

The Vladivostok Accord left unresolved or ambiguous two important issues. First, a precise definition and classification of heavy bombers was excluded. In particular, the Soviet Backfire bomber was not classified as a heavy bomber, although some U.S. analysts claimed it had all the characteristics and capabilities of other intercontinental bombers that were so designated.[27] Soviet negotiators, however, denied a strategic mission for the plane.

The second ambiguity was the constraint placed on air-to-surface missiles. Soviet officials claimed the limitation agreed at Vladivostok included all air-launched missiles with the specified ranges. This definition included the modern American cruise missiles then beginning deployment. Kissinger argued in early 1975 that the restriction applied only to air-launched ballistic missiles. These differences over the Backfire bomber and U.S. cruise missiles would plague SALT II negotiations through 1979.

As SALT II negotiations continued after Vladivostok, Soviet negotiators generally retained their commitment to the structure of the 1974 accord, while U.S. negotiators produced a number of position changes and new proposals.[28] The most dramatic U.S. shift was the submission and subsequent repudiation of a "deep cuts" proposal in March 1977.

In January 1977, shortly after his inauguration, President Jimmy Carter asserted his commitment to seek a rapid conclusion to SALT and then to move from that treaty to a new agreement embodying significant arms reductions. For all practical purposes this meant concluding a treaty based on the Vladivostok Accord, leaving the difficult issues of cruise missiles, the Backfire bomber, and intermediate-range nuclear forces for the next set of negotiations.[29]

In March, however, U.S. negotiators proposed an agreement for deep cuts in strategic arsenals. The aggregate ceilings of the Vladivostok Accord would be reduced by as many as 600 launchers. Subceilings on multiple warhead missiles would be reduced to between 1,100 and 1,200 and broadened to include further sublimits on MIRVed ICBMs (550) and on the Soviet "modern large ballistic missile launchers," or MLBMs (150). Intercontinental ballistic missile deployments would be frozen, and testing of new ICBMs, including mobile land-based missiles, would be banned. Long-range nuclear cruise missiles (with ranges over 2,500 kilometers) would be banned, and those of shorter range carried on strategic bombers would be counted under the multiple warhead subceilings.[30]

Only slight adjustments to U.S. programs would have been required under this "deep cuts" proposal. Soviet forces, however, would sustain major reductions in deployed ICBMs and modernization programs, generally because land-based missiles comprised nearly two-thirds of the Soviet arsenal.[31] With some justification, Soviet leaders perceived the plan as "unbalanced." Soviet leaders rejected the new U.S. proposal and maintained their commitment of the Vladivostok Accord.

Negotiations resumed in May with a new U.S. treaty structure essentially based on Vladivostok. The major issues that had to be resolved were setting numerical ceilings, defining and controlling heavy ICBMs, establishing verification rules and procedures, and defining constraints on modernization.

Basic problems on numerical ceilings were resolved by September 1977 when the United States proposed a nested series of ceilings including a new sublimit on multiple warhead ICBMs. Inclusion of the new subceiling was prompted by U.S. recognition that a direct limit on MLBMs was not negotiable and that the expansion of MIRVs to all Soviet missiles posed a greater strategic-military prob-

lem for the United States than MIRVed heavy missiles alone. The U.S. proposals set a total launcher limit at 2,160 (10 percent below Vladivostok), a MIRV
launcher ceiling of 1,320 (which would include cruise missile–carrying
bombers), a limit of 1,200 MIRVed missiles, and a ceiling of 800 multiple warhead ICBMs.

The Soviet response in September 1977 was to accept the outline of the proposal but to raise the numbers—2,250 total strategic systems, 1,250 multiple
warhead missiles, and 850 MIRVed ICBMs. By the end of 1978 the final numerical limits were agreed. The Soviet grand total of 2,250 was retained (thus
requiring fewer retirements of older weapons). MIRVed systems, including
cruise missile–carrying bombers, were limited to 1,320, and the ceiling for multiple warhead missiles was set at 1,200, both from the September U.S. proposal.
The number of permitted multiple warhead ICBMs was set at 820, splitting the
difference between the positions.

The American retreat from its objective of reducing Soviet heavy missiles
meant that roughly 300 of these weapon systems would remain in the Soviet arsenal. Since the beginning of SALT, the Soviet Union had refused to accept a
separate and special limitation on these missiles. In SALT II, however, Soviet
negotiators agreed that no more should be added and accepted a definition distinguishing between heavy and light missiles with reference to existing Soviet
missile types.

American concerns for verification centered on three issues—establishment
of an agreed database, counting rules for MIRV launchers, and the practice of
coding, or encryption, of data transmitted during missile flight tests. The principle of verification by national technical means had already been established in
previous SALT agreements, and the Carter administration had no desire to push
for intrusive inspection measures. The U.S. concerns reflected desires to
strengthen unilateral technical capabilities by closing several loopholes.

An agreed database of strategic weapons was a nonnegotiable point for the
U.S. Congress. Initially, Soviet negotiators maintained that all necessary data
was already obtainable by accepted techniques, such as satellite reconnaissance.
They then attempted to link a concession on the database to U.S. concessions on
cruise missiles. Beginning in September 1977, however, Soviet negotiators offered specific information about their country's forces, without demanding a
U.S. counterconcession. Disclosure of some types of information, such as the
multiple warhead loadings of ballistic missiles, was given reluctantly. A complete
set of agreed information was established by the spring of 1979.

Because SALT II would explicitly limit MIRVed missiles, the treaty required
procedural rules for counting these weapons. Soviet negotiators conceded to
two American points by September 1977. First, they agreed that any missile
tested with multiple warheads would be counted as a MIRV missile, regardless
of whether actual deployments carried single or multiple warheads. One obvious effect of this agreement was to encourage the deployment of MIRVed,
rather than single warhead missiles, which would create some continuing strate-

gic and military problems. Soviet negotiators also agreed to count all launchers at a given location as MIRVed, even if only a portion of them were actually deployed in this way.

The question of coded telemetry was more difficult to resolve. Secretary of State Cyrus Vance and Foreign Minister Gromyko reached a general understanding in early 1978 that encryption could impede verification. Each adversary monitored the missile tests of the other and collected the data transmitted back to the test facilities on its own electronic surveillance equipment. Such electronic eavesdropping was tolerated as a necessary part of national technical means of verification. Since each side maintained an interest in avoiding the other's unwarranted accusation of treaty violation, both countries acknowledged the legitimacy of data collection. Vance and Gromyko agreed that data encryption would be prohibited whenever it impaired verification capabilities.

The U.S. Director of Central Intelligence, Stansfield Turner, however, thought this language was too permissive. Concerned by what he considered excessive data encryption of a Soviet missile test in July 1978, he demanded the explicit Soviet agreement that the specific level of encryption employed in the tests was not acceptable. Vance, under orders from President Carter, reopened the issue and protested the July flight test. The result was a reciprocal stiffening of the Soviet position.[32] Eventually, the United States relaxed its demands, and a compromise was reached to include treaty language that reinstated the Vance-Gromyko understanding.

New types of weapons systems and the modernization of older ones posed significant challenges for the SALT negotiations because both sides were actively pursuing new developments and improving existing weapons. The SALT II agreement broke new ground in its attempt to control the pace of weapon modernization and qualitative change. The lessons of failing to control multiple warheads under SALT I were not lost on American negotiators. Technological progress threatened to undermine whatever strategic stability was achieved by numerical limitations. The negotiations on modernization revolved around prohibitions and definitions of new types of missiles. Each side sought to preserve a particular weapon then in development—a solid fuel replacement for the Soviet single-warhead SS-11, and the MX ICBM, a MIRVed replacement for U.S. Minuteman missiles. Both parties placed their modernization limits in the draft treaty's protocol, which had a shorter duration than the main document.

American proposals initially prohibited modernization except for one new MIRV missile. Soviet positions allowed an exemption only for a new single warhead missile. Neither side changed its position until April 1978. In April, U.S. negotiators offered two proposals. One plan banned, in the protocol, all new types of missiles. The other plan allowed, in the main treaty document, one exemption to the prohibition, which could be either a single or multiple warhead missile. Soviet negotiators at first responded with a treaty ban that permitted only the single warhead exemption. They then offered a total ban in the main treaty document. Apparently, they were willing to forgo the SS-11 replacement in exchange for a prohibition on MX. The treaty eventually met the U.S. position and retained the right to develop either a new single or multiple warhead missile, whether mobile or in a fixed deployment.

Defining what constituted a new type of weapon involved an additional series of offers and trades. For most of 1978, Soviet negotiators accepted the U.S. position that "new" involved a change of plus or minus 5 percent in various physical parameters of a missile. At the end of 1978 the Soviet position changed to a demand of plus 5 percent or minus 20 percent. The U.S. negotiators rejected this position as too permissive of significantly different missiles and held to their plus or minus five position and identified a large number of relevant parameters, including the number of stages and the fuel type. In March 1979, Vance proposed a trade-off in which the 5 percent variable was maintained, but the number of relevant parameters was limited to length, diameter, launch-weight, and throw-weight. Soviet negotiators accepted this compromise.

The 1979 Agreement

The SALT II treaty, signed in Vienna, Austria, on 18 June 1979, imposed limited but important constraints in several areas. First, the treaty formalized the numerical limits on launch vehicles, including strategic bombers as well as ballistic missiles. Each party was restricted to the equal aggregate limits on launchers (missiles and bombers) of 2,400, which would be reduced to 2,250 by 1980. Beneath the overall ceilings, sublimits restricted each side to no more than 1,320 ICBMs, SLBMs, MIRVed air-to-surface ballistic missiles (ASBMs), and bombers equipped with nuclear cruise missiles. Only 1,200 ICBMs, SLBMs, or ASBMs equipped with MIRVs were permitted, and MIRVed intercontinental ballistic missiles were limited to 820.

Second, in a departure from SALT I, the new treaty created limits on qualitative improvements to the strategic arsenals. Only one new type of "light" ICBM was allowed to be flight-tested, and this restriction meant that new missiles as large as the Soviet SS-18 could not be developed. Furthermore, the treaty prohibited upgrading older weapons or the conversion of older silos to hold new missiles.

Finally, in an effort to bring the fractionation race under control, SALT II devised means to constrain the proliferation of warheads throughout the two arsenals. Because the verification measures would rely on national technical means, supplemented by diplomatic exchanges of disagreements through the Standing Consultative Commission created by SALT I, the new treaty developed counting rules to limit MIRVs. A missile would be counted as having the maximum number of warheads with which it had been tested, even if the actual missile deployments carried fewer weapons. In practical terms, this approach provided a fair amount of flexibility for each side actually to continue increasing the size of its arsenals if it chose.

CONCLUSIONS: RECIPROCITY, INITIATIVE, AND AGREEMENT

Bargaining behavior based on a strategy of reciprocation such as tit-for-tat appeared to be a necessary condition for agreement. Significantly, American negotiators were not the only ones making concessions or taking the initial steps toward compromise. Often Soviet alterations of previously firm positions were key to moving negotiations forward. When the United States responded with counterconcessions, negotiations often ended in agreement. When the United States responded negatively, failure commonly resulted.

The pattern of unreciprocated concessions makes an initiative strategy harder to support. At certain points unilateral restraints or novel concessions prodded agreement. But at other points the initiatives did not produce the expected result. Given the larger concession-convergence pattern, however, and the need for some kind of initial move, the potential value of an initiative strategy increases.

Throughout the SALT negotiations concessions were exchanged, recalling the bargaining in the test ban talks, although these often were "package deals" of linked issues. At the general level, the United States tied agreement on ABM limits to restrictions on offensive weapons, even though an ABM agreement was more readily accessible. Soviet concession on this linkage came in the first half of 1971. At the same time, the Soviet Union dropped its demands for inclusion of U.S. nuclear systems based in Western Europe in return for U.S. exclusion of specific limits on heavy Soviet ICBMs. This series of concessions broke a deadlocked pattern of mutual noncooperation that had persisted for several months.

Not all concessions were cooperative moves reciprocated by the bargaining partner; a pure tit-for-tat strategy did not prevail. Several concessions, in which the minimum position of one side accommodated the maximum demands of the other were not reciprocated—for example, the U.S. allowances on the numbers of Soviet ICBMs and SLBMs that entered the Interim Agreement and the American willingness to permit the retention of Soviet heavy missiles in SALT II.

In addition, not all defections brought retaliation in kind. Soviet negotiators did not retreat from their acceptance of the initial U.S. proposal to eliminate anti-ballistic missiles, even though the American positions shifted through several other options clearly favoring U.S. interests. The Soviets did not escalate their demands; nor did they retreat from a position that would have required them to dismantle an existing ABM site. They simply waited for an equitable solution to reemerge.[33]

The Soviet-American negotiating experience points to several conclusions. First, the importance of reciprocated concession making was clear. As many bargaining theories suggest, the willingness of each side to respond favorably to concessions or overtures of compromise made by the opponent drove the process toward agreement. Reciprocal behavior, most prominently in concession making, was an important element of successful negotiations. Axelrod's theory predicts that cooperation can permit each side to gain mutual advantages in circumstances when mutual competition is less preferred. The "shadow of the future" between the United States and the Soviet Union, or the probability of continuing interaction through arms control or arms racing, was prominent throughout these negotiations. There was little chance that either side would cease to be a world power. Thus, each seemed likely to seek some form of accommodation with the other at most times.

Issue linkages were important features of bargaining strategies for reciprocal concession making. During the SALT negotiations in particular, in which a large number of items related to the central strategic forces of each side were on the table, the packaging of compromises was a key to success. In 1970, for example, Soviet insistence that French and British nuclear forces be included in offensive limitations was dropped in return for American acquiescence to several hundred very large Soviet ICBMs. Similarly, in 1978 U.S. negotiators agreed to constraints on range limits for air-launched cruise missiles in return for Soviet acceptance of a freeze of warhead numbers on SS-17 and SS-19 ICBMs.

Failed negotiations were characterized by bargaining strategies often described as "tough"—extremely high opening bids, retractions of offers that had elicited concessions, or the unwillingness to explore indications of compromise. This does not mean, however, that tough bargaining did not occur during those negotiations that were ultimately successful. For example, Soviet negotiators retreated from compromising positions during the test ban negotiations in 1962, and U.S. negotiators retracted offers in 1970 to limit ABMs to one national site each, or to none, after Soviet acceptance. The significant difference between these episodes and those negotiations in which tough bargaining prevailed lay in the fact that in the former, tough moves were not reciprocated with similar actions. A downward spiral of retreat and intransigence was avoided by the willingness of one side to maintain its commitment to compromise long enough for the other to reverse direction. This pattern is a departure from the pure tit-for-tat strategy of reciprocation offered by Axelrod. Cooperation theory suggests that cooperation can be best promoted by a strategy that "punishes" noncooperation by responding in kind. As Axelrod noted, one of the dangers of tit-for-tat is that noncooperation is as easily reinforced as cooperation. A key challenge for the strategy as a means of promoting cooperation, therefore, is how to avoid this spiral of defection

One solution to tit-for-tat's defection problem is to make it more "forgiving." Axelrod noted that in his computer tournaments a strategy of responding only after two instances of defection actually did better than the straight tit-for-tat. Throughout the successful U.S.-Soviet negotiations we see a pattern of forgiveness that differs from a tit-for-tat strategy. There was, however, no consistent pattern that would suggest a specific alternative strategy for these negotiations. The willingness of either side to stand by the concessions it had already made appeared to be rooted in domestic politics.

Finally, some examples of national restraint and bargaining initiatives helped to begin patterns of mutual compromise. Initiative strategies also promoted forgiving behavior. Restraint appeared to facilitate success in several cases, contrary to the claims that U.S. self-restraint amounted to "unilateral disarmament" and damaged American security. The U.S. restraint in the Limited Test Ban negotiations clearly was an important prod toward agreement. Soviet restraint in the ABM negotiations facilitated agreement by dampening slightly the military competition. In addition, U.S. restraint was a policy option that was consciously rejected during the MIRV limitation exchanges; and it was arguably one that could have encouraged success. On the whole, however, initiative tactics or strategies were not used widely in either testing or strategic arms limitation efforts. Notable examples were Kennedy's declaration of a unilateral moratorium on testing in 1963, the Soviet pause in ABM construction between 1970 and 1972, and the Soviet acceptance of on-site inspection for verification in the 1978 test ban negotiations.

On some occasions when new initiatives were taken, however, the opposing negotiators subsequently retreated from previous positions and the negotiations ended in failure. This occurred after Soviet concessions in the 1954 disarmament talks, in the face of American and British efforts to restart test ban talks in 1961, and after the Soviet concessions on inspection in the 1978 test ban talks. The bargaining signal sent by the Soviet ABM building pause in 1970 was ambiguous and not clearly related to immediate bargaining moves. Importantly, the stereotyping of Soviet negotiation style—high demands, intransigent responses, refusal to take the initiative—frequently was inaccurate, and the stereotype may well have impaired the development of efficacious bargaining strategies.

NOTES

1. Data on the evolution of U.S. and Soviet nuclear arsenals are available in various sources, including official Soviet and American documents. The standard nonpartisan source is the annual *Military Balance*, published by the International Institute of Strategic Studies in London. Thomas B. Cochran, William M. Arkin, and Milton M. Hoenig produced a series entitled *Nuclear Weapons Databook* beginning in 1984 (Cambridge, MA: Ballinger). All figures from all sources should be treated as estimates, even if they are considered fairly accurate estimates.

2. "Hard-point" defense refers to defense of ballistic missile silos and associated launch facilities, which are generally "hardened" against nuclear blast and radiation effects and require high accuracy to destroy. So-called "soft" targets, like cities, are very easy to destroy and therefore much more difficult to defend successfully.

3. See John Barton and Lawrence Weiler, *International Arms Control* (Stanford: Stanford University Press, 1976); Bernard Bechhoefer, *Postwar Negotiations for Arms Control* (Washington: Brookings Institution, 1961); Seyom Brown, *Faces of Power: Constancy and Change in United States Foreign Policy from Truman to Reagan* (New York: Columbia University Press, 1983); Robert Divine, *Blowing on the Wind* (New York: Oxford University Press, 1978); Matthew Evangelista, "Cooperation Theory and Disarma-

ment Negotiations in the 1950s," *World Politics* 42 (July 1990): 502–529; John Gaddis, *Strategies of Containment: A Critical Appraisal of Postwar American National Security Policy* (New York: Oxford University Press, 1982); United Nations, *The United Nations and Disarmament* (New York: United Nations, 1967).

4. United Nations, *UN and Disarmament*, p. 51.

5. Brown, *Faces of Power*, pp. 96–98.

6. Barton and Weiler, *International Arms Control*, p. 80.

7. See Barton and Weiler, *International Arms Control*; Duncan Clarke, *The Politics of Arms Control* (New York: Free Press, 1979); United Nations, *UN and Disarmament*; United States Arms Control and Disarmament Agency (ACDA), *Documents on Disarmament, 1964* (Washington, DC: U.S. Government Printing Office, 1965).

8. Quoted in ACDA, *Documents on Disarmament, 1964*, p. 372.

9. The literature on SALT is vast. As a sample see Coit D. Blacker and Gloria Duffy, eds., *International Arms Control: Issues and Agreements*, 2nd ed. (Stanford: Stanford University Press, 1984); Brown, *Faces of Power*; Philip J. Farley, "Strategic Arms Control, 1967–1987," in *U.S.-Soviet Security Cooperation: Achievements, Failures, Lessons*, ed. Alexander George, Philip J. Farley and Alexander Dallin (New York: Oxford University Press, 1988); Raymond Garthoff, *Detente and Confrontation: American-Soviet Relations from Nixon to Reagan* (Washington, DC: Brookings Institution, 1985); Fen Olser Hampson, "SALT I: The Interim Agreement and ABM Treaty," in *Superpower Arms Control: Setting the Record Straight*, ed. Albert Carnesale and Richard N. Haass (Cambridge, MA: Ballinger, 1987); Seymour Hersh, *The Price of Power: Henry Kissinger in the Nixon White House* (New York: Summit Books, 1983); Henry Kissinger, *The White House Years* (Boston: Little, Brown, 1979); John Newhouse, *Cold Dawn* (New York: Holt, Rinehart and Winston, 1973); Gerard Smith, *Doubletalk: The Story of SALT I* (New York: Doubleday, 1980); and Thomas Wolfe, *The SALT Experience* (Cambridge, MA: Ballinger Publishers, 1980).

10. See Ashton Carter and David N. Schwartz, eds., *Ballistic Missile Defense* (Washington, DC: Brookings Institution, 1984) for historical, contemporary, and technical discussions of American and Soviet ballistic missile defense programs.

11. See Abram Chayes and Jerome Weisner, eds., *ABM: An Evaluation of the Decision to Deploy an Antiballistic Missile System* (New York: Harper and Row, 1969); Morton Halperin, "The Decision to Deploy ABM: Bureaucratic and Domestic Politics in the Johnson Administration," *World Politics* 25 (October 1972): 62–95; Frederick Morris, "ABM," in the *Report of the Commission on the Organization of the Government for the Conduct of Foreign Policy* (the Murphy Commission), Appendix K (Washington: Government Printing Office, 1975); Burton K. Rosenthal, "The Formation of SALT Negotiating Positions," in Murphy Commission *Report*.

12. Blacker and Duffy, *International Arms Control*, pp. 221–223.

13. Hersh, *The Price of Power*, pp. 338–339.

14. Garthoff, *Detente and Confrontation*, pp. 150–155; Garthoff, "Negotiating with the Soviets: Some Lessons from SALT," *International Security* 1 (Spring 1977); Smith, *Doubletalk*.

15. Garthoff, *Detente and Confrontation*, pp. 133, 134, 136–342; Smith, *Doubletalk*, pp. 154–178.

16. Smith, *Doubletalk*, pp. 165–166.

17. Alton Frye, *A Responsible Congress* (New York: McGraw Hill, 1975), p. 64.

18. For the most comprehensive account see Ted Greenwood, *The Making of MIRV* (Cambridge, MA: Ballinger, 1976).

19. Hersh, *Price of Power*, pp. 154–155.

20. See Smith, *Doubletalk*, pp. 175, 457, 471–472; Hersh, *Price of Power*, pp. 165–166.

21. Smith, *Doubletalk*, pp. 222–246.

22. Ibid., p. 415.

23. Ibid., pp. 411–413.

24. Hersh, *Price of Power*, pp. 342–343, 537.

25. Garthoff, *Detente and Confrontation*, pp. 418–420.

26. Ibid., pp. 443–444.

27. See House Committee on International Relations, *The Vladivostok Accord: Implications for U.S. Security, Arms Control and World Peace*, 94th Cong., 1st sess., 1975, Hearings, pp. 84–85.

28. See Barry Blechman, ed. *Rethinking U.S. Strategic Posture* (Cambridge, MA: Ballinger, 1983); Seyom Brown, *Faces of Power*; Stephen J. Flanagan, "SALT II," in Carnesale and Haass, *Superpower Arms Control;* Garthoff, *Detente and Confrontation;* Strobe Talbott, *Endgame: The Story of SALT Two* (New York: Harper & Row, 1979); and Wolfe, *SALT Experience*.

29. Talbott, *Endgame*, p. 42.

30. Wolfe, *SALT Experience*, pp. 221–222.

31. Ibid., pp. 223–226.

32. Garthoff, *Detente and Confrontation*, pp. 818–820.

33. Ibid., pp. 146–183.

6

Negotiating the 1987 Treaty on Intermediate-Range Nuclear Forces

The first major arms control achievement of the 1980s was the 1987 Treaty on Intermediate-Range Nuclear Forces.[1] Signed by Presidents Mikhail Gorbachev and Ronald Reagan in Washington on 8 December 1987, the INF Treaty marked a dramatic departure from both the tenor of arms control bargaining only a few years earlier and from the major treaties of the past. Unlike SALT II, which sought primarily to regulate the arms race in strategic offensive weapons, the INF Treaty committed both sides to dismantle and destroy all land-based nuclear missiles with flight ranges between 500 and 5,500 kilometers. This meant eliminating a total of 2,695 missiles, plus their launchers and support facilities. Many of these missiles were no more than ten years old. For the United States, the 689 Pershing 2 IRBMs and ground launched cruise missiles that were to be destroyed had only been deployed since December 1983. These American missiles, plus the Soviet SS-20 intermediate-range ballistic missiles (IRBMs), had been at the heart of tension and controversy between the United States and the Soviet Union, and among the American and West European publics, for the first half of the decade. The Soviet missiles had become evidence to conservative political forces in the United States and Europe that Soviet leaders would exploit the loopholes of political détente and would actively seek military advantage over NATO. Imminent deployment of the American missiles rallied a quiescent peace movement in the United States and Western Europe, the activists being concerned with the missiles as symbols of the dangerous excesses of a continuing nuclear arms race. Politically, conservative parties controlled the governments of the three key NATO countries, the United States, Great Britain, and West Germany. Peace movements mobilized popular power in the streets and through local politics and referendum campaigns. In the end, no small amount of political capital was spent to deploy the very missiles that were to be systematically destroyed under the INF Treaty.

Furthermore, elimination of these weapons was to occur under a detailed plan specifying rights of inspection and observation, as well as procedures for their actual destruction. The treaty and its inspection protocol permitted each side to make as many as twenty inspections of declared missile bases and support facilities, on notice as short as sixteen hours, during the initial three years of implementation. Each side also was permitted to witness the destruction of the missiles, as well as to maintain continuous monitoring of the entry and exit from the missile production facilities in Utah and Russia.[2]

If nothing else, this agreement raised serious questions about the apparent virtues of the bargaining strategies employed in previous decades. Former top Pentagon arms control expert Richard Perle, for example, presented the major lessons of the negotiations: tough bargaining, patience, and commitment to a single best position were the effective methods for making the Soviet Union concede at the negotiating table.[3] He made the argument succinctly:

However one regards the INF Treaty, it is the treaty that Ronald Reagan set out to get in 1981. His will and resolve and that of our allies has vindicated the judgment that the Soviets could be pressed to abandon their intermediate missiles in exchange for ours.[4]

The INF Treaty appeared to support these claims. Each of the treaty's major achievements—elimination of an entire class of nuclear weapons systems and extensive verification measures, including on-site inspections—represented almost total Soviet embrace of American positions. The apparent simplicity and obviousness of Perle's claims was probably one reason that even Democratic critics of Reagan's arms control policies generally were silent.

The central negotiating issue of the INF talks involved the question of how many U.S. and Soviet weapons would remain after an agreement was reached. Related issues included what kinds of weapons would be limited, the geographical application of limitations, and the inclusion of non-U.S. NATO nuclear forces in the agreement. Almost all of these issues ultimately were resolved in favor of the United States. A careful examination of the negotiating process suggests, however, that the result may not have been determined by the virtues of the tough bargaining approach of the Reagan administration. Indeed, much of the bargaining showed more evidence of the virtues of mutual concessions and even initiatives than of toughness. Significantly, Gorbachev's initiatives, especially during 1987, challenged the American attachment to its own tough proposals.

BACKGROUND TO THE NEGOTIATIONS

The SS-20 IRBM was first deployed by the Soviet Union in the latter half of 1976 and became operational a year later.[5] The SS-20 replaced aging medium-range missiles, some of which were among the original weapons deployed in the early years of the missile race. The new missiles dramatically improved Soviet technology—they were solid fueled, they had a rapid response time, they were mobile, they were far less vulnerable to preemption, and they carried three accurate independently targetable warheads.[6] From NATO's perspective, the SS-20 changed the nuclear balance in Europe and placed at risk the nuclear deterrent forces of the alliance, including the independent strategic forces of Britain and France. Furthermore, the advent of strategic parity between the superpowers eroded Western Europe's confidence in American guarantees and highlighted disparities in the European balance.

West German Chancellor Helmut Schmidt, in an address to the International Institute for Strategic Studies in October 1977, pointedly directed attention to these concerns.[7] He suggested that the Western alliance must take steps to rectify the situation through both military and diplomatic measures. By the end of 1979, NATO reached a decision that called for a "two-track" response. On the one track, the alliance would deploy new American ground-launched cruise missiles (GLCM) and Pershing 2 intermediate-range ballistic missiles to modernize its own aging deterrent forces. Both new missiles provided significant technological advantages. The GLCMs were modern versions of the German V-2 rockets used in World War II. Using microelectronics and advanced jet engines, however, GLCMs could fly close to the ground for very long ranges and strike their targets with great accuracy. Although the missile was capable of carrying either conventional or nuclear munitions, only nuclear versions were planned for European deployment.[8] Pershing 2 IRBMs extended the range and increased the accuracy of the Pershing 1 and 1A missiles already deployed. These improvements allowed deployment further away from the conflict front, thus improving survival, and gave NATO planners a larger set of targets. Both missiles provided the capacity to strike targets within the Soviet Union, as well as within the Warsaw Pact states.

The SS-20 deployments contributed to the erosion of détente that began in about 1975 and accelerated toward the end of the decade. Following the 1979 NATO decision to deploy new U.S. intermediate-range missiles, Soviet leaders maintained a public posture favoring arms control negotiations and opposing American "militarism." They argued that the new American weapons would upset the military balance in Europe (since the SS-20s were only modernizations of existing weapons) and therefore were "unacceptable."[9] In October 1979, just before NATO's decision, Brezhnev seemed aware of the political damage caused by the SS-20 and offered to reduce IRBM deployments if NATO did not deploy new missiles. Otherwise, he warned that American deployments would "preclude negotiations."[10] At brief meetings in the fall of 1980, Soviet negotiators proposed a freeze of the status quo—no further Soviet deployments and no new NATO missiles.[11] At the time the Soviet Union had deployed about 200 SS-20s in the western Soviet Union and in Soviet Asia.[12]

FROM OPENING BIDS TO IMPASSE

The basic Soviet position, outlined in February 1981, involved a moratorium on deployments of nuclear weapons with ranges exceeding 1,000 kilometers "intended for use" in a European conflict. The thrust of the 1981 Soviet proposal was to prevent the deployment of new American missiles on the basis that nuclear equality already existed in Europe. To argue this, Soviet leaders included British and French nuclear forces, as well as carrier-based American nuclear-capable fighters and NATO-dedicated U.S. Poseidon submarines.[13]

American proposals for INF limitations from the Reagan administration came on 18 November 1981. In a speech broadly painting the dangers of the Soviet threat, Reagan offered a "zero-zero option." The United States would cancel its deployment plans (the American zero) in exchange for the elimination of all Soviet IRBMs deployed in Europe and Asia (the Soviet zero). The sweeping plan was characterized by American policy makers as "real" arms control, calling for the global elimination of an entire class of nuclear delivery systems. When the zero option was presented in negotiations in February 1982, the United States also called for a freeze on shorter-range INF (SRINF) that the Soviet Union had deployed in Eastern Europe (the SS-12/22, SS-23 IRBMs).[14]

At the opening round of INF talks in February 1982, Soviet negotiators tabled a proposal for staged reductions of nuclear weapons systems, including some aircraft, first to 600 delivery systems, then to 300 in a second phase. In May, General Secretary Brezhnev announced a unilateral freeze on SS-20s deployed or under construction in Europe.[15]

In July 1982 the United States began to move away from absolute zero and toward a compromise that would preserve some deployments for each side. American negotiator Paul Nitze opened an informal (and unauthorized) negotiation with counterpart Yuri Kvitsinsky. The "walk-in-the-woods" formula involved a trade of reduced numbers of SS-20 IRBMs (75 launchers with 225 warheads) in exchange for zero Pershing 2 IRBMs and 284 ground launched cruise missiles (72 launchers with four GLCMs per launch system). Both the U.S. and Soviet governments subsequently repudiated this formula.[16]

The Soviet Union also offered deeper reductions in its deployed forces, although as a way of forestalling any new American weapons. In December, the new general secretary, Yuri Andropov, offered to cut Soviet forces in Europe to equal British and French nuclear systems. This arrangement would still have maintained Soviet superiority in warheads because SS-20s were MIRVed, whereas British and French missiles (at the time) were not. In May 1983, however, Andropov indicated willingness to reduce his SS-20s to match these NATO allies' missile warheads.[17]

Another shift of the American positions away from zero came in the spring of 1983. From the beginning of the internal American debates in 1981, a "zero-plus" alternative existed.[18] Proponents of this alternative considered some deployment of U.S. INF to be necessary for NATO security. In other words, U.S. INF deployments were justified not simply as a response to Soviet SS-20s, but as an essential element in the whole NATO strategic structure of flexible response. Even if all SS-20s were removed, NATO would still want some INF deployments to strengthen the coupling of the United States with European defense.[19]

In the spring of 1983, European allies of the United States, particularly Belgium, the Netherlands, and West Germany, also were facing rising domestic pressure for progress on arms control that would reduce or obviate the need for deployment. European domestic problems were passed along to the alliance leader. In March the United States offered an interim proposal in which American deployments and Soviet reductions would be set to an equal number of both missiles and warheads.

During the fifth round of negotiations (between May and July 1983) the United States proposed global equality of warheads at a level between 50 and 450.[20] On 29 June 1983 President Reagan promoted the interim agreement, saying that if the Soviets would not accept zero, "OK, then a reduction as far as you will go."[21] In September the White House stated in a press release that the United States was seeking "more flexibility" in its negotiating stance, and would find acceptable an agreement that specified "equal rights and limits."[22]

Soviet positions consistently referred to the nuclear balance in Europe. By calculated omission the Soviets sought to maintain their deployments of SS-20s in Asia. Gradually, their positions shifted to accept that INF removed from Europe would not be relocated either east of the Ural Mountains or to Asia, and in August 1983 they allowed that European SS-20s would be destroyed.

In the fall, during round six of the talks, American negotiators amended their position again, accommodating somewhat the Soviet desire to preserve their missiles in Asia. Warhead equality would be applied only to Europe if the Soviets froze the number of SS-20s deployed in Asia at 108.[23] American willingness to accept continued Soviet SS-20 deployments in Asia after September 1983 raised concerns among Asian allies, especially Japan. In an address to the Japanese Diet in November, President Reagan offered reassurance, stating the "global reductions will not adversely affect the security of Asia."[24] The president's speech reiterated assurances given to Prime Minister Yashuhiro Nakasone a year before.[25] A subsequent U.S. proposal in November 1985 called for the reduction of Asian SS-20s from 170 to 85.[26] But the United States did not step back from the position of accepting some SS-20 deployments in Asia until mid-1987. This was at least partly due to American recognition that the Soviets were unwilling at the time to make more than token reductions in Asia.[27] From the beginning of 1986 the Soviet position clearly accepted deep cuts in their European INF forces. From the end of the year through 1987 they accepted the idea of INF elimination in Europe, with 100 additional INF warheads allowable for each side, of which their deployments would be in Asia. Thus, despite gradual concessions on numbers, Soviet negotiators refused global elimination of INF until mid-1987.

Also during round six of negotiations, in the fall of 1983, Soviet negotiators restated their position—zero new American deployments, reduction of European SS-20s to 140 (the number they claimed for British and French nuclear missiles), and a freeze on SS-20s in Asia (then at about 170).[28] As the deadline for American deployment neared, with little indication that the United States was willing either to delay or to countenance any deal that prohibited some deployment, Soviet positions on the future of the talks hardened.

American negotiating changes offered in the final months before the scheduled deployment of Pershing 2s and GLCMs did not persuade Soviet negotiators to continue talking. Fulfilling their threats that U.S. deployments and negotiations were incompatible, the Soviets walked out of INF talks in late November 1983 and refused to set new dates for either START or conventional force limitation talks.

Formal negotiations on nuclear arms did not resume until early 1985, when combined Nuclear and Space Talks (NST) began in January. During 1984 each side engaged largely in public posturing. Both professed a desire to see a resumption of talks and an improvement in U.S.-Soviet relations. But neither could accept the other's position, and the behavior of both governments sent inconsistent signals. Within the Soviet Union, the second leadership transition in two years was under way. Konstantin Chernenko became the Party's general secretary following Yuri Andropov's death in February. Chernenko urged renewed dialogue in a speech in March and then in May announced increases in Soviet ballistic missile submarine patrols near North America. In September, Foreign Minister Andrei Gromyko denounced U.S. policy in a speech at the United Nations, and then in October Chernenko expressed optimism about U.S.-Soviet relations. Similarly, on the American side, the administration alternately charged Soviet violations of existing arms treaties and urged the resumption of talks for new agreements.

Near the top of the Soviet agenda was to bring the American SDI program into the nuclear bargaining process. Resumption of the INF talks was affected because these became bundled into a broader negotiating agenda that included strategic offensive arms, and, if the Soviet position prevailed, space-based weapons. In January and July 1984 the Soviet Union rejected American suggestions for combined INF-START negotiations. Similarly, the United States rejected Soviet calls for space weapons talks. By November, the two sides finally moved together on this procedural question. They announced a new round of negotiations, including all three issues, to begin in the new year.

In the spring of 1985 the Soviet Union had its third new leader since Brezhnev's death in 1982. Mikhail Gorbachev, the youngest member of the Politburo, became the general secretary, and subsequently president of the Supreme Soviet and chairman of the Defense Council. Gorbachev was expected to follow some of Andropov's leads in terms of reforming Soviet industry and economic efficiency. There also were indications of his willingness to make compromises on offensive strategic arms in order to reach an arms control agreement. In December 1984, for example, Gorbachev addressed the British Parliament and asserted the readiness of the Soviet Union to make significant reductions in its nuclear forces, and calling for a ban on "space weapons."

Throughout 1985, Soviet negotiators maintained their definition of strategic weapons as those that could strike the homeland of the adversary, which again served to justify the lower numbers of SS-20s that the Kremlin apparently was willing to accept. In April, Gorbachev announced a unilateral freeze on new SS-20 deployments and proposed that the U.S. reciprocate. This marked a shift in Soviet positions to the acceptance of some American INF missiles. In October the Soviets tabled a new proposal calling for staged reductions and eliminations. The first phase would be a moratorium on new deployments; Soviet figures placed then current forces at 243 SS-20s and 209 U.S. INF. In the second phase Pershing 2s would be eliminated, and GLCMs would stay at 120 to 130. Soviet SS-20s would be reduced to about 100 systems, or 300 warheads, numbers the Soviet leadership claimed to be equal to the combined U.S., British, and French forces. Soviet negotiators claimed a warhead balance in Europe existed at 729 (if French and British forces were counted). The plan would exclude aircraft from the first stage and freeze SRINF.[29]

During this round of the talks, American proposals called for equal launcher numbers of 140 and equal warhead numbers of 420.[30] This proposal would have allowed the deployment of 108 Pershing 2s and 32 cruise missile launchers (128 missiles) with room to grow and would have required reductions of Soviet SS-20s from 270 launchers and 810 warheads.[31] The distance moved in the evolving American positions can be seen when this proposal is compared with the "walk-in-the-woods" formula of 1982. In the earlier proposed deal, the Soviets would have retained only 75 SS-20 launchers, while American forces would have consisted of 284 GLCMs and no Pershing 2 IRBMs. Obviously, by the end of 1985, American policy makers were more committed to the Pershing IRBM and more willing to accept the presence of the modern Soviet counterpart.

Gorbachev opened a new public relations campaign on arms control in January 1986 with a call to eliminate all nuclear weapons by A.D. 2000, in which the first stage would eliminate all INF in Europe. At the time, 243 SS-20s were deployed in the so-called European zone, which leaders indicated extended quite far into central Siberia. This number was roughly equal to the deployments in place when Brezhnev announced the first Soviet deployment moratorium in March 1982. Soviet SS-20s in Asia (about 170) would not be affected during the first phase of Gorbachev's plan.[32]

Significantly, the plan also dropped the requirement for counting French and British forces in the first round and implicitly marked official acceptance of the goal of global elimination, although couched in the rhetoric of a grand and unlikely scheme. In February Soviet leaders indicated that a separate INF treaty, unconnected to either strategic force reductions or ballistic missile defense issues, was acceptable.

American bargaining positions were revised again in the fall of 1986, when the United States indicated it was willing to pursue elimination in stages. A new interim agreement would permit 100 INF warheads on each side in Europe, plus

100 Soviet INF warheads in Asia, and 100 American INF warheads maintained in the continental United States.[33]

A framework for an INF treaty emerged from the summit talks in Reykjavik, Iceland, in October. The meeting was conceived as a "pre-summit summit," and General Secretary Gorbachev arrived prepared for serious bargaining, maintaining his position that the Soviets be allowed some INF in Asia, although at a sharply reduced level (100 warheads in place of the 510 already deployed). Soviet agreement to an INF treaty, as well as strategic arms reductions, remained linked to restrictions on SDI. President Reagan's refusal to make that key concession resulted in acrimony and mutual accusation as the meetings ended. The general outline of the agreement, however, was used when negotiations resumed in January 1987.

FROM REYKJAVIK TO A TREATY

The final months of bargaining on the INF treaty revealed an important discrepancy between dramatic Soviet concessions toward Western positions and reactions within the United States and the Western alliance. Instead of deriving satisfaction from the Soviet policy changes, the alliance was put in turmoil by concessions from the Kremlin.

An INF treaty appeared within grasp at the Reykjavik summit in October 1986, despite Soviet linkage of INF with strategic defense issues. At the end of February 1987, Gorbachev separated the issues, and an INF treaty gained its own momentum. The Reykjavik framework called for the elimination of INF from Europe, Soviet retention of 100 SS-20 warheads in Asia, American retention of 100 INF warheads in the continental U.S., and a freeze on shorter-range intermediate-range nuclear forces (a repeat of the U.S. position of February 1982).

In the West, NATO concerns began to focus seriously on the security implications of the emerging agreement—eliminating the new American missiles that had been deployed to more firmly couple the United States to European defense, numerical disparities of shorter-range INF favoring the Soviet Union, chronic conventional force imbalances, the problem of verifying the residual 200 INF warheads, and the continued presence of Soviet INF in Asia without compensating American forces. Soviet concessions toward the Western policy positions adopted in 1981 stimulated, perhaps belatedly, considerations of the consequences of a zero option on INF. Richard Nixon and Henry Kissinger, Caspar Weinberger, and General Bernard Rogers (Supreme NATO Commander) all expressed criticisms of the emerging treaty in March and April 1987. Members of the British, French and German governments also raised concerns.

Gorbachev increased the Western dilemma in April by proposing elimination of SRINF. Secretary of State George Shultz, supported by German Chancellor Helmut Kohl, argued in Moscow for an American "right to match." The United States and NATO SRINF would be created by removing a booster stage from

Pershing 2 missiles that were withdrawn. The Pershing 1b missiles thus created would then be transferred back to West Germany to replace the older Pershing 1a. A Soviet draft treaty presented in April specifically prohibited this conversion.[34]

The second zero of SRINF sharply divided the West German government. Chancellor Kohl sided with conservative opponents of the proposal. But he faced strong internal and external pressures. German public opinion contained a strong antinuclear current, as shown by the popular and electoral success of the Green party in state and federal elections. In addition, Kohl's coalition partners in the government, the Free Democratic Party, were more moderate on arms control and nuclear reductions than were Kohl's own Christian Democrats. Finally, the chancellor recognized the evident desire in Washington for an INF agreement now that one seemed within reach. In the end, Kohl acquiesced to these forces and supported the elimination of short-range forces.

British and French officials also were unenthusiastic about the second zero and were prepared to take a tough line on SRINF before the Gorbachev offer.[35] Eliminating SRINF would leave short-range battlefield nuclear weapons deployed only in Germany, thus heightening German fears of becoming an isolated nuclear battlefield in a European conflict. This was Kohl's argument against the proposal and the reasoning behind his support for both the U.S. right to match Soviet SRINF and contingent Warsaw Pact conventional force reductions.[36] London and Paris, however, feared that this situation would encourage Germany to pursue the "third zero"—elimination of tactical nuclear weapons. In effect, Britain and France feared undercutting German commitment to the alliance's nuclear deterrent posture and continuing nuclear weapons modernization. Both fears were supported by Bonn's behavior through early 1988.[37]

General Rogers argued pointedly in April 1987 that eliminating SRINF was a bad idea militarily. He recommended instead that the United States deploy additional short-range missiles in Europe.[38] Rogers's argument rested on his interpretation of NATO military requirements for deterrence under the doctrine of flexible response. Eliminating all nuclear missiles, he argued, would remove the alliance's ability to strike Warsaw Pact targets in a conflict. The effect would be to weaken the West's deterrent posture and invite Soviet "intimidation and blackmail."[39] The potential failure of the United States to actually employ nuclear weapons in the defense of Europe had been a matter of debate for over twenty years and was one of the justifications for the new American INF deployments in the 1980s.

Other American critiques of the treaty focused on the security and verification problems of the residual warheads.[40] Richard Nixon and Henry Kissinger argued that the framework was flawed, in part because it permitted thirty or so SS-20s in Asia. They also called for unilateral conventional force reductions by the Warsaw Pact as a prerequisite for American agreement. Defense Secretary Weinberger argued that he would like to see "all of the weapons go." Retaining small residual forces, he argued, complicated both security planning and the verification demands for the treaty.[41]

American negotiators held to the "right to match" formula until July. On 25 July, Gorbachev announced that the Soviet Union would "proceed from the concept of 'global double zero' " (elimination of both INF and SRINF) and that elimination of Soviet missiles in Asia was not linked to reciprocal reductions or restriction of American forces in the Far East.[42] This shift by Moscow diffused mounting Western criticisms and set the stage for the final compromises.

Politically, it was no longer tenable for either the United States or its European allies to hold out for the right to deploy new missiles when Moscow was offering to eliminate nuclear weapons in which it held a distinct numerical advantage. Negotiating attention turned to the problems of seventy-two West German Pershing 1a missiles for which the United States controlled the warheads. This issue was resolved by a German commitment to destroy the missiles at the end of the U.S.-Soviet dismantling process.[43]

The treaty signed on 8 December 1987 was a watershed in U.S.-Soviet arms control efforts. For the first time the countries agreed to measures that required them to eliminate two entire classes of nuclear weapons systems. Significantly, these were not weapons for which retirement was imminent in any case. Nor were they weapons deployed or planned for regions in which the parties had little interest. The weapons to be removed and destroyed by the INF Treaty were among the most modern systems either side had deployed—weapons in which each had invested substantial economic resources to develop and, in the case of the United States, substantial political resources to deploy. Furthermore, the elimination was global—no ballistic nuclear missiles with ranges greater than 500 kilometers and less than 5,500 kilometers would remain in the Soviet or American arsenals when the treaty provisions were fully implemented.

Verification measures to ensure compliance with the treaty were the most extensive ever written. Each side gained rights to witness the destruction of the missiles taken out of service by the other party. To guarantee that no additional missiles were produced clandestinely, each side was permitted to monitor the materials entering and leaving the designated production facilities of its adversary by maintaining an inspection team on site at the factories. Over the course of the next five years, each side conducted several inspections of production facilities and witnessed the destruction of hundreds of missiles. In a symbolic gesture, Presidents Bush and Gorbachev signed the first START agreement in 1991 with pens made from weapons destroyed under the INF process.

CONCLUSIONS

The final months of the negotiations illustrated that the American reversion to the predeployment zero option was deeply troubling to the Atlantic alliance. The difficulty with which American policy makers and European allies came to accept the expanded version of their own proposals, handed to them by significant Soviet compromises, suggested that these concessions from the Kremlin were not extracted by a tough American negotiating stance. Instead, the general wariness of European alliance members toward the zero option and preference for some deployments were apparent in the American bargaining positions from 1983 through 1987. "Hanging tough," in the actual process of bargaining, rather than simply in public statements, was not a consistent American position. The United States modified its offers to accommodate both allies' concerns and Soviet interests and, until Reykjavik, was committed to a stance that permitted deployments of both American and Soviet missiles.

Accommodating allies' concerns was consistent with the desire in Washington to deploy the new weapons as well as with a general antipathy toward arms control within the Reagan administration. Hostility toward arms control on the part of many top appointees was reflected in the approach to and the substance of U.S. negotiating positions.[44] The zero option presented in late 1981 was politically astute, insofar as it calmed European political nerves about U.S. commitment to arms control. However, the proposal also represented a victory for the hard-line bargainers in the Department of Defense in that it rejected "negotiability" as a criterion for judging offers.[45] These officials sought to ensure deployment of the new missiles by presenting a position that was patently unacceptable to the Soviet Union.

Not all members of the administration agreed with this approach to the negotiations. Paul Nitze, then chief INF negotiator, reportedly stated in late summer 1982 that "it was inconceivable that the Soviets would ever accept a proposal that required them to dismantle every last one of their most modern intermediate range missiles; that was simply asking, and hoping for, too much."[46] General Rogers testified in 1988 that "No one with whom I spoke on either side of the Atlantic at the time [the zero option] proposal was made believed that it would be accepted by the Soviets." His arguments favoring deployment on military grounds paralleled strategic political opinions in both Europe and the United States. Rogers argued that NATO's 1979 decision was "sold to the publics on both sides of the Atlantic as a means by which to capture the Soviet SS-20 missiles that were being deployed." In Rogers's opinion, NATO needed new intermediate-range nuclear forces in the mid-1970s irrespective of the SS-20s. "The fact that they were being deployed only made it more urgent for NATO to get on with its decisions."[47]

Helmut Schmidt's address in 1977 (which produced the political momentum leading to the 1979 decision) called attention to both the benefits of arms limitations and the alliance's need to maintain the military capabilities for deterrence.[48] Within the Reagan administration several policy makers argued against the zero option on similar grounds.[49] European leaders who saw the military logic of new INF deployments, however, were ensnared by more ambivalent public attitudes. One factor in the growth of the anti-INF movement in European publics in the early 1980s was the obverse of their leaders' desires to couple the United States to Europe—the people feared becoming a nuclear battlefield in which the superpowers waged war but remained untouched.[50]

   Collapse of negotiations in 1983 resulted largely from the Soviet hard line on preventing any new American INF deployments. Progressive Soviet offers and unilateral actions to reduce European SS-20 forces were aimed at preventing U.S. deployment, not at reaching a new bilateral balance. Significantly, by the fall of 1983, the positions of both sides had converged on agreement to permit around 100 SS-20s in Europe and slightly fewer in Asia. But the two sides were far apart on the critical question of how many U.S. forces would be permitted in Europe. To get some new missiles deployed, the United States was willing to live with some SS-20s; Soviet leaders continued to see new American missiles as unacceptable. Soviet political calculations that they could play to European public opinion by portraying the United States as the revisionist power turned out to be wildly optimistic.

   American policy makers, therefore, continually modified their offers in the face of pressure from allies, Soviet intransigence, and internal bureaucratic struggles. The key shifts were the decisions in the fall of 1983 to permit some Soviet INF if they were matched by U.S. systems and the acceptance of residual Soviet forces in Asia. These positions were more than tactical bargaining shifts, despite public statements that zero was the only real goal. They represented important accommodations to Western allies' concerns and the outcomes of bureaucratic battles. They were not evidence of hanging tough on the original position.

   Relatively comfortable with the deployments, and having paid a fairly high political price to get them, NATO's leaders were caught by their own promises when faced with Soviet concession in 1986 and 1987. In the end, Rogers argued, "political credibility [of NATO's European leaders] took a higher priority than that of the deterrence of NATO [sic]."[51] While his analysis of the treaty's strategic failings is open to question, he correctly identifies the motivation for agreement and the source of the alliance's discomfort.

   Thus the manner, timing, and motivations for shifts in American negotiating positions did not fit well with a model of how a tough bargaining strategy should work. Ironically, some of the U.S. shifts bear a closer resemblance to Kissinger's détente strategy, in which American concessions to the Soviet Union were offered in advance as enticements for good behavior, rather than as rewards after the fact.[52] Furthermore, Soviet initiatives taken in 1986 and 1987 significantly transformed the bargaining process and made a much more far-reaching agreement possible.

NOTES

   1. The official name for the treaty is Treaty Between the United States of America and the Union of Soviet Socialist Republics on the Elimination of Their Intermediate-Range and Shorter-Range Missiles. Much of the discussion in this chapter is based on William B. Vogele, "Tough Bargaining and Arms Control: Lessons of the INF Treaty," *Journal of Strategic Studies* 12 (September 1989): 257–272.

2. The text of the treaty and protocols is reprinted in full in *Arms Control Today* 18 (January/February 1988), special supplementary section.

3. Senate Committee on Foreign Relations, *The INF Treaty,* pt. 3, 100th Cong., 1st sess., Hearings, 1988, p. 5. See also Caspar Weinberger, "Arms Reductions and Deterrence," *Foreign Affairs* 66 (Spring 1988): 700–720; George Shultz in Committee on Foreign Relations, *The INF Treaty,* pt. 1, pp. 4–11; Kenneth Adelman made similar arguments earlier in "Arms Control With and Without Agreements," *Foreign Affairs* 63 (Winter 1984/1985): 240–263.

4. Senate Committee on Foreign Relations, *The INF Treaty,* pt. 1, p. 5.

5. Raymond Garthoff, *Detente and Confrontation: American-Soviet Relations from Nixon to Reagan* (Washington, DC: Brookings Institution, 1985), p. 856 fn 16.

6. For discussions of the Soviet decision to deploy the SS-20 see Garthoff, *Detente and Confrontation,* pp. 870–886; Jonathan Haslam, *The Soviet Union and the Politics of Nuclear Weapons in Europe, 1969–1987* (Ithaca: Cornell University Press, 1990), pp. 58–88.

7. See Garthoff, *Detente and Confrontation,* pp. 855–856.

8. For background on cruise missiles see Richard K. Betts, ed., *Cruise Missiles: Technology, Strategy, and Politics* (Washington, DC: Brookings Institution, 1981); Kostas Tsipis, "Cruise Missiles," *Scientific American,* February 1977.

9. Jonathan Dean, *Watershed in Europe* (Cambridge, MA: Lexington Books, 1987), pp. 118, 126.

10. Strobe Talbott, *Deadly Gambits* (New York: Knopf, 1984), pp. 30–40. Also see David N. Schwartz, *NATO's Nuclear Dilemmas* (Washington, DC: Brookings Institution, 1983), p. 238.

11. Talbott, *Deadly Gambits,* p. 42.

12. Garthoff, *Detente and Confrontation,* p. 856 fn 16.

13. Talbott, *Deadly Gambits,* pp. 84–89; Dean, *Watershed in Europe,* pp. 128–129.

14. Dean, *Watershed in Europe,* p. 131.

15. Dean, *Watershed in Europe,* p. 131.

16. Talbott, *Deadly Gambits,* pp. 115–132.

17. Dean, *Watershed in Europe,* p. 133.

18. Talbott, *Deadly Gambits,* pp. 56–70.

19. For background on these arguments in the period leading up to the 1979 NATO decision, see Schwartz, *NATO's Nuclear Dilemmas,* pp. 201–240. Also Dean, *Watershed in Europe,* p. 121.

20. *Arms Control Today,* "News and Negotiations," 13 September 1983: 5.

21. *Weekly Compilation of Presidential Documents,* 29 June 1983, p. 957.

22. *Weekly Compilation of Presidential Documents,* 12 September 1983, p. 1238.

23. *Arms Control Today,* "News and Negotiations," 13 October 1983: 5.

24. *Weekly Compilation of Presidential Documents,* 11 November 1983, p. 1556.

25. Talbott, *Deadly Gambits,* p. 177.

26. Dean, *Watershed in Europe,* pp. 141–142.

27. *Arms Control Today,* "News and Negotiations," 16 October 1986: 21.

28. Dean, *Watershed in Europe,* p. 134; *Arms Control Today,* "News and Negotiations," 13 October 1983: 5.

29. See Dean, *Watershed in Europe,* pp. 140–141; *Arms Control Today,* "News and Negotiations," 15 October 1985: 14.

30. *Arms Control Today*, "News and Negotiations," 15 (October 1985): 13–14.

31. Dean, *Watershed in Europe*, pp. 141–142.

32. See Garthoff, "The Gorbachev Proposal and the Prospects for Arms Control," *Arms Control Today* 16 (January/February 1986): 5; Dean, *Watershed in Europe*, p. 144.

33. *Arms Control Today*, "News and Negotiations," 16 (October 1986): 21.

34. Jesse James, "Controversy at Short Range," *Arms Control Today* 17 (June 1987): 13.

35. James M. Markham, "Missile Diplomacy: Europe Prepares," *New York Times*, 2 April 1987: A3.

36. James M. Markham, "West German Foes of Missiles See Victory Close," *New York Times*, 21 April 1987: A6; Serge Schmemann, "Bonn's Coalition Agrees to Endorse Missiles' Removal," *New York Times*, 2 June 1987: A1.

37. James M. Markham, "Bonn's Tactical Stand Worries Some NATO Allies," *New York Times*, 9 October 1987: A6; Julie Johnson, "Unity Stressed at NATO Summit but Tough Issues Are Unresolved," *New York Times*, 4 March 1987: A1; Markham, "In Europe, Reaffirmation," *New York Times*, 4 March 1987: A8.

38. Michael R. Gordon, "Commander of NATO Is Opposed to Ridding Europe of All Missiles," *New York Times*, 21 April 1987: A6. See also Paul Lewis, "General Sees Missile Plan as a Mistake," *New York Times*, 24 June 1987: A3.

39. Lewis, "General Sees Missile Plan as a Mistake."

40. Leon Sigal, "The Long and the Short of It: Allied Ambivalence About a Zero INF Deal," *Arms Control Today* 17 (May 1987): 10–13; James, "Controversy at Short Range"; Bill Keller, "Shultz in Soviet, Presses for Pact," *New York Times*, 14 April 1987: A1; Gordon, "Commander of NATO." See also *Arms Control Today*, "News and Negotiations," in issues of April, May, and June 1987.

41. See John Markham, "A Europe of Two Minds," *New York Times*, 3 March 1987: A1; Markham, "Missile Diplomacy: Europe Prepares"; Bill Keller, "West in a Quandary," *New York Times*, 16 April 1987: A1; *Arms Control Today*, "Momentum Builds Toward INF Accord," 17 (June 1987): 22.

42. Philip Taubman, "Gorbachev Agrees to U.S. Suggestion for a Missile Ban, " *New York Times*, 23 July 1987: A1; Taubman, "A Sense of Strategy," *New York Times*, 26 July 1987: IV3; Steven V. Roberts, "Reagan Optimistic on a Soviet Pact to Curb Missiles," *New York Times*, 29 July 1987: A1.

43. Serge Schmemann, "Bonn's Coalition Agrees to Endorse Missiles' Removal," *New York Times*, 2 June 1987: A1; Michael Gordon, "U.S. Said to Endorse Soviet Ideas for Compromise on Missile Cut," *New York Times*, 1 July 1987: A1; Michael Gordon, "Moscow to Consider Compromise in Disputes with Bonn over Missiles," *New York Times*, 3 August 1987: A1; Paul Lewis, "Soviet Says Pershing Missiles are Main Impediment to Pact," *New York Times*, 7 August 1987: A1.

44. See Kenneth Oye, "Constrained Confidence and the Evolution of Reagan Foreign Policy," in *Eagle Resurgent? American Foreign Policy in the Reagan Years*, ed. Kenneth Oye, Robert Lieber, and Donald Rothchild (Boston: Little, Brown, 1987), pp. 6–7, 27–30; Barry Posen and Stephen W. Van Evera, "Reagan Administration Defense Policy: Departure from Containment," in Oye, Lieber, and Rothchild, eds. *Eagle Resurgent?*, pp. 75–114.

45. Talbott, *Deadly Gambits*, pp. 8, 69, 70.

46. Ibid., p. 144.

47. Senate Committee on Foreign Relations, *The INF Treaty*, pt. 3, p. 11.

48. See Schwartz, *NATO's Nuclear Dilemmas,* p. 1.

49. Talbott, *Deadly Gambits,* pp. 56–70.

50. See Dean, *Watershed in Europe,* pp. 3–28; Talbott, *Deadly Gambits,* p. 23.

51. Senate Committee on Foreign Relations, *The INF Treaty,* pt. 3, p. 22.

52. Seyom Brown, *Faces of Power Constancy and Change in United States Foregin Policy from Truman to Reagan* (New York: Columbia University Press, 1983), pp. 332, 353–357.

7

Strategic Arms Reduction Talks: 1982–1991

On 31 July 1991, Presidents George Bush and Mikhail Gorbachev signed the first START agreement.[1] The treaty was a remarkable achievement in many ways. Nuclear weapons—the warheads, bombs, and cruise missiles—would be reduced by about a third. Most affected by the treaty would be land-based intercontinental missiles, of which the Soviet Union had a significant advantage. Far more lightly affected (even, in some ways, privileged) would be the nuclear weapons carried on long-range bombers, of which the United States had a numerical and technological edge. Like the INF agreement of 1987, START I created a detailed system of intrusive inspection rights and responsibilities. In the new treaty, however, inspection provisions would apply even to the remaining nuclear arsenal, meaning that each side was permitted to examine directly the operational weapons systems of its opponent.

Neither president could have predicted the course of events that would transpire in the next eighteen months, and probably neither expected their commitments to seek further reductions to be fulfilled so soon. Momentum to reduce nuclear forces increased in September 1991, when President Bush announced unilateral reductions in the American arsenal. Bush announced that the United States would redeploy all tactical nuclear weapons from overseas to the continental United States, including all tactical nuclear weapons on American surface ships and attack submarines. Furthermore, the United States would terminate its two mobile ICBM programs, remove from alert status over 1,000 ICBMs and SLBMs, as well as all strategic bombers. President Gorbachev responded quickly, saying the Soviet Union would destroy all remaining land-based tactical nuclear weapons (almost 10,000) and withdraw tactical nuclear warheads from surface ships and submarines. The Soviet Union would also unilaterally cut its strategic warheads to 5,000 (1,000 fewer than the START treaty prescribed), remove almost 1,100 strategic warheads from alert status, and halt development of various land- and bomber-based weapons.[2]

Gorbachev's political power and the Soviet Union's existence both were at an end, however. In December 1991 the Soviet Union splintered into independent republics. Eleven of the fifteen former republics, including the four new states that inherited the Soviet nuclear arsenal, formed the Commonwealth of Independent States and agreed to place all nuclear weapons under a single joint military command. Furthermore, over the next several months, each new state (except Russia) agreed to give up its nuclear arms and join the Nuclear Nonproliferation Treaty as a non-nuclear party. With the agreement of Russia, Kazakhstan, Ukraine, and Belarus to join START, the treaty could be ratified and the next START treaty signed and implemented.

The START II treaty was signed by President George Bush and Russian President Boris Yeltsin on 3 January 1993.[3] This treaty banned all land-based ballistic missiles with multiple warheads and reduced the total allowable number of all strategic nuclear weapons to between 3,000 and 3,500 each. Whereas START I tended to favor bombers by discounting their weapons capacity (by counting each bomber as if it carried a smaller number of weapons than was its actual capacity), START II counted the number of weapons actually deployed on each plane. The end result was a treaty that deeply cut both parties' nuclear arsenals, requiring the retirement of many modern, deployed weapons. By 1993, however, this dramatic progress in nuclear disarmament remained jeopardized by political tension and instability in Russia and backtracking on the NPT commitments made by Ukraine.

Equally as remarkable as the substantive achievements of START was the difference between the prospects for any kind of arms control agreement in 1981 and the negotiating process a decade later. The path by which negotiators traveled to START was as different from previous efforts as was the treaty. Notably, both the United States and the Soviet Union adopted bargaining strategies that departed significantly from those of their predecessors. Like the INF treaty, START was settled largely, although not entirely, on American terms. Understanding the bargaining patterns will help answer the question of whether it was the tough posture adopted by the Reagan and Bush administrations that pried open the Soviet concessions or whether the Soviet concessionary strategy created a new dynamic that was essential for agreement.

DEEP REDUCTIONS VERSUS SALT

In the 1980 U.S. presidential campaign, SALT II was one of the whipping boys. Substantively, the treaty made important but modest progress in regulating the nuclear competition. As a result, political support in the United States was decidedly tepid. Liberal arms control advocates decried it as too permissive of the new weapons programs on the Pentagon wish list, such as the MX ICBM. Conservatives charged that the treaty failed to reduce the Soviets' advantage in throw-weight because it allowed them to retain their heavy MIRVed ICBMs. Politically, the treaty could not withstand the consequences of the Soviet invasion of Afghanistan in December 1979. Charges of American weakness and inferiority in the face of numerous threats ranging from the Soviet military to militant students in Iran pushed traditional arms control into political oblivion. The most vocal private organization lobbying against SALT, the Committee on the Present Danger, called the treaty fatally flawed and demanded a military buildup to rectify the alleged U.S. inferiority.

Ronald Reagan won the presidency on such a mixed wave of public sentiment. Virtually all of the top personnel dealing with arms control in the Departments of State and Defense, and in ACDA, came from the Committee on the Present Danger or were closely associated with it. The new administration's anti-Soviet rhetoric began early on. In January 1981, Defense Secretary designate Caspar Weinberger testified that renewal of the ABM Treaty past 1982 was not automatic. Alexander Haig, the new secretary of state, accused the Soviet Union of promoting terrorism and of being the main source of insecurity in the world. Haig also stated that arms control talks could not be pursued at the expense of the strength of the Western alliance. In February, President Reagan called for meetings to discuss cuts in nuclear arms. He rejected the SALT treaty as unbalanced and detrimental to American interests. From the American point of view, "real" arms control required significant reductions by the Soviet Union in the weapons of greatest concern to the United States—large land-based ballistic missiles with multiple warheads. Nevertheless, although the State Department held that the United States was not legally bound by the unratified SALT II agreement, the United States would continue to adhere to the treaty limits pending a review of strategic plans and negotiations.

The American strategic review lasted until the spring of 1982. Over the year political pressures for greater engagement on arms control increased within the United States and NATO. Domestically, a grassroots movement emerged demanding a freeze on all nuclear weapons production, testing, and deployment by both the United States and the Soviet Union. Throughout 1981, partly in response to bellicose statements from Reagan administration officials and the apparent disinterest of the administration with any arms control, the freeze movement spread rapidly. By the end of the year public debate had merged with congressional interest and in early 1982 began to produce legislative freeze proposals.[4] In addition, arms control policy making was obstructed by bureaucratic debates within the administration among officials who sought to abandon SALT and arms control altogether and those who saw at least political necessity (if not strategic virtue) in negotiations.[5] The result was that the National Security Council did not even have its first meeting devoted to START until April 1982.[6]

In the rest of the Atlantic alliance, a similar process of grassroots mobilization focused on NATO's planned deployment of new intermediate-range nuclear missiles. Like the motivation for domestic American pressure, Washington's apparent abandonment of arms control and the loose talk about fighting and win-ning a nuclear war generated deep concern in the European publics and in their capitals. Movement on the INF issues came first (see Chapter 6), and negotiations began at the end of 1981. The cumulative effects of these changes in public sentiment would produce a return to the arms control arena on strategic arms in the spring of 1982.

At the end of March, President Reagan called on the Soviet Union to join the United States in making deep cuts in their strategic arsenals. In the meantime, however, he still characterized the nuclear balance as lopsided, saying the Soviet Union had a "definite margin of superiority" and pledged that the U.S. buildup would continue.[7] By May the administration was completing a proposal to put forward. On 9 May, the president called for new arms control measures in a speech at Eureka College. He called for new "Strategic Arms Reductions Talks," which would work for new measures that would do more than limit the strategic arsenals in the manner of SALT. He outlined two phases:

At the end of the first phase of START reductions I expect ballistic missile warheads— the most serious threat we face—to be reduced to equal ceilings at least a third below current levels. To enhance stability I would ask that no more than half of those warheads be land based. . . . In the second phase we will seek to achieve equal ceilings on other elements of our strategic nuclear forces, including limits on ballistic missile throw-weight at less than current American levels. At both phases we will insist on verification procedures to ensure compliance with the agreements.[8]

Expressed in terms of the hardware of strategic forces, the American proposal called for a common ceiling of 850 long-range missiles carrying no more than 5,000 warheads. No more than 2,500 of the warheads could be deployed on land-based missiles. The proposal imposed no limitations on strategic nuclear bombers or on air-launched cruise missiles.

The American proposal was an assortment of new and old concepts, as well as the product of intellectual and political struggles inside Washington.[9] But in two important ways the plan differed from previous efforts. First, it shifted the principal unit of account from launchers to warheads. Although it employed the launcher ceiling device that had become central to SALT, the real objective of the proposal was to reduce the numbers of warheads. For many in the Reagan administration, SALT II's failure to address the warhead imbalance on land-based ballistic missiles was one of the previous treaty's critical flaws. Second, the plan sought what appeared to be dramatic reductions in the nuclear arsenals.

The deep cuts only appeared mutual, however. They cut deeply into Soviet ICBM forces but barely affected the American arsenal. At the time, the United States had deployed about 2,200 warheads on its ICBM force, while the USSR had about 6,000. The disparity reflected the historical evolution of the two arsenals in which each had, over time, maximized its own geographical comparative advantage. With its large land mass and restricted warm water ports, the Soviet strategic forces had emphasized land-based missiles. Furthermore, Soviet missiles generally were larger than American forces—and thus could carry more warheads.[10]

Soviet reaction was negative, perhaps predictably. Leslie Gelb, for example, reported prior to Reagan's speech:

Administration analysts were told not even to consider the acceptability of any new plan to Moscow, just to lay out what was best for the United States and let Moscow make a counter offer. . . . State Department officials say the real aim of Eugene V. Rostow, director of the Arms Control and Disarmament Agency, and Richard N. Perle, Assistant Secretary of Defense for Policy, is to make unacceptable offers that Moscow will refuse, proving that arms control will not work. Defense Department officials say that Richard Burt, director of the State Department's Bureau of Politico-Military Affairs, is trying to bend to West European fashions for détente and secretly reconstitute the old approach to arms control.[11]

In August, Soviet negotiators presented their response to the American proposals. Their proposal called for an equal ceiling of 1,800 bombers and missiles combined. In addition, the Soviets called for the prohibition of all forms of cruise missiles with ranges exceeding 600 kilometers. The aggregate numbers represented a cut from the ceilings accepted by Moscow in SALT II (which placed ceilings at 2,250), but they were far higher than the American position. The Soviets also rejected the structure of subceilings that the Americans had presented. Furthermore, their call for cruise missile prohibitions clearly was aimed at the INF negotiations, in which ground-launched cruise missiles were one of the primary issues. Prohibiting long-range air-launched cruise missiles (ALCMs) also targeted the American advantage in these weapons and broadened the restrictions contained in the SALT II protocol.[12] American policy makers and negotiators rejected the Soviet plan.

By the beginning of 1983, intimations of shifts within the Reagan administration emerged. Edward Rowny reportedly suggested including sea-launched cruise missile limitations in the American position. This would be a concession in principle to one of the Soviet points of August 1982 and was presented as a way to show "U.S. seriousness."[13] No substantive changes were made in the American position, however, and the sides remained deadlocked. Each blamed the other for stalling and said that progress would depend on a change in the attitude of the other side.[14]

In June, both parties presented new proposals. The Soviets called for staged reductions to 1,800 missiles and bombers by 1990. Of these, 1,080 missile launchers could carry multiple warheads, of which 680 could be land based. Strategic bombers carrying cruise missiles would be limited to 120 planes. The Soviet position represented a modest change toward the United States with regard to missile sublimits and the acceptance by implication of some ALCMs. Under this proposal the Soviet Union would be permitted to keep all of its heavy and modern medium-range ICBMs. However, in the context of increasing tensions over INF in Europe, Soviet negotiators stated that the proposal would be withdrawn if NATO deployed its GLCM and Pershing 2 missiles in the fall as scheduled.

The June Soviet proposals also marked a modest concession toward the United States position of warhead limitation, at least in principle. However, the Soviet position did not specify numerical ceilings except to say that these should be below the current U.S. level. Lest this be taken as a major concession, the Soviet counting procedure included all American forward-based forces or short- and intermediate-range weapons deployed as bombs, land-based missiles or on aircraft carriers—effectively eliminating the Soviet advantage in long-range strategic warheads.[15]

The U.S. draft treaty in June expanded existing American proposals. The overall ceiling of 5,000 warheads remained, of which 2,500 could be deployed on land-based ballistic missiles. Of the warheads permitted by the draft treaty, only 210 could be deployed on Soviet MIRVed ICBMs, and only 110 of these could be on Soviet heavy missiles. At the time, the Soviet Union had deployed 308 SS-18 heavy ICBMs with ten warheads each. Furthermore, throw-weight was to be reduced to the current U.S. level about 4.5 million pounds. The American treaty increased the overall ceiling on missile launchers from 850 to 1,200 and included bombers in the reduction process (the bomber limit was set at 400 each, including the Soviet Backfire bomber). Weapons carried on bombers, however, would be discounted, so that one bomber counted as one "warhead," regardless of the actual weapons loading.

Substantial reductions in Soviet weapons continued to be the centerpiece of the American draft treaty, with few corresponding cuts on the American side. For example, ceilings on heavy ICBMs applied only to the Soviet arsenal since the United States had neither these weapons nor any plans to build them. Similarly, throw-weight reductions required as much as a two-thirds cut by the Soviets (from approximately 12 million pounds), while requiring no change or even permitting an increase by the United States.[16]

Domestic pressures on the American administration, however, prompted revisions in the U.S. stance. The freeze movement maintained a momentum of criticism about official policies and proposals. In Congress proposals emerged for a middle ground that would permit modernization of the strategic arsenal— especially the perennially contentious MX ICBM—and create more flexibility in the negotiations. The key proposal called for a "build down" of nuclear forces in which old weapons would be replaced at a rate of less than one for one.[17] In October the United States offered a double build down plan in the negotiations. The new scheme called for aging bombers to be replaced at a rate of one for one, submarine-launched ballistic missile warheads at a rate of two for every three removed, and land-based ballistic missile warheads at a rate of one for every two removed from service. Minimum annual reductions of 5 percent were required until the ceiling of 5,000 warheads was reached. The second part of the build down plan called for annual reductions of ballistic missile throw-weight to the level of 4 to 5 million pounds.[18] Soviet negotiators rejected the new plan as "vague, obscure, and unclear," and claimed it was an invidious effort to propel the arms race to a dangerous qualitative level.[19]

At the end of December 1983, START negotiations fell victim to the Soviet protests over NATO's INF deployments. The session ended with no date set for resumption. For the next year, each party engaged in a process of posturing and proposals aimed at restarting the negotiations. In addition, the military and political context began to be influenced by American plans to develop a space-based missile defense system. Both Moscow and Washington had some interest in negotiating, but the changing balance of military forces and strategies shifted the issues they brought to the table.

THE STRATEGIC DEFENSE CHALLENGE

For the first few years of the Reagan administration the American military buildup continued, but it did not generate any dramatic departures from previous military plans. The differences lay more in the quantity and speed with which new weapons were acquired than with their novelty. Reagan policies moved the MX ICBM and the Trident D-5 SLBM through production and closer to deployment, but these systems were already in the pipeline in 1980. In fact, the Reagan administration ultimately was unable to resolve the problems associated with mobile basing modes for the MX and by 1985 settled for placing fifty of the new missiles in existing Minuteman silos in Wyoming.

Soviet and American strategic arsenals did not undergo fundamental change during the 1980s. Offensively, the Soviet military acquired somewhat larger numbers of nuclear weapons (bombs and missile warheads) than the United States, while remaining within the permissive limits of SALT II.[20] Both American and Soviet strategic programs continued to modernize, moving toward systems with greater accuracy and survivability.

Offensive strategic force modernization in the United States produced new submarine platforms (the Ohio class Trident submarine) and new generations of long-range bombers (the B-1 supersonic bomber, and the B-2 bomber employing radar defeating "stealth" technology). On board the Trident submarine, the Trident 2 SLBM (D-5) was deployed in late 1986. This new SLBM was designed to be as accurate as land-based ICBMs.[21] Each Trident submarine carried eighteen SLBMs, with up to fourteen warheads each (on the D-5 missiles). Although over 300 feet long, the Trident was much quieter than existing Poseidon submarines and therefore was less vulnerable to detection. Because its larger size also increased its range and patrol time, American submarine-based deterrent forces became even more survivable than before. These advances gave the United States an invulnerable counterforce capability that no land-based deployments could match. Finally, air-launched cruise missiles were deployed on B-52 strategic bombers, with 131 bombers converted by December 1986, providing a substantial new capability for the air-breathing leg of the American triad. The effect of programs on both sides was to increase counterforce capabilities and numbers of weapons.

In March 1983, however, Ronald Reagan added a new element to the calculations of military and strategic balance. In a nationally televised speech, the president called upon scientists to develop a defensive shield that would render nuclear weapons "impotent and obsolete." Three years later, Reagan characterized his 1983 speech in this way:

Back in 1983, I challenged America's scientific community to develop an alternative to our total reliance on the threat of nuclear retaliation, an alternative based on protecting innocent people rather than avenging them; an alternative that would be judged effective by how many lives it could save, rather than how many lives it could destroy.[22]

With a sweeping proclamation the president reversed traditional nuclear doctrine that rested on the assumption of mutual deterrence under the conditions of mutual assured destruction. Given the tremendous destructive potential of nuclear weapons, strategists had assumed that anything less than a perfect defense made little sense. This logic led to the conclusion that only the willingness and capability to undertake a nuclear exchange, even after an initial attack, could deter a nuclear war in the first place. Security, in Winston Churchill's well-known phrase, became the "sturdy child of terror." Deterrence through threats of mutual annihilation, however, was morally uncomfortable to many in and out of the government, including President Reagan. Thus, in his call for a new defense the president asked if it was not better to protect one's citizens than to be able to act only in revenge and retaliation. Reagan's assertion of the moral superiority of defense over retaliation (or offense) was almost precisely the argument made by Soviet Premier Alexei Kosygin to President Lyndon Johnson at their meeting in Glassboro, New Jersey, in 1967. At that time, the failure of the Soviet Union to accept the American logic of the offense-defense linkage provided the final motivation for Johnson to initiate the U.S. ABM program.

American SDI programs also presented a potentially dramatic shift in the rate of change for defensive forces. The United States had mothballed its ABM installation at Grand Forks, North Dakota, as soon as it was finished. The Soviet Union had maintained and modernized its ABM system surrounding Moscow and had developed new missile defense radars (at least one of which, at Krasnoyarsk, appeared to violate the ABM treaty). Both sides had continued to fund research related to defense, but at relatively modest levels. The return of the United States to a major BMD commitment, with all of the advantages of more advanced American technology, promised to reinvigorate a defensive arms race. All of the problems for stable deterrence that arose during the ABM debates would then be renewed. In particular, new U.S. programs suggested the potential for seriously threatening Soviet assured-destruction retaliatory capabilities acquired since 1968. This change was especially threatening to the Soviets when combined with American offensive force improvements. One of the Soviet responses, in turn, could have been to pursue more active offensive systems programs and improvements.

This element of change in the military balance, therefore, became the central issue in both policy making and bargaining choices. General Secretary Yuri Andropov immediately denounced the U.S. defensive plan as an attempt to disarm the Soviet Union. At the end of April he called for an international ban on space weapons. Within a year, however, negotiations for offensive reductions were linked to questions of strategic defense. By the end of 1984 Soviet concessions on offensive force reductions, necessary for U.S. agreement, became firmly tied to American concessions on SDI restrictions. Both sides initially took extreme positions. Soviets demanded the prohibition of even laboratory testing of strategic defenses, a more restrictive provision than the ABM treaty contained. Americans argued that the 1972 treaty permitted testing and development of ballistic missile defenses based on exotic technologies and proposed offensive limits that cut deeply in Soviet ICBM forces while marginally affecting American systems.

FORMING THE SDI CONNECTION AND
RESUMING TALKS

Although formal negotiations ended with the December 1983 Soviet walkout, both sides jockeyed to resume talks through 1984. In January, Edward Rowny stated that the United States would consider merging the INF and START talks to create a new comprehensive vehicle for negotiations. Before the INF deployments, after all, Soviet positions in START often sought to limit INF, by counting forward-based forces as strategic weapons, for example. Soviet leaders rejected Rowny's proposal, however. Their primary interest and concern was the SDI challenge.

In June, Moscow offered to begin talks on space weapons, although not in the context of broader negotiations; Washington rejected separate talks on space. By the fall, however, the American desire to reduce the Soviet offensive arsenal began to converge with the Soviet desire to restrict SDI. On 22 November, Soviet and American officials announced that they would resume negotiations in the new year under broad-agenda umbrella talks. At the end of December, each side made conciliatory statements toward the other. Mikhail Gorbachev, in an address to the British Parliament, signaled the readiness of the Soviet Union to make significant concessions on offensive arms in exchange for controls on missile defenses. American officials similarly reported that the United States was willing to make concessions on SDI. A pattern soon developed, however, in which Moscow would firmly link offensive reductions (including asymmetrical cuts in the USSR arsenal) with strict limits on strategic defenses, and the United States would suggest that SDI was on the table for trading—but then would firmly refuse any linkage.

When the Nuclear and Space Talks began in March 1985, American positions on offensive arms remained unchanged—a 5,000-missile warhead ceiling, of which 2,500 could be on ICBMs. Soviet negotiators made a general proposal for 25 percent reductions in launchers and began to press more firmly for controls on space-based weapons.[23] By May, negotiators had made no progress on either offensive or defensive limitations. Gorbachev characterized the talks as fruitless and blamed the American commitment to SDI as the main obstacle to achieving reductions.

In September, the Soviet approach shifted. At the end of August hints began to emerge from Moscow of a willingness to make significant concessions on offensive arms—up to 40 percent reductions—conditioned on an end to the SDI program. The American response was to adopt a tougher line on SDI.[24] At the end of September, Gorbachev officially proposed 50 percent cuts in "nuclear charges," plus a ban on all new types of offensive weapons and space weapons. He also proposed that no more than 60 percent of the deployed warheads could be on launchers of any one basing mode.[25] Secretary of State George Shultz asserted that the United States would not stop work on SDI, even in exchange for cutting Soviet arms in half.[26] Other U.S. officials rejected the Soviet offer on the grounds that it required the abandonment of the American programs for the MX ICBM, the Trident D-5 SLBM, and the B-2 strategic bomber, but it would not affect such Soviet programs as the SS-25 mobile ICBM, which was already being deployed.[27] Nevertheless, as the first U.S.-Soviet summit since 1979 approached, some reactions in Washington indicated a softening line as other officials suggested that the Geneva talks could have a "positive outcome."[28]

American policy was confused.[29] On the one hand, translating the Soviet proposals on offensive cuts into numbers of warheads yielded an overall ceiling of 6,000 warheads and an implied ICBM ceiling of 3,600 warheads. The first number was close to the American position, although the second remained much higher. In anticipation of the summit, both U.S. positions were revised upward in October, so that they called for an overall ceiling of 6,000 warheads and a ballistic missile ceiling of 3,000 warheads.[30] At the Geneva summit in November 1985, Reagan and Gorbachev agreed on a total ceiling of 6,000 warheads, of which 4,500 could be on ballistic missiles. They could not agree, however, on a separate sublimit on ICBM warheads.[31]

On the other hand, American negotiators were very ambivalent about their willingness to limit SDI and very reluctant to abandon the goal of direct limits on throw-weight. Although some U.S. officials indicated that SDI activity might be confined to research, others opposed any restraints. The official position remained that reductions in offensive arms could not be contingent upon defensive limits because SDI was seen as inherently stabilizing for a strategic environment of deep offensive cuts.[32] In any case, the Soviet position on space weapons did not indicate whether Moscow envisioned a comprehensive ban or one that would prohibit deployment while permitting some forms of research.[33] To the extent that Soviet positions called for a complete prohibition of any research or development of strategic defenses, the negotiators contradicted their stated commitment to the "traditional" interpretation of the ABM treaty, which permitted research. Similarly, the United States continued to call for direct reductions of throw-weight, while the Soviet proposals would make these a function of numerical reductions.

Finally, in November, the United States proposed a ban on mobile ICBMs, an item that so far had been left out of the negotiations.[34] The American position seemed somewhat disingenuous, given the persistent efforts to build the MX ICBM in a mobile platform. But it clearly was a reaction to the recent Soviet deployments of the SS-25 ICBM in a road-mobile platform and the MIRVed SS-24 ICBM on a rail-based platform, and it reflected an American desire to reverse the imbalance.[35] Overall, American positions tended toward the view expressed by Defense Secretary Caspar Weinberger in January 1986: "Moscow's willingness to accept an agreement, I think, will be determined primarily, if not only, by its judgment about what the U.S. will do in the absence of an agreement."[36]

Gorbachev seized the public stage on arms control again on 15 January 1986 with a set of sweeping proposals to eliminate nuclear arms by the year 2000. At least two elements of the plans made concessions to the United States. First, the plan implied the separation of INF from strategic arms talks, thus making resolution of the former issues more likely. Furthermore, Gorbachev began to clarify the Soviet demand for a ban on SDI. He stated clearly that offensive arms reductions were only possible if the United States renounced "development, testing, and deployment" of space weapons. First Deputy Foreign Minister Georgi M. Korniyenko subsequently noted that this did not imply a ban on "basic research," which presumably could continue under the terms of the 1972 ABM treaty.[37] Basic research remained undefined, although the new Soviet position appeared to be an effort to satisfy American desires to continue the investigation of space-based defense, if not the desire to move to early deployment.

By beginning to offer distinctions in terms of research and development phases for SDI, the Soviets were engaging in a major domestic debate in Washington. Interpretation of the ABM treaty had become a major row between the administration and the Senate. Administration officials argued that the 1972 treaty should be interpreted broadly. Their position held that research was very broadly permitted and that prohibitions of new types of missile defense technology should be narrowly construed to those named in the treaty. Some senators, among them Sam Nunn, argued just the reverse—that a "strict" or traditional interpretation of the treaty was warranted in accordance with the understanding of the treaty as offered at the time of ratification.[38] The Soviet position, therefore, was moving toward the Senate leaders' strict interpretation. In May the Soviet SDI position became more elaborate. They proposed that each party to the START treaty agree to refrain from withdrawing from the ABM treaty for fifteen to twenty years and that each side agree to abide by a strict interpretation of its provisions.[39]

In June 1986, Gorbachev formally separated INF and strategic arms in the Soviet bargaining positions. At the same time, however, he introduced a new warhead ceiling of 8,000, which included sea-launched cruise missiles (SLCMs). The new ceiling effectively raised the ICBM ceiling to 4,800 warheads.[40] Including SLCMs represented a move away from the previous position of a total ban on cruise missiles. The effect was to place cruise missiles generally within the negotiating arena for potential limitation, or preservation, as the United States desired. The United States, however, was not interested in bringing sea-launched cruise missiles into the negotiations.

In response, the United States revised its proposals for numerical ceilings upward once more. New positions offered in August increased the warhead ceiling to 7,500, with 5,500 on ballistic missiles and 3,300 on ICBMs. Of the ICBM warheads, no more than 1,650 could be on heavy missiles, mobile land-based missiles, or missiles with six or more warheads. American negotiators thus tabled, by implication, an alternative to their ban on mobile ICBMs—at least partly in recognition that the Soviet Union was unlikely to give up the newly deployed SS-24 multiple warhead mobile missile. Still remaining outside the U.S. limitation proposals, however, were bombers, ALCMs, and sea-launched cruise missiles.[41]

In September, Gorbachev began to scale back the Soviet position on adherence to the ABM treaty, proposing a nonwithdrawal period of "up to fifteen years," rather than fifteen to twenty.[42] At the Reykjavik summit the following month the Soviet position shifted downward again to call for a ten-year period. Reagan accepted the Soviet position on a period of nonwithdrawal, and the leaders agreed in principle to observe the ABM treaty for a period of ten years. Nevertheless, the definition of what research was permissible under a strictly observed ABM treaty, the crux of the argument over SDI, remained unresolved.

At Reykjavik the leaders made progress in shaping the general terms of the agreement. They agreed to overall limits of 6,000 warheads to be deployed on 1,600 bombers and missiles. Bombers, and therefore ALCMs, returned to the negotiations, as they had been both in SALT and in Soviet START positions. (How to count the weapons carried on bombers subsequently would become an issue for debate.) Furthermore, the Soviet Union agreed to cut its force of SS-18 heavy ICBMs by half, from 308 to 154 (reducing its number of warheads on heavy ICBMs to 1,540). Finally, submarine-launched cruise missiles were taken out of the strategic arms reduction talks and were to be resolved separately.[43] These points were notable, first, for the acceptance by Washington of inclusion of bombers in the reduction process, and second, for the agreement by Moscow to an aggregate ceiling that was below the most recent American proposal. Soviet negotiators, however, refused to discuss sublimits of the kind desired by the Americans.

But the summit itself was highly contentious. The two leaders appeared to agree to dramatic commitments to either eliminate all nuclear weapons in ten years or to eliminate ballistic missiles in ten years. American officials contended that the president was interested only in eliminating ballistic missiles in so short a time, but the Soviets charged a "massive disinformation campaign" on the part of Washington aimed at disguising the scope of the potential agreement.[44] In either case, such sweeping new agreements collapsed over SDI. Gorbachev's effort to bind reductions in offensive forces to restriction on defensive systems met a stone wall with Reagan. As Reagan put it, "In effect, he was killing SDI. . . . I told him I had pledged to the American people that I would not trade away SDI."[45] That pledge was made in August when the president said, "our response to demands that we cut off all testing and close shop is : no way. SDI is no bargaining chip. . . . And the research is not, and never has been, negotiable."[46] One American analyst commented that intentionally or not, Reagan's attachment to strategic defenses saved the United States from entering a strategically ill-advised reduction process, which it probably would have had to abandon.[47] The Soviet refusal to sever the link between offensive reductions and SDI would remain a major item of contention.

Negotiating progress through most of 1987 remained impaired by each party's adherence to its post-Reykjavik positions. Below the 6,000-warhead ceiling, the United States continued to demand a limit of 4,800 ballistic missile warheads, with only 3,300 permitted on land-based missiles, of which 1,650 would be allowed on heavy ICBMs, mobile missiles, or those with six or more warheads. For their part, the Soviets maintained their desire to have a freedom to mix the distribution of warheads among basing modes, even though they were willing to take 50 percent cuts in SS-18s. In September 1987, Moscow modified this stance somewhat by formally proposing a sublimit ceiling of 1,540 warheads on SS-18 heavy missiles and a restriction of 60 percent of the deployed warheads to any single basing mode (echoing their position from the previous year). In practice, this meant a land-based missile warhead ceiling of 3,600 warheads.

Soviet negotiators departed from their resistance to specific sublimits in October when they presented new, detailed comprehensive proposals of offensive reductions tied to an explicit commitment to nonwithdrawal from the ABM treaty. The Soviet package included a limit of 3,000 to 3,300 ICBM warheads (with only 1,540 on heavy missiles), 1,800 to 2,000 submarine-launched ballistic missile warheads, and 800 to 900 air-launched cruise missiles. These ceilings were quite close to the proposed American restrictions: 4,800 ballistic missile warheads, with 3,300 on land-based missiles, of which only 1,650 could be on mobile, heavy, or missiles carrying six or more warheads. The American difficulty with the Soviet plan, however, was that it was too restrictive of U.S. submarine-based forces. In other words, while the Soviets had previously argued for a freedom to mix warheads across all platforms, so as to maintain their comparative advantage of geography, the United States wanted to be able to mix ballistic missile warhead platforms, reflecting its emphasis on sea-based forces. At a meeting in November, Secretary of State George Shultz and Soviet Marshall Sergei Akhromeyev agreed to a ballistic missile warhead ceiling of 5,100, with the freedom to mix between land-based and submarine-based platforms. In December, at the Washington summit, Reagan and Gorbachev moved these limits down.

Thus, at the end of 1987, agreement on the structure of offensive reductions stood as permitting no more than 1,600 strategic delivery vehicles, with 6,000 warheads overall, 4,900 of which would be on ballistic missiles, with a ceiling of 1,540 warheads on heavy land-based missiles. The leaders committed their governments to finding a "mutually acceptable solution" to the problem of limiting long-range nuclear sea-launched cruise missiles but would not count them against the 6,000-warhead limitation. Furthermore, Gorbachev agreed to the goal of throw-weight limitation, although not through direct restrictions as the United States had desired since 1982. The Joint Statement made at the end of the summit read in part, "that as a result of the reductions the aggregate throw-weight of the Soviet Union's ICBMs and SLBMs will be reduced to a level approximately fifty percent below the existing level, and this level will not be exceeded by either side."[48]

Nevertheless, differences remained about other limitations. The United States dropped its sublimit of 1,650 warheads on heavy missiles, but kept the 3,300 ICBM warhead sublimit. The Soviet Union, in turn, dropped its separate ICBM and SLBM limits and increased the permitted number of air-launched cruise missiles to 1,100. They differed on both the counting rules for ALCMs and the range that would include or exclude the weapons from treaty limits. Finally, Soviet negotiators continued to demand an explicit provision in START committing each party to observe the traditional understanding of the ABM treaty.

Although the December 1987 summit seemed to generate momentum for strategic arms talks, negotiations slowed down in the first months of 1988. The unresolved issue of SDI testing was the key obstacle. By the end of March, Secretary of State George Shultz admitted that START and defensive limitations could not be entirely separated, and he said he thought that differences on SDI could not be set aside to facilitate resolution of offensive issues. He noted that the two negotiations should be "completed more or less at the same time so the two things move in parallel." Shultz's position reflected a recognition that Moscow was not going to let go of the connection, and it would probably be detrimental to American interests to proceed under conflicting assumptions of what behavior was acceptable.[49] When Reagan and Gorbachev met for their fourth summit, in June, the central disputes remained unresolved. As one reporter put it, "The United States offered no compromise suggestions to limit [testing of defensive systems] at the summit. The Russians held firm to their demands for strict limits."[50]

Modest progress was made on the methods to verify limits on mobile ICBMs. The U.S. proposals, suggesting limited deployment areas and prior notice of movements out of these areas for maintenance or training, were reportedly accepted by the Soviets. Negotiators disagreed on the size of the deployment areas—the United States called for an area of 25 square kilometers, while the Soviets argued for a region of about 100 square kilometers.[51] The leaders also agreed that strategic bombers "equipped only for nuclear gravity bombs and

SRAMs will count as one delivery vehicle against the 1600 limit and one war-head against the 6000 limit."[52] Nevertheless, the summit's accomplishments were very modest. And as the American presidential election neared, it became increasingly unlikely that the remaining issues could be resolved during the Reagan presidency.[53]

Ronald Reagan could claim the INF treaty as a landmark agreement achieved under his administration, but START eluded him. Nor did George Bush's victory in the American presidential election move the negotiations closer to conclusion. In fact, one of the first acts of the new administration was to delay the resumption of negotiations, scheduled for February 1989, while strategic positions and policies were reviewed.[54] Negotiations did not begin until June, and even then major issues remained unresolved in American policy, including the linkage of START and ABM, counting procedures for ALCMs, and deployment constraints for mobile ICBMs.[55]

During the first session of negotiations Bush placed a new issue on the table. The administration proposed, in "general form," several measures designed to develop verification techniques in advance of the completed treaty. These measures included advance notification of significant exercises involving strategic forces, prohibition of tests of depressed trajectory missiles, establishing permanent on-site monitoring of mobile ICBM production facilities, experiments and trials with "tagging" mobile ICBMs and inspecting warheads on other ballistic missiles, commitment to a comprehensive data exchange similar to the INF treaty provisions, and a ban on encryption of telemetry data transmitted during missile tests.[56] Since the beginning of negotiations in the early 1980s, the United States had demanded far more intrusive verification measures than any previous treaty had contained. The argument for undertaking these experiments and agreements before other issues were resolved was twofold. First, the practical question of how to verify limitations or reductions was closely tied to the political question of what to limit. In the 1970s, for example, the choice to count launchers rather than warheads reflected, in part, the capabilities (and limitations) of national technical means of verification. Similarly, the question of how low a testing threshold might be depended on the sensitivity and reliability of national seismic measurements, if these were to be the exclusive means of verification. Negotiators were loath to accept a limitation if they had no confidence in the means to monitor compliance. By this token, the American call for intrusive inspection measures was a logical requirement if actual deployed warheads were to be the unit of account. Second, given the precedent of the INF treaty, on-site inspections and other cooperative verification arrangements clearly were going to be included in the START treaty. Technical details and specific rules and procedures, therefore, would have to be resolved sooner or later. Better to work on these issues in advance rather than during the final hours of negotiations, according to the American view.

Victor Karpov, head of the Soviet delegation to the talks, stated Soviet acceptance of some of these proposals in an interview in the *Washington Post*. He ac-

cepted outright the plans to develop tags for mobile ICBMs and the goal of banning telemetry encryption. He called the proposals for data exchange, exercise
notification, and warhead inspection trials "reasonable." However, he suggested
that any on-site monitoring should be both comprehensive and reciprocal, including bombers, ALCMs, and SLCMs.[57] When Foreign Minister Eduard Shevardnadze met with U.S. Secretary of State James Baker in September in
Wyoming, they signed agreements to move the verification measures process
forward. The Agreement on Verification and Stability Measures stated: "The
purpose of the above measures is to conduct pilot trials with the aim of subsequently refining, during negotiations, the verification procedures to be included
in the Treaty."[58]

The ministerial meeting also brought U.S. and Soviet negotiators closer together on several other issues. On the question of limits to mobile ICBMs, the
Soviet Union accepted limits on both numbers and restrictions of these weapons
to designated areas. In June 1986, the Soviets had proposed a verification
scheme for mobile missiles that included several items, such as the designated
areas and provisions for periodic visibility and display of the missiles. This early
willingness to find acceptable verification techniques probably accounted for
the U.S. implicit acceptance of mobile missiles in September 1986, despite their
standing position favoring a ban.[59] Official Soviet acceptance of a U.S. verification plan in 1989 led Baker and Shevardnadze to announce that the United
States was withdrawing its proposal to ban the missiles.[60]

More importantly, the Soviet Union dropped the requirement for a defense
and space treaty as a condition for an offensive arms accord. Leading up to the
ministerial meeting, the ABM gap remained. Richard Burt, head of the American delegation, stated that the U.S. goal was to "preserve our options to deploy
advanced defenses," and Under Secretary of State Reginald Bartholomew asserted that the Bush administration supported the broad interpretation of the
ABM treaty.[61] On the Soviet side, Karpov had stated that the Soviet Union could
not accept the American position on ABM, and negotiator Yuri Nazarkin stated
flatly that "a treaty on fifty percent cuts in strategic offensive weapons can be
concluded only if the Anti-Ballistic Missile Treaty is observed."[62] In the Joint
Statement of the Baker-Shevardnadze meeting, however, the "sides agree to
drop the approach of a non-withdrawal commitment" as part of the START
treaty.[63] Shevardnadze stated that the Soviet Union was "ready to sign and ratify
the START treaty even if, by the time it is completed, an agreement on the
ABM problem will not have been reached, provided, of course, that both sides
would continue to comply with the ABM treaty as signed in 1972."[64] Removing
the condition for a space treaty created the possibility of an agreement on offensive reductions.

Bush and Gorbachev met on a ship in the Mediterranean off the coast of
Malta for a "nonsummit" summit in December 1989. They each declared that
the Soviet-American relationship was at a historic moment. Bush stated that "we
can realize a lasting peace and transform the East-West relationship to one of

enduring cooperation." Gorbachev asserted that the presidents agreed that "the world leaves one epoch of Cold War, and enters another epoch."[65] They pledged to hold an "arms control summit" in June 1990. At the end of 1989, the distance on several important issues, including strategic defense, was closing.

THE ENDGAME OF START I: 1990–1991

Although Soviet negotiators had stepped back from demanding either a parallel treaty on strategic defenses or a specific nonwithdrawal clause in the START treaty, they did not fully abandon the linkage of SDI and offensive reductions. As the endgame of START began, Soviet negotiators "continued to demand an agreed statement permitting either side to withdraw from START if the other side violated the traditional interpretation of the ABM treaty."[66] The Bush administration opposed inclusion of this statement, at least in part because the basic issue of what constituted permissible behavior under the traditional interpretation remained contested. American negotiators wanted only the more generic clause permitting withdrawal when the "supreme national interests" were violated.

Negotiators remained divided on other issues as well. At the Malta summit, Gorbachev continued to press for inclusion of sea-launched cruise missiles in START and for the states to undertake talks on naval arms limitations generally. Counting methods for ALCMs also differed. Moscow wanted to count each deployed cruise missile with a range exceeding 600 kilometers as one warhead and to use on-site inspections for verification. American negotiators wanted a counting rule similar to that employed in SALT, whereby each bomber would be counted as if it carried ten cruise missiles, even though it potentially could be loaded with a larger number of weapons. This counting rule would eliminate on-site inspection of bombers and would apply only to cruise missiles with ranges exceeding 1,500 kilometers. On the question of numeric constraints on nondeployed missiles, American negotiators sought controls that applied to the entire missile inventories of each side. Their concern was to prevent the emergence of a future Soviet advantage made possible by maintaining rapid replacement capacities for the relatively low number of deployed missiles that remained after reductions. The Soviets argued that only nondeployed mobile missiles should be counted, since only these posed a significant military threat through rapid deployment. They were willing, however, to prohibit storage of all nondeployed missiles near launch sites. Finally, the two sides agreed on the principle of prohibiting the encryption of telemetric data during missile tests, but they could not agree on the details of how and when during flight these data should be broadcast free of coding.[67]

When James Baker met with Eduard Shevardnadze and Mikhail Gorbachev in Moscow in early February 1990, several of these issues were resolved. They agreed to adopt the U.S. counting rule approach to limiting ALCMs. American bombers would be counted as if they carried ten warheads (although they could carry up to twenty), Soviet bombers would be counted as if they carried eight (although their maximum load was twelve), and all future ALCM-capable bombers on either side would be counted as ten. This method provided a substantial advantage for the United States because it discounted the actual weapons that could be carried on bombers, a leg of the strategic forces in which the United States held a traditional advantage. No agreement was reached, however, on the matter of the range criterion for cruise missiles, although the United States was prepared to consider limits on missiles with ranges exceeding 1,000 kilometers, instead of 1,600 kilometers.

Sea-launched cruise missiles were to be handled by means of periodic declarations of the actual number of deployed nuclear SLCMs, an American position that the Soviets accepted. In turn, the United States was willing to consider this declaration "politically binding." As with the ALCM issue, differences remained on what ranges to include in the limitation, although the positions were reversed. The United States wanted to count all SLCMs with ranges exceeding 300 kilometers, while Soviet leaders wanted to count only those missiles with ranges beyond 600 kilometers. The differences, again as in the case of the ALCM issue, reflected the differences in capabilities between the sides—the United States wanted to protect its shorter-range air-launched missiles from constraints and simultaneously place restrictions on the shorter-range sea-launched cruise missiles, in which the Soviet Union had an advantage. Finally, Baker agreed to the Soviet position regarding nondeployed missiles, and the treaty would only count these for mobile land-based missiles.[68]

At the June summit, Presidents Bush and Gorbachev issued a joint statement that recapitulated the existing agreed terms for the treaty, but it was unclear whether the treaty would be signed that year. In numerical terms, United States and Soviet leaders agreed to the following framework. Strategic launchers (land- and sea-based ballistic missiles and long-range bombers) would be limited to 1,600 each. The total number of accountable warheads (including ballistic missile warheads, air-launched cruise missiles, and non-ALCM-carrying bombers) would be set at 6,000 for each side. Within the overall ceiling, only 4,900 warheads would be permitted on ballistic missiles, of which 1,540 would be permitted on heavy ICBMs and 1,100 on mobile land-based ballistic missiles. The counting rule approach to bombers and air-launched cruise missiles was reaffirmed so that all non-ALCM-carrying bombers would count as one warhead against the 6,000 ceiling. American and Soviet ALCM-capable bombers would be counted as ten warheads and eight warheads per bomber, respectively. The United States conceded to the Soviet desire to include all air-launched cruise missiles with ranges exceeding 600 kilometers.

Several other important issues were included as agreed elements of the future treaty. On throw-weight limitations the Joint Statement reiterated the previous Soviet position:

The aggregate throw-weight of the deployed ICBMs and SLBMs of each side will be limited to an agreed level which will be approximately fifty percent below the existing level of the aggregate throw-weight of deployed ICBMs and SLBMs of the Union of Soviet Socialist Republics as of a date to be determined.

Sea-launched cruise missiles would be handled outside the START treaty, through politically binding unilateral declarations. As on the air-launched cruise missiles, the United States conceded to the Soviet position on ranges, accepting inclusion of all SLCMs with ranges exceeding 600 kilometers. Specifically prohibited in the Joint Statement were new heavy ICBMs, heavy SLBMs, mobile launchers for heavy ICBMs, new types of ICBMs and SLBMs with more than ten warheads, capabilities for rapid reload of launchers, flight testing of depressed trajectory missiles, and MIRVed long-range air-launched cruise missiles.

Following the model of the INF Treaty, the Joint Statement declared that compliance with the provisions of the prospective START treaty would be verified through on-site inspections (including short-notice inspections), national technical means, the prohibition of encrypted telemetry during missile flight tests, an exchange of information on the size and disposition of each other's strategic forces, and a comprehensive agreement on deployment restrictions for mobile ICBMs, including the use of "tags" and other measures developed during the joint verification experiments.[69]

Despite these important points of agreement, James Baker noted three major issues that remained unresolved, in addition to several lesser items. The major issues involved flight-test constraints on Soviet SS-18 heavy ICBMs, the status of the Soviet Backfire bomber (one of the vexing problems left over from SALT II), and the noncircumvention clause for the treaty. Additional issues included verification procedures for mobile ICBMs, defining accountable throw-weight, counting rules for future types of ballistic missiles, rules for "downloading" MIRVed ICBMs (that is, reducing the number of warheads that could be carried in a reentry bus designed for more), numerical limits on nondeployed mobile ICBMs, and a sublimit on ICBM warheads. The endgame, in other words, involved a fair amount of devilish details needing attention and resolution.

By the end of the year, the three main issues that Baker had identified in June were resolved in principle, but the prospects for completing the treaty in early 1991 dimmed, largely because of remaining problems with the lesser issues and also because of developments outside the START process. The major obstacles were overcome by a combination of compromise on SS-18 flight test restrictions and, in the case of the Backfire bomber and the noncircumvention clause, agreement to make unilateral statements that would not be contested by the other side, but which did not have the status of formal treaty items.[70] The United States abandoned its efforts to impose flight-test restrictions on the SS-18 ICBM. In November 1985, the United States had first proposed a ban on all flight tests, modernization, and production of the heavy SS-18. This effort was consistent with the American goal of severely constraining, and ideally eliminating, the Soviet advantage in heavy missiles. At that time, and when it resurfaced in the START endgame, the Soviet response was categorically negative. Even when the United States modified its position in early 1990 to permit limited flight tests on existing types of SS-18s and to phase out production over several years, the Soviets were not interested.[71] They said essentially that the United States should be satisfied with the 50 percent cuts they were already willing to make.[72] At the end of 1990, American negotiators gave up the goal of a flight-test ban. In turn, the Soviets agreed not to increase the throw-weight or launch-weight of the SS-18 beyond the current version, known as Mod 5.

On 28 January 1991, the summit meeting scheduled for February was postponed until midyear. In addition to the continuing lack of closure on several important issues pertaining to the treaty itself, two developments external to the nuclear negotiations created problems. Unrest and secessionist sentiments in the Soviet republics was creating general political instability in the Soviet Union and threatening the processes of political reform undertaken by Gorbachev. The most acute crisis emerged in January 1991 in the Baltics. The previous year each of the Baltic republics (Lithuania, Latvia, and Estonia) had declared its independence and asserted the sovereignty of its own laws and governments. They had all begun to engage in acts of defiance against the central government in Moscow, including encouraging draft resistance of Baltic youth and the defection of Baltic nationals from the Soviet armed forces. Popular elections brought independence parties and coalitions into power. During 1990 the response of the Moscow government was to apply sanctions, such as curtailing fuel supplies, to coerce the republics back into line. By January 1991 these measures by Moscow had failed to have the desired result. In Lithuania, Soviet special forces troops attempted to gain control of the government in Vilnius directly. Crowds of nonviolent popular resisters, coordinated to some extent by the Lithuanian government, blockaded the parliament building and the television station. Several people were killed and wounded when the Soviet troops opened fire.[73]

The heavy-handed efforts of pre-Gorbachev style repression failed to reverse the independence movements in the Baltics. Arguably, these movements were strengthened both in their resolve and in their sense of their capacities to resist repression. The anti-reform tactics of the Soviet government, however, raised serious questions about the future of Mikhail Gorbachev and the willingness of the Soviet government to make binding commitments in the START process.

The second issue involved interpretation of the Treaty on Conventional Forces in Europe (CFE) signed in Paris by the members of NATO and the Warsaw Alliance on 19 November 1990. The CFE treaty was a historic document, designed to undo the militarized confrontation between the Cold War alliances in central Europe. Under its terms thousands of troops and tanks would be withdrawn from the various states and regional theaters.[74] Dispute over whether or not to count approximately 5,500 artillery pieces deployed in Soviet naval infantry units held up the potential for the treaty's ratification until June 1991, and START thus became a hostage to both the process of political turmoil in the Soviet Union and disagreement on another major arms control agreement.

With the CFE issues settled by a compromise in early June, START negotiations regained momentum. In the next two months negotiators worked to fashion compromises on the remaining issues: defining new types of missiles, downloading MIRVed missiles, verifying mobile missile deployments and monitoring their production, and ensuring access to the relevant telemetry data from missile flight tests.[75]

The 1991 START Agreement

The START I agreement, signed on 31 July 1991, built on the agreed framework of the 1990 Joint Statement. It required that by the end of seven years each side must have reduced its strategic nuclear arsenal to 1,600 strategic nuclear delivery vehicles. The treaty permitted a maximum of 6,000 "accountable" strategic nuclear warheads, 4,900 of which could be deployed on ballistic missiles. Soviet heavy ICBMs, one of the enduring American strategic concerns since the 1970s, were to be reduced by half and their modernization halted. The treaty permitted 1,100 deployed warheads on land-based mobile missiles, and required the total throw-weight of all ballistic missiles to be reduced to no more than 3,600 metric tons (roughly 7.9 million pounds).[76]

The START agreements also contained two provisions that, in broad strategic terms, began to reverse the progress of both sides toward more accurate MIRVed counterforce weapons and encouraged both de-MIRVing and mobility as a means to increase survival. Land-based missiles carrying multiple warheads could be downloaded, or have their warhead loadings reduced, up to a total of 1,250 warheads at any one time on three existing types of ICBMs, including the Minuteman III and the SS-18 (Article 3, section 5). Reductions of warheads on the two named ICBMs, however, required destruction of the existing reentry bus and replacement with a new warhead carrier. Economic and strategic logic informed these provisions. In economic terms, it was less expensive to reduce the warhead loading on existing MIRVed missiles than to replace the entire missile and launcher with a new system. This was a key argument put forth by Soviet negotiators. Strategically, however, it was necessary to prevent the future possibility that warheads, once removed, could easily be replaced by a regime bent on overturning the treaty restrictions. Thus, START made a critical step backward from the relentless pursuit of MIRVed missiles that had characterized the nuclear competition for twenty years. Signed just eighteen months after START I, START II prohibited MIRVed ICBMs entirely.

The second mutual strategic adjustment toward enhanced stability was the set of provisions permitting, within certain limits, mobile land-based launchers. On the one hand, permitting mobile ICBMs, despite the quixotic efforts of the United States to ban them, reflected strategic reality. The Soviet Union had deployed two types of mobile ICBMs by 1991, one of which was MIRVed. And the United States had long desired the production of some type of mobile missile, which by 1991 looked increasingly like the single warhead Midgetman. Furthermore, the survival advantages of mobility increased mutual stability and made the reductions of warheads on fixed Soviet missiles more palatable to Moscow and the Soviet military. Mobile missiles did receive various restrictions, however. Article IV restricted the number of permissible nondeployed ICBMs for mobile launches to 250 each (while nondeployed missiles for fixed launchers remained unrestricted), as well as specified restrictions on movements, tests, and storage of these missiles. Article VI specified restrictions on the deployment areas for mobile ICBMs, including the number of permissible structures, the land area of deployment zones, and notice for relocation.

The START agreement of July 1991 thus prescribed substantial reductions in each superpower's strategic arsenal, although not exactly equal reductions. Soviet ICBM warheads were to be cut by one-half, while warheads on U.S. land-based missiles would be reduced by about a third. Preferential treatment was given to those weapons considered to have the least threatening counterforce capabilities and the highest probability for survival in a nuclear attack. Thus American advantages in cruise missiles, bomber technology, and submarine capabilities were reinforced. Soviet advantages in large, high payload, multiple warhead ICBMs were greatly diminished. By one estimate, the United States was allowed to retain about 11,000 of its 12,000 warheads deployed on intercontinental weapons systems. Comparable Soviet forces were to be reduced from 11,000 to 8,500.[77]

Reducing warheads also marked a departure from previous arms control efforts in three important ways. First, it required the retirement of almost all of the older, but still useful, nuclear delivery systems, plus the removal of some new systems. Dismantling older systems was the most cost-effective way to reduce the warhead arsenal. Second, structural differences between Soviet and American nuclear forces required the Soviet Union to make disproportionate cuts. This resulted from the fact that the strictest limitations applied to land-based missile warheads, which comprised roughly two-thirds of the Soviet strategic force. For the second time since serious arms control began in 1969, the Soviet Union agreed to remove far more weapons than the United States in order to reach the goal of actual numerical equality.

Third, reductions in warheads rather than in the delivery systems required extensive direct verification. The 1987 INF Treaty established the precedent for an intrusive inspection system and had provided a great deal of experience with cooperative verification methods. By the time START was signed in July 1991, all of the missiles specified for elimination under the INF accord had been destroyed. Inspection and verification of strategic arsenals, because they were so much larger, required an unprecedented degree of cooperation. START differed from INF, however, in that the warheads on deployed missiles would be subject to counting and verification under START, whereas the INF treaty prescribed that missiles and their launchers be removed from deployment and destroyed. Each of those latter procedures could be observed with limited threat to the requirements for keeping strategic secrets. In this regard, the verification experiments were valuable exercises in how to observe and count. By mid-1990, Soviet and American experts had completed six trial inspections of missiles and bombers, including the U.S. MX and the Soviet SS-18.[78] Article VIII of the START treaty established procedures for the exchange of a comprehensive database and mutual notification, through the Nuclear Risk Reduction Centers, of tests and exercises. Article X prohibited various forms of encryption or other electronic deception in the broadcast of telemetric data during missile flight tests. Article XI established general rights and requirements for warhead inspections, monitoring of production facilities, and periodic exhibitions of weapons. Two additional protocols to the treaty provided more specific rules and procedures.

The START agreements provided the framework for substantial reductions and substantive restrictions on the nuclear deterrent forces of both sides. In many areas, the treaty broke new ground in methods to adjust the strategic behavior of the competitors in order to realize greater stability and, therefore, security through cooperation. Furthermore, START was seen as the first in a series of arms reduction treaties. This expectation was carried forward first in the reciprocated unilateral reductions of the fall 1991 and subsequently in START II.

CONCLUSIONS

Concluding a survey and analysis of bargaining in the START negotiations requires attention to the general issues that concern this study—the pattern of exchanges that comprise the negotiations. In START, did tough bargaining tend to promote concessions or frustration? Were concessions (and retractions) reciprocated in some more or less equivalent way? And did unilateral initiatives in the bargaining compromises lead directly to agreements or did they promote a more favorable environment for the negotiations? Closely related to these general issues is the question of the role of SDI in the START negotiations. The U.S. and Soviet positions on strategic defenses were important indicators of the bargaining approaches employed by each side.

Tracing the pattern of exchanges through the START negotiations reveals that although the major concessions were made by the Soviet Union, American negotiators engaged in various adjustments toward the Soviet positions that made agreement possible. In other words, whether one compares the terms of the treaty with the opening positions of each side or looks at the movement in positions at various times, it is hard to detect strong evidence to validate the tough bargaining approach.

The endpoint for some issues in the treaty was closer to the original Soviet position than to that of the United States. For example, the launcher total (1,600) was almost double the original U.S. proposal (850) and still a third larger than the total of 1,200 in the June 1983 revisions. Significantly, Soviet proposals began at 1,800 launchers and always included bombers, which the United States sought to exempt until June 1983.

Several points of agreement resulted from mutual compromises. Regarding air-launched cruise missiles, the initial positions of the United States and the Soviet Union were exclusion from limits and a total ban on all cruise missiles, respectively. By 1983, ALCMs and bombers were brought back into the negotiation process for potential limitation. The arguments then turned to the proper ways to count the weapons against the overall ceilings and what classes of ALCMs to include. Eventually, the Soviets accepted the counting rule proposed by the Americans and the United States accepted that the limitations should apply to all ALCMs with ranges exceeding 600 kilometers (as opposed to the more restrictive cutoff of 1,500 kilometers originally pursued). Similarly, the United States dropped its call for a ban on mobile ICBMs, even though the prospects for congressional approval of any land-mobile basing system were remote, in return for detailed restrictions on deployment zones.

On three issues central to the initial U.S. positions the outcomes of the bargaining were mixed, as are the lessons for bargaining strategies. First, the United States demanded that the unit of account for strategic arms control change from launchers to warheads. This reflected a view that counting launchers, although technically easier for the purposes of treaty verification, required liberal counting rules with respect to weapons. Under the SALT II structure, for example, both sides had a great deal of room to increase the number of warheads they targeted at the other. Given the much greater throw-weight of Soviet missile forces, and therefore the greater potential for warhead proliferation, American analysts felt that the threat was not sufficiently well contained. Counting warheads directly, on the other hand, could create more precision and greater balance in the standoff of strategic forces. Counting warheads, in turn, required much more intrusive and cooperative verification measures. On both of these issues the American position was pursued consistently and eventually prevailed. By 1987, the precedent for intrusive verification was set with the INF treaty, and by 1989 Soviet leaders had accepted that numerical limits on warheads should be the central feature of START.

Dramatic constraints on Soviet missile throw-weight was the second key element of the original START goals. The success of the American bargaining strategy is somewhat harder to judge. In the first place, the START treaty specified throw-weight limitations of about 8 million pounds. In this sense, the U.S. goal of an explicit restriction was fulfilled. However, the number was at least 50 percent higher than the original targets. Second, explicit throw-weight limits did not play a central role in the bargaining positions offered by the United States after 1983. Instead, attention turned to settling questions of warhead ceilings. Soviet negotiators, once they accepted the general objective measuring force reductions by warheads, argued consistently that any throw-weight reductions would be a consequence of weapons reductions and not negotiated separately. Gorbachev's agreement in 1990 to throw-weight limits at approximately half of the Soviet force capabilities reflected more the direction of warhead reductions than a willingness for an explicit measurement. Furthermore, one should interpret the final number (7.9 million pounds) as meaning either that the Soviet forces preserved more than half of their aggregate missile throw-weight or that the initial American estimates (of about 11.5 million pounds) were almost 4 million pounds too low. This is a large error for a variable about which so much concern was expended.

Finally, there is the question of the role of SDI in the START bargaining process. Some policy makers and analysts argued that SDI was the key to extracting concessions on offensive weapons from the Soviets. Kerry Kartchner argues that "the steadfast U.S. commitment to pursue SDI, even at the cost of progress in arms control, was responsible for most of the apparent flexibility in Soviet START policy after 1986."[79] Taking a perspective that sees weapons programs as the essential sources of bargaining leverage, Kartchner continued:

The central mystery of the START experience is why the United States achieved all that it did, given the poor state of U.S. bargaining leverage. . . . The only plausible explanation is that U.S. cruise missile production and the SDI program provided whatever bargaining leverage the United States brought to bear in the negotiations.

The Reagan administration assertions to the effect that SDI had brought the Soviets back to the negotiating table . . . were essentially validated by the START experience.[80]

Jack Mendelsohn and James Rubin, on the other hand, argued that the Soviet return to the bargaining table in 1985 responded to their need to reverse the failed policy of trying to mobilize European opinion against the INF deployments and also reflected the new leadership of Mikhail Gorbachev in the Kremlin.[81]

What did the bargaining record show? In support of the argument made by Kartchner, American negotiators did not retreat from their position that SDI should not be included in an offensive agreement, even though some policy makers hinted at offensive-defensive trade-offs in late 1984, and Shultz acknowledged in 1988 that the two negotiations should proceed in parallel. The closest the United States came to a concession on SDI was when Reagan accepted at Reykjavik the principle of a ten-year period during which neither side would withdraw from the ABM treaty. Furthermore, the United States did not move on SDI when the Soviets offered to cut strategic forces by half in 1986.

After 1986, Soviet positions gradually evolved from seeking a complete ban on strategic defenses and space weapons, to a START provision promising non-withdrawal from the ABM treaty for a specified time, to a START article that asserted the so-called traditional interpretation of the ABM treaty, to a unilateral statement. In the end, the START treaty signed in 1991 was accompanied by a Soviet statement making explicit Moscow's linkage of START and defensive limitations:

This Treaty may be effective and viable only under conditions of compliance with the Treaty between the U.S. and the USSR on the Limitation of Anti-Ballistic Missile Systems, as signed on May 26, 1972. The extraordinary events referred to in Article [XVII] of this Treaty also include events related to the withdrawal by one of the Parties from the Treaty on the Limitation of Anti-Ballistic Missile Systems, or related to its material breach.[82]

In this sense, the United States achieved its objective of preserving SDI from any explicit limitations either in START or in a separate treaty. On the other hand, the Soviets were equally clear that they considered extensive development and deployment of SDI by the United States grounds for leaving the START treaty. Whether this posture was a bluff that could be called by an American administration determined to proceed with new strategic defenses was never tested.

NOTES

1. See text of the START Treaty, *Arms Control Today* 22 (November 1991), special supplement.

2. See "Factfile: Comparisons of U.S. and Soviet Nuclear Cuts," *Arms Control Today* 22 (November 1991): 27–28; also texts of speeches by George Bush and Mikhail Gorbachev in *Arms Control Today* 22 (October 1991): 3–6.

3. See "Summary of START II Treaty," *Arms Control Today* 23 (February 1993).

4. See Douglas C. Waller, *Congress and the Nuclear Freeze Movement: An Inside Look at the Politics of a Mass Movement* (Amherst: University of Massachusetts Press, 1987), pp. 21–73; Pam Solo, *From Protest to Politics* (Cambridge, MA: Ballinger, 1987).

5. Strobe Talbott, *Deadly Gambits* (New York: Knopf, 1984), pp. 222–233.

6. Ibid., p. 246.

7. Bernard Gwertzman, "Reagan Calls for Dramatic Slash in Nuclear Arms, " *New York Times,* 1 April 1982: A1.

8. "Text of President Reagan's Address on Nuclear Policy and East-West Issues," *New York Times,* 10 May 1982: A14.

9. See Talbott, *Deadly Gambits*, pp. 233–277.

10. Lloyd Jensen, *Bargaining for National Security* (Columbia: University of South Carolina Press, 1988), p. 210.

11. Leslie H. Gelb, "U.S. Forging New Concept to Curb Strategic Arms," *New York Times,* 2 May 1982: A16.

12. Talbott, *Deadly Gambits,* p. 297; Leslie H. Gelb, "Offer By Moscow to Curb Bombers and Missiles Cited," *New York Times,* 1 August 1982: A1.

13. William Beecher, "U.S. Weighing Modification in Arms Stance," *Boston Globe,* 7 January 1983: A1.

14. "Arms Negotiators Return to Geneva," *New York Times*, 1 February 1983: A8.

15. Kerry M. Kartchner, *Negotiating START: Strategic Arms Reduction Talks and the Quest for Strategic Stability* (New Brunswick, NJ: Transaction Publishers, 1991), p. 106.

16. Ibid., 133–134.

17. Alton Frye, "Strategic Build Down: A Context for Restraint," *Foreign Affairs* 62 (Winter 1983/1984): 293–317.

18. Kartchner, *Negotiating START,* p. 106; Talbott, *Deadly Gambits,* pp. 333–342.

19. Talbott, *Deadly Gambits*, p. 34. See also Kartchner, *Negotiating START*, p. 108.

20. Michael R Gordon, "The Last Arms Accord?" *New York Times*, 16 July 1991: A1.

21. The range of the D-5 SLBM was 4,000 to 6,000 nautical miles, depending on the number of warheads it carried, carrying 10 to 14 warheads with an accuracy of 400 feet CEP. (CEP refers to the "circular error probable," or the circle around a target into which 50 percent of the warheads are expected to fall.) By comparison, the C-4 SLBM on the Poseidon submarines had a range of 4,230 to 7,400 nautical miles, carrying 8 warheads with an accuracy of 1,500 feet CEP; the MX ICBM carried 10 warheads over a range of 6,000 to 7,000 nautical miles with accuracies of less than 400 feet CEP. See Thomas B. Cochran, William M. Arkin, and Milton M. Hoenig, *Nuclear Weapons Databook. Volume I: U.S. Nuclear Forces and Capabilities* (Cambridge, MA: Ballinger, 1984), pp. 121, 142–146.

22. Ronald Reagan, "SDI: Progress and Promise," 6 August 1986, *Current Policy* 858 (Washington, DC: United States Department of State, 1986).

23. Kartchner, *Negotiating START,* p. 106.

24. Hedrick Smith, "U.S. Strategy of Toughness: A Counter to the Russians, " *New York Times*, 25 August 1985: A1.

25. Richard Bernstein, "Gorbachev Urges Arms Agreement with Europeans," *New York Times*, 4 October 1985: A1; Kartchner, *Negotiating START,* pp. 110–111.

26. Bernard Gwertzman, "Shultz Says New Soviet Offer Won't Halt 'Star Wars' Work," *New York Times*, 30 September 1985: A1.

27. Hedrick Smith, "U.S. Officials Say Soviet Arms Plan Is Not Balanced," *New York Times*, 1 October 1985; Paul H. Nitze, "The Nuclear and Space Arms Talks: Where We Are After the Summit," 5 December 1985, *Current Policy* 770 (Washington, DC: United States Department of State, 1985).

28. Bernard Weintraub, "U.S. Says Soviet Offer Could Be a Beginning," *New York Times*, 9 October 1985: A7.

29. Leslie Gelb, "U.S. Officials Reveal Disunity on Arms Goals," *New York Times*, 25 October 1985: A1.

30. Nitze, "Nuclear and Space Arms Talks"; Kartchner, *Negotiating START,* p. 142.

31. "The Arms Proposals: A Balance Sheet," *New York Times*, 13 November 1985: A11.

32. Nitze, "Nuclear and Space Arms Talks."

33. Bernard Gwertzman, "U.S. Seems Puzzled by Soviet Stance on Space Weapons," *New York Times*, 22 November 1985: A1.

34. Nitze, "Nuclear and Space Arms Talks."

35. Kartchner, *Negotiating START,* p. 154.

36. Bill Keller, "Weinberger Says Military Budget Cuts Would Imperil Arms Talks," *New York Times*, 10 January 1986.

37. Serge Schmemann, "Moscow Amplifies Latest Arms Plan," *New York Times*, 19 June 1986: A13.

38. See Matthew Bunn, *Foundation for the Future: The ABM Treaty and National Security* (Washington, DC: Arms Control Association, 1990), pp. 58–73, especially 61–68.

39. Philip Taubman, "Top U.S. Officials Arrive in Moscow for Talks on Arms," *New York Times*, 11 August 1986: A1.

40. "Bargaining over Arms: How the Kremlin and White House Proposals Compare," *New York Times*, 3 July 1986: A8.

41. "Reagan Is Looking to Arms Progress," *New York Times*, 18 September 1986: A15.

42. Michael R. Gordon, "Arms Goals: Flexibility and Firmness," *New York Times*, 3 September 1986: A3.

43. Thomas W. Netter, "Geneva Arms Talks Resume," *New York Times*, 16 October 1986: A11; Thomas W. Netter, "Parley in Geneva Adjourns," *New York Times*, 13 November 1986: A7; Kartchner, *Negotiating START*, p. 116; Jack Mendelsohn and James P. Rubin, "SDI as Negotiating Leverage," *Arms Control Today* 16 (December 1986): 8.

44. Ronald Reagan, "Report from Reykjavik," 13 December 1986, *Current Policy* 875 (Washington, DC: United States Department of State, 1986); Philip Taubman, "Soviet Blames U.S. for Talks Failure," *New York Times*, 13 October 1986: A1; Michael T. Kaufman, "Soviet Official Suggests Minutes of Summit Talks May Be Released," *New York Times*, 27 October 1986: Al.

45. Reagan, "Report from Reykjavik."

46. Reagan, "SDI: Progress and Promise."

47. James Schlesinger, "Reykjavik and Revelations: A Turn of the Tide?" *Foreign Affairs* 65 (America and the World 1986): 426–437. See also Michael Mandelbaum and Strobe Talbott, "Reykjavik and Beyond," *Foreign Affairs* 65 (Winter 1986/1987): 215–235.

48. Excerpts from the Joint Statement issued on 10 December 1987, reprinted in *Arms Control Today* 18 (January/February 1988):16.

49. Michael R. Gordon, "Reversal on 'Star Wars,'" *New York Times*, 25 March 1988: A1.

50. Michael R. Gordon, "Hope, but No Promises," *New York Times*, 2 June 1988: A17.

51. Ibid.

52. Excerpts from the Joint Statement, "Joint Document: 'Realistic Approach' to Reducing Nuclear Risks," *New York Times*, 2 June 1988: A17.

53. Michael R. Gordon, "Shultz and Shevardnadze Confer; Soviets Suggest Interim Arms Pact," *New York Times*, 23 September 1988: A1.

54. Michele Flournoy, "START Talks Delay as Bush Administration Review U.S. Positions," *Arms Control Today* 19 (January/February 1989): 29.

55. Thomas E. Halverson, "First Bush Defense Budget Reveals Program Cuts, Strategic Decisions," *Arms Control Today* 19 (May 1989): 21.

56. James P. Rubin, "As START Resumes, Bush Pushes Early Verification, " *Arms Control Today* 19 (August 1989): 24–25.

57. Rubin, "As START Resumes," p. 25.

58. Reprinted in *Arms Control Today* 19 (October 1989): 24–25.

59. See Kartchner, *Negotiating START*, pp. 155–157.

60. Excerpts of the Joint Statement of 23 September 1989 in *Arms Control Today* 19 (October 1989): 22.

61. Rubin, "As START Resumes," p. 25.

62. Matthew Bunn, "START Progress Slow; Baker and Shevardnadze to Meet," *Arms Control Today* 19 (September 1989): 28.

63. Excerpts in *Arms Control Today*, p. 22.

64. Quoted in James P. Rubin, "Baker, Shevardnadze Generate Arms Control Progress," *Arms Control Today* 19 (October 1989): 26.

65. Quoted in James P. Rubin, "Malta Summit Makes Waves: Leaders to Seek START, CFE Pacts in 1990," *Arms Control Today* 19 (January 1990): 21–22.

66. Matthew Bunn, "Major START Disputes Remain," *Arms Control Today* 20 (February 1990): 30.

67. Rubin, "Malta Summit Makes Waves."

68. See Matthew Bunn and Lee Feinstein, "Baker and Shevardnadze Clear START Roadblocks," *Arms Control Today* 20 (March 1990): 21–22; excerpts from the Joint Ministerial Statement of 9 February 1990, *Arms Control Today* 20 (March 1990): 28; Spurgeon Keeny, Jr., "Moscow, Ottawa, and the Ascent to the Next Summit," *Arms Control Today* 20 (March 1990): 3–4.

69. "Joint Statement on the Treaty on Strategic Offensive Arms," reprinted in *Arms Control Today* 20 (June 1990): 22–33.

70. See Dunbar Lockwood, "February START Summit Uncertain as Negotiations Inch Toward Finish," *Arms Control Today* 21 (January/February 1991): 23–24.

71. Matthew Bunn, "SS-18 Modernization: The Satan and START," *Arms Control Today* 20 (July/August 1990): 13–17.

72. Robert Pear, "In Arms Talks, Devil Is in the Details," *New York Times*, 21 May 1990: A14.

73. See Olgerts Eglitis, *Nonviolent Action in the Liberation of Latvia,* Monograph Series no. 5 (Cambridge, MA: Albert Einstein Institution, 1993); also Adam Roberts, *Civil Resistance in the East European and Soviet Revolutions,* Monograph Series no. 4 (Cambridge, MA: Albert Einstein Institution, 1991).

74. See the special supplementary section containing the text of the CFE Treaty in *Arms Control Today* 21 (January/February 1991).

75. See Dunbar Lockwood, "START Work Intensifies," *Arms Control Today* 21 (July/August 1991): 22; Andrew Rosenthal, "Bush Seeks Unity on U.S. Arms Stand," *New York Times*, 7 June 1991: A1.

76. Article II, "Treaty Between the United States of America and the Union of Soviet Socialist Republics on the Reduction and Limitation of Strategic Offensive Arms" (START Treaty), reprinted in *Arms Control Today* 21 (November 1991).

77. Jack Mendelsohn and Dunbar Lockwood, "Factfile: Estimated Strategic Forces Under START," *Arms Control Today* 21 (April 1991): 30–31. The disparity in the effects of START favoring the United States result from the combination of different initial force structures and the counting rules employed. Counting rules discount heavily the warhead load of strategic bombers. Soviet ballistic missile warheads would be reduced by about half; the same American forces would be cut by about a third.

78. Dunbar Lockwood, "Missile Glasnost," *Arms Control Today* 20 (July/August 1990): 26.

79. Kartchner, *Negotiating START,* p. 254.

80. Ibid., p. 269.

81. Mendelsohn and Rubin, "SDI as Negotiating Leverage."

82. Statement by the Soviet Union, dated 13 June 1991, reprinted as "START Supplement" in *Arms Control Today* 21 (November 1991): 23.

8

Stepping Back from the Cold War

Nuclear arms negotiations were at the center of the historic transformations ending the cold war. The arms control agreements achieved by the end of 1991 did not end the cold war. Arguably, the cold war ended on 8 November 1989, when the Berlin Wall collapsed physically, politically, and metaphorically. But the end of the cold war is also hard to imagine without these arms control achievements. This reflects a simple truth: for reasons that may be both rational and irrational, states (and their leaders) are reluctant to trust their adversaries, even when those adversaries are actively seeking a new and cooperative relationship, and even when the sincerity of particular leaders is largely accepted. Hedging one's bets against future revisionism is always advised. Hence, achieving a firm and presumably binding agreement that specifies rights and obligations often is desirable.[1]

States do alter their relationships from foe to friend. The United States and Canada gave up their military hostility long ago. Great Britain and France shifted from pointed rivalry to alliance between the end of the nineteenth century and the First World War. And the states of Western Europe accepted the Federal Republic of Germany into a collective security system after the Second World War. These changes are important and should not be trivialized. But neither should one overlook the fact that the transformations they implied took a long time. It took many decades, for example, for the U.S.-Canadian relationship to become less hostile and militarized than it was in the beginning. The Rush-Bagot Treaty of 1812, an arms control agreement that is generally admired for its durability, was in fact routinely violated for several decades.[2] Changes between the other states occurred under pressures of external security threats. Even in those circumstances, the transformation from adversaries to allies was difficult. British policy before the First World War wavered between attraction and aversion to Germany, depending in part on the party in power in London.[3] Richard Rosecrance has observed correctly that the British-French-Russian alliance of the time was as much a result of Germany's "casting off" potential allies as it was of the other states "balancing" German power.[4] Similarly, integration of the Federal Republic into the Atlantic alliance faced significant resistance from France and required substantial restrictions on German sovereignty over its armed forces. By comparison, the transformation of the cold war confrontation between the United States and the Soviet Union was breathtakingly swift.

Nuclear arms control agreements were one of the key elements of this contemporary transformation. Negotiations, in turn, were the main instruments for achieving these agreements. The major premise of this book is that the manner in which negotiations were conducted—the bargaining approaches or strategies employed—significantly influenced whether, and how well, the negotiations succeeded.

BARGAINING STRATEGIES AND ARMS AGREEMENTS

In order to examine the fit between the theoretical propositions about how bargaining behavior influences negotiating outcomes, as well as the related prescriptions for how to negotiate, especially in adversarial security relationships, I outlined three distinctive models of bargaining as the analytical framework for this study. The three models of bargaining (treated loosely as bargaining strategies) were neutral reciprocity, initiatives, and tough bargaining. A bargaining strategy of neutral reciprocity (or tit-for-tat) responds to the previous move of the bargaining partner, so that concessions are rewarded with comparable concessions and defections (retractions or inaction) receive the same in turn. Tit-for-tat assumes that rational bargainers in a relationship that resembles the prisoner's dilemma game can recognize the utility of mutual cooperation for their long-term maximization of gains. An initiative strategy undertakes unilateral efforts to reduce the tension that is assumed to be impairing the parties' abilities to cooperate, reach agreements, or at least dampen the dangerous effects of their hostility. A strategy of initiatives assumes that the environment for cooperation can be improved when one side takes steps to alter the structure of conflict, as well as the image of the relationship maintained by the other side, between the adversaries. Tough strategies seek to apply the maximum pressure possible in order to extract concessions from the bargaining partner by making extreme demands, resisting the reciprocation of concessions, and even escalating positions in response to concessions. This approach assumes that negotiations are decided by the capacity of one side to wield, or threaten to wield, greater power than the other.

Two broad patterns emerge from the negotiations examined in this book. First, in each negotiation, the initiative behavior and the acceleration of concession making came from the Soviet side of the table. Although the Soviets sometimes induced reciprocal concessions in response, their concessions were not usually met in kind. Second, despite the high stakes rhetoric about hanging tough, American negotiators frequently engaged in bargaining that was closer to the process of reciprocal compromise characteristic of tit-for-tat. These patterns are important both for the light they shed on Soviet negotiating styles at the end of the cold war and for what they suggest about the theoretical arguments of bargaining strategies that framed this inquiry.

Bargaining Patterns

The bargaining patterns and outcomes of negotiations in the 1980s can be summarized in terms of the individual negotiations and considered in terms of the interactive effects with the larger political and security situation. Individually, each negotiation revealed a slightly different pattern that is worth reviewing.

Negotiations on nuclear testing produced the most dramatic example of deliberate and sustained initiatives. They also were the least productive negotiations. For its part, the Soviet Union proceeded as if it were guided by Osgood's map for undertaking unilateral initiatives—they clearly stated their objectives, detailed the actions they would take, invited reciprocity, maintained their course in the face of opposition, and accepted significant costs. American negotiators, however, consistently rejected calls for reciprocity. Soviet negotiators reluctantly ended their moratorium after a year and a half but remained willing to reimpose it in the pursuit of a comprehensive test ban agreement. With the failure of their initiatives to elicit any positive response, the Soviets agreed to enter very limited negotiations on verification improvements to the existing Threshold Test Ban and Peaceful Nuclear Explosions treaties. The outcomes of these limited negotiations reflected a modest degree of mutual compromise, but largely they satisfied American desires. American bargaining strategy in these talks was the toughest among the three nuclear negotiations of the 1980s.

The INF negotiations, on the other hand, revealed the greatest willingness to engage in reciprocal compromise. The various alterations of the original zero option that occurred through 1983 reflected two facts. First, important interests within the U.S. government and within the Atlantic alliance desired the deployment of some new intermediate-range missiles. Second, there was a sense that Soviet acceptance of the zero option was unlikely. General Bernard Rogers stated this explicitly in testimony in 1988, and the sentiment was attributed to Paul Nitze as early as 1982. The uncompromising position adopted by the Soviet Union on any new NATO deployments encouraged a series of compromises by the United States up to 1983 (although not on the central concession of forgoing new missiles). The Soviet tough stand, however, also produced the collapse of all arms control talks at the end of 1983. Conversely, the dramatic series of Soviet concessions and initiatives in 1986 and 1987 had the consequence of driving the agreement beyond the original zero option, somewhat to the discomfort of American and European leaders. Soviet concessions also produced verification provisions that went further than the United States had really thought possible (resulting in some discomfort among American military leaders). The progress of the INF negotiations provides the best evidence among these cases for the benefits of a reciprocal bargaining strategy and of the power of initiatives to transform the bargaining process.

Bargaining in the START negotiations produced a more mixed pattern than either of the other arms control efforts. In some ways START looked much like the INF bargaining—the pattern of positions suggested reciprocal changes and a mutual willingness to make adjustments. These patterns show up in the various revisions of the numbers of weapons that would be allowed, inclusion of bombers and air-launched cruise missiles, the final resolution of the throw-weight issue, and the question of modernizing heavy ICBMs. In other ways, especially on strategic defenses, the positions adopted by the United States closely conformed to the prescriptions of a tough bargaining strategy, and the outcomes seemed to validate this approach. The United States successfully kept SDI and the ABM treaty out of START. And, despite George Shultz's prediction that offensive and defensive negotiations must move toward resolution in parallel, no treaty on strategic defense was signed or imminent when START was completed in 1991.

Nevertheless, SDI did not go away in the negotiations. After a series of concessions, Moscow finally resorted to the instrument of a unilateral statement, articulating clearly its understanding of the interdependence of offense reductions and defensive restraints. After the collapse of the Soviet Union in 1991, SDI lost much of its compelling attraction. When George Bush offered unilateral initiatives in September 1991, he tried to revive SDI, but neither Russia nor the United States Congress responded with much enthusiasm; SDI thus rapidly became a solution in search of a problem. The emerging strategic relationship between the United States and Russia, as well as between Russia and its European neighbors, would be the most important factor in determining the fate of SDI.

Although the United States obtained almost all of its major objectives in each negotiation, it would be a mistake to attribute this to the adoption of a tough bargaining approach or strategy. The mistake would not simply be one of misplaced attribution, but potentially one of serious error for the guidance of future policies.

American negotiators clearly were firm and committed bargainers—much the same as many past practitioners describe the Soviet Union's traditional approach. The U.S. policy makers tended to hold to certain key objectives that defined, for them, American strategic and national security interests. No one who studies bargaining or who advises parties to a negotiation would suggest that core interests should be sacrificed in the interest of achieving an agreement. Roger Fisher and William Ury, for example, perhaps the foremost advocates of nonconfrontational negotiating approaches, state that a person or group can only negotiate effectively if the "best alternative to a negotiated agreement" is clearly defined.[5] Similarly, Charles Osgood counseled that initiatives should be significant but should not undermine or jeopardize fundamental security interests.[6] Telling a firm commitment to basic interests from a tough bargaining approach may be difficult. Nevertheless, certain kinds of behavior are prescribed by a tough strategy that distinguishes it in practice from an approach that may be firm but flexible.

Tough strategies are based on a power-political view of bargaining relationships that sees little hope and even less virtue in processes of mutual accommodation. The underlying norms are self-interest and self-help, and the basic currency of the relationship is power. Agreement, if it is to occur at all, will be sought by a process of extracting the greatest possible concessions from the adversary. The instrument for this task is the assertion by one side of the capability and willingness to manipulate greater power resources than the other. Thus, the adversary will either be forced to go along, or no agreement will be concluded. In either case, the outcome is desirable because actions have been based on unilateral definition and pursuit of self-interests, a prudent course in the dangerous world of states. A tough strategy typically manifests itself in negotiations by extremely high opening positions, the absence of initiating concessions, and a general unwillingness to reciprocate the opponent's concessions. A tough strategy may go so far as to raise demands in response to concessions, because concessions are taken to be indicators of weakness and, therefore, opportunities to exploit. Any concessions made in negotiations are likely to be minor and not on fundamental issues in the talks. Only in the testing talks did something close to this strategy dominate the pattern of exchanges.

Learning, Bargaining, and Change

The interaction of bargaining across these negotiations, as well as within the larger political and security relationship of the superpowers, suggests another window on the effects of bargaining strategies for promoting cooperation. Nuclear arms control negotiations took place within a larger process of political change in the Soviet Union that cannot be ignored. From the perspectives of both learning theories and initiative perspectives on adversarial bargaining, the broader context was important in two ways. First, learning theories focus on general cognitive maps, or images by which people assess their experience. Attitudes toward nuclear arms control are embedded in, or connected to, attitudes and images of the specific nuclear balance, the overall military balance, the military and nuclear balance in specific theaters of confrontation, beliefs about the goals of the other's military and foreign policy behavior, and beliefs about the nature of the other's political system and decision-making processes.[7]

Decision makers learn, in the sense of altering their images of the adversary or the situation, when they are confronted with experience that challenges the validity of those beliefs and the reliability of their images to guide their choices. Thus, the larger political relationship interacts with the specifics of the negotiations to support or disconfirm the reigning cognitive maps.

In behavioral terms, what is happening in the political and strategic relationship outside the arms negotiations will have important influences on the process.

Historically, arms control has always been linked to the larger political relationship, but the specific mechanisms of that linkage, or even the direction of causality, are not clear. For example, one might assume arms control agreements would be more easily reached in climates of good or improving relations. The arms control record offers some support for this position. The Limited Test Ban Treaty was signed as the superpowers repaired relations following the Cuban missile crisis, and SALT I is generally associated with the mid-1970s era of détente. Conversely, crucial conflict events disrupted or damaged various arms control efforts that appeared to be moving forward. Test ban negotiations were curtailed abruptly when the U-2 spy plane of Francis Gary Powers was shot down over the Soviet Union in 1960, and the Soviet invasion of Afghanistan in late 1979 effectively killed SALT II's chances for U.S. ratification.

But the record does not reveal whether warming trends in the cold war were necessary for arms agreements or just a facilitator for them. Nor is the direction of causality clear. Consider the Cuban crisis. Both leaders were chastened by their brush with nuclear war, and each determined to pursue arms control more vigorously because of the crisis. Furthermore, Kennedy and Khrushchev (as well as Nixon and Kissinger a decade later) saw arms control as a kind of bellwether of the overall relationship. Arms control agreements in this view would be necessary for improving the relationship; the latter could not happen without the former.

Learning theories and initiative approaches to negotiating suggest that the direction of causality runs from the political relationship to the negotiations. In addition, they suggest that the mechanism of change involves the challenges to the cognitive maps or belief systems of decision makers posed by the environment they confront. Osgood's notion of GRIT rests on the assumption that policy change in the adversary will follow from cognitive change, which results from experience with the deliberate acts of tension reduction undertaken by the actor employing GRIT. The function of initiatives in GRIT is to undermine the adversary's presumption that the initiator does not desire a reduction in tensions. If actions speak louder than words, then the actions of the initiator should provide powerful evidence of good faith. These actions substantively alter the political environment, thus, Osgood argues, facilitating the negotiation of formal measures to reduce tension and reverse the arms race.

We have seen that many of the dramatic and specific initiatives taken by the Soviet Union within the nuclear negotiations went largely unreciprocated. Judging by the agreements that marked the ends of negotiations on all three issue areas, we found it hard to argue that these negotiating initiatives produced substantive changes in American positions. An alternative question is whether initiatives taken by the Soviet Union in other arenas of competition improved the environment for nuclear arms control negotiations. On this point the evidence is more positive.

Except for the test ban moratorium, the major unilateral military and security initiatives undertaken by the Soviet Union were the withdrawal from Afghanistan and the unilateral reductions of conventional forces in Europe. In April 1988, Moscow and the United States cosigned as guarantors bilateral accords between Afghanistan and Pakistan. The accords provided a vehicle for withdrawing Soviet troops and disengaging from the protracted war. In effect, the Soviet Union was conceding that its effort to crush an insurgency by Muslim and nationalist guerrillas against the Communist government in Kabul had failed.[8] Ten years of war had produced only a grinding military stalemate, political instability in Afghanistan, and severe problems of morale and performance in the Soviet armed forces. The situation was not unlike the American experience in Vietnam. Insofar as Soviet involvement in Afghanistan was seen by the West as symptomatic of Moscow's tendencies to adventurism, unilaterally pulling out challenged that view through unequivocal action. Similarly, Soviet leaders began to retract support for various client governments or insurgent forces engaged in conflicts that had strong links to the cold war system. They reduced support to Vietnam, Mozambique, Ethiopia, Angola, Nicaragua, and Cuba. Each of these states was told, essentially, to tend to their own economic troubles, resolve their ongoing political conflicts, and find new diplomatic relations with other states.

Dramatic changes also overturned the military and political status quo in Europe, beginning in December 1988. In a speech to the United Nations General Assembly on 7 December 1988, Gorbachev announced significant unilateral reductions of Soviet troops and withdrawal of many Soviet troops from the allied states in Eastern Europe. By the end of 1990, he pledged to cut Soviet armed forces by 50,000 troops (about 10 percent) and to reduce by 10,000 the number of tanks in the area from the Atlantic to the Urals, 5,000 of which would be removed from East Germany, Hungary, and Czechoslovakia. Significantly, these moves were not tied to any progress in the ongoing negotiations to reduce conventional forces in Europe.[9] The major Soviet allies in Europe accompanied Gorbachev's "preemptive concession" with their own announcements of force reductions, generally on the order of 10 percent cuts in defense budgets and troops.[10]

By the end of 1989, Moscow stood by while East Germans voted with their feet and then with their hands in a wholesale rejection of the GDR's Communist regime. During the summer a flood of East Germans pressed for refugee status and transit through Hungary into Austria and then to the Federal Republic. Facing mounting pressure, Hungary ignored treaty commitments with the GDR and permitted Germans to cross its border as the first sections of the iron curtain fell. Popular anti-regime protests emerged into public visibility throughout the Warsaw Pact, often despite governments' attempts at forceful repression. The Soviet "new thinking" and policies of perestroika and glasnost were spreading through the alliance. Short of turning back the clock on Soviet reforms, Moscow could not support the reimposition of orthodoxy as it had in Czechoslovakia in 1968.

Still, most Western observers, and apparently American government officials, did not recognize the magnitude of the changes underway. Nor did they predict the unification of the two German states in the near future. Jeane Kirkpatrick argued in early 1990, for example, that a unified Germany within NATO would be unacceptable to Moscow and that a neutral Germany outside NATO would be unacceptable to the United States.[11] Nevertheless, in July Gorbachev and West German Chancellor Helmut Kohl agreed that a united Germany would remain within NATO, with its troops reduced to 370,000.[12] Notably, this was an agreement made between Moscow and Bonn, without the mediation of the United States. In November the treaty on Conventional Forces in Europe was signed in Paris by all members of NATO and the Warsaw Treaty Organization.

All of these events stemmed from initiatives undertaken by the Soviet Union as part of sweeping alterations of traditional policies. The cumulative effect, combined with initiatives within the nuclear negotiations, began to affect the attitudes of American policy makers toward the desirability and feasibility of arms agreements. Shortly before the meeting between Bush and Gorbachev near Malta in late 1989, James Baker, secretary of state, made these observations:

It would be folly indeed to miss this opportunity. . . . Soviet new thinking in foreign and defense policy promises possibilities that would have been unthinkable a decade ago, such as deep, stabilizing cuts in strategic forces and parity in reduced conventional arms in Europe.

Any uncertainty about the fate of reform in the Soviet Union, however, is all the more reason, not less, for us to seize the present opportunity. For the works of our labor—a diminished Soviet threat and effectively verifiable agreements—can endure even if *perestroika* does not. If the Soviets have already destroyed weapons, it will be difficult, costly, and time consuming for any future Kremlin leadership to reverse the process and assert military superiority.[13]

Until 1989, however, changes in the images of the Soviet Union and arms control held by American leaders are hard to detect. Keith Shimko, for example, employed the methods of content analysis and operational codes to study systematically the attitudes of Caspar Weinberger, George Shultz, Richard Perle, Richard Burt, and President Reagan as these were expressed in public documents and statements.[14] His analysis revealed that the attitudes expressed by all of these actors on the question of how the Soviet Union responded to different bargaining approaches were generally the same—each policy maker expressed the view that Soviet leaders tend to exploit indications of restraint on the part of their adversaries but back down in the face of firmness. Arms negotiator Edward Rowny articulated this view clearly in late 1986 and early 1987:

For public consumption, the Soviets profess that they are flexible. They have a special talent for recycling their more shopworn offers and reintroducing them as if they constituted new and substantive concessions. . . . But in practice, we can only reach a deal with them when we have something significant to give up. . . . At the table, they are anything but flexible. . . . The Soviets do not deal in bargaining chips. They do not make concessions in the spirit of give-and-take or as a sign of good will. Rather, they consider unilateral concessions to be a mark of contemptible weakness.[15]

... a third requirement for negotiating with the Soviets [is contained in] the classic warning: "beware of Greeks bearing gifts." The Soviets only grudgingly acknowledge the necessity of making trades; they consider compromise a weakness. . . . The Soviets are masters of eleventh hour negotiations—that is, they will wait until the last moment before agreeing with us.[16]

Rowny's image of the Soviet bargaining style is interesting for two reasons. First, it is clearly consistent with a prescription for tough bargaining. Nevertheless, by mid-1986, the United States already had shown a willingness to make reciprocal compromises on some issues in START and in the INF talks. Second, by September 1986, his characterization was perhaps better applied to the United States than to the Soviet Union. It was the Soviet Union that had maintained a unilateral moratorium on nuclear testing for the previous year (while the United States refused entreaties to suspend testing or to join testing negotiations). Furthermore, the Soviet Union had begun to make significant concessions in START, articulating a willingness to accept dramatic asymmetrical cuts in offensive forces in return for constraints on strategic defense. At about the same time as Rowny's 1986 speech, George Shultz stated that the United States would not trade away SDI, even in exchange for 50 percent reductions in Soviet offensive arms. Thus, although Rowny's characterization suffers somewhat as a valid empirical statement, it did express a dominant attitude among American policy makers.

Shimko also suggested that the images held by these top five policy makers did not change and that, at least for the hard-liners (Shimko's characterization of Weinberger and Perle), their images tended to guide policy preferences. Reagan's attitudes toward arms control did seem to shift in his second administration. Shimko argues, however, that this was a shift to a parallel set of beliefs on the part of Reagan reflecting a faith in the Enlightenment notion that rational discussion can resolve most differences, not an adjustment in Reagan's images of the Soviet Union. In other words, the president seemed to maintain two somewhat contradictory sets of attitudes regarding bargaining with Soviet leaders, neither of which were very deep or internally coherent. Reagan appeared simply to shift to the set more compatible with reality at the end of his presidency.[17]

Perhaps the explanation for the persistence of American images at odds with the "objective" evidence in arms control negotiations is the fundamental difficulty of changing images. Although scholars studying the role of learning in foreign policy suggest mechanisms by which various forms of learning, including cognitive shifts, occur, they are understandably silent about how long the process can take.[18] The reasons for this apparent lack of precision are clear. On the one hand, beliefs, images, or attitudes about specific issues like arms control are characteristics of individuals and embedded in complex individual personalities. No general theory can predict with precision how long any particular process of individual change will take. On the other hand, government policies are almost always the product of collective decision making in which interpersonal dynamics will interact with individual styles and beliefs. In a collective setting, there may not be any incentive for an individual to change his or her mind, and there may be strong incentives to resist change. This sort of situation is suggested in Matthew Evangelista's analysis of John Foster Dulles and the Soviet initiatives for comprehensive disarmament in the 1950s. Contrary to the predictions of GRIT, Dulles's failure to respond positively to the Soviet moves was conscious and deliberate, not the result of misinterpretation of the actions. According to Evangelista's account, Dulles recognized the importance of the Soviet behavior and understood its purpose. But he refused to alter his notion of how to fulfill American national security interests.[19]

It is difficult to prescribe, therefore, how long a state should maintain an initiative strategy before expecting it to pay off in an alteration of the adversary's behavior, and perhaps its leaders' attitudes. An answer of "a good long time" to the duration question does not inspire confidence for a leader contemplating taking the political risks of an initiative strategy. Nevertheless, there was some evidence in the U.S.-Soviet arms control interactions of policy adaptation and shifts in bargaining approaches as the scope of political changes settled in. By mid-1986, for example, after a year or so of the Soviet unilateral test moratorium, the American rationale for continuing testing increasingly emphasized the need to maintain reliability of the nuclear stockpiles, rather than dismissing the moratorium as a public relations campaign with no military importance.[20] Soviet signature to the INF treaty, and equally important, the mutual Soviet-American experience with implementing the treaty's provisions through 1988 and 1989 substantially changed the boundaries about what kinds of agreements were possible, rather than just desirable. Finally, as Gorbachev began to carry out the unilateral reductions of conventional forces in Europe that he promised at the United Nations in December 1988, skeptical American security analysts had to adjust their presumptions about whether these offers were genuine. More generally, Western analysts began to accept the fact that Soviet pronouncements about changing their military doctrines to be "defensively oriented" and organized around the concept of "sufficiency" had substantive validity.[21]

Following START I, a new willingness emerged on the part of the United States to pursue new reductions through mutual or unilateral initiatives. Generally, a new commitment to arms control, perhaps motivated by challenges emerging to the reform processes in the Soviet Union, replaced the rhetoric of toughness at the end of the Bush administration.

From START I to START II

Just after the START I treaty was signed, conservative Communist party and military leaders attempted a putsch in the Soviet Union. Mikhail Gorbachev was vacationing in the Crimea when declarations of martial law and announcements of Gorbachev's replacement were announced. The putsch attempt failed within three days, for reasons that ranged from the incompetence of its planners, to insubordination in the military forces charged with carrying out the takeover, to nonviolent resistance by civilians and reformist political leaders in Leningrad (St. Petersburg) and Moscow.[22] But in the outcome, President Gorbachev's political power and reputation were deeply damaged. For its part, the United States government had tied its post–cold war policies closely to the fate of Gorbachev, most recently with the START I treaty. Thus, in October, President Bush made a dramatic unilateral gesture of arms control.

Rather than waiting for negotiations to work their way to a second START treaty, in which weapons reductions would be even more substantial, Bush announced that the United States would remove all tactical nuclear weapons from surface ships, withdraw nuclear forces from overseas, and stand down from alert status over 2,000 strategic ballistic missiles and all of the U.S. strategic bombers. At this time, Bush proposed no further reductions in strategic warheads beyond START I. He did propose, however, the elimination of all ICBMs with multiple warheads, and he terminated the rail-garrison MX ICBM program and the road mobile-basing plans for the single warhead Midgetman.

Gorbachev quickly matched many of the U.S. reductions moves and went beyond others. He stated that the Soviet Union would destroy all tactical and battlefield nuclear weapons based on land and would remove them from naval forces. Mirroring the American initiatives, Gorbachev stated that 503 ICBMs, including 137 MIRVed ICBMs, would be removed from alert, and submarines carrying 92 single warhead SLBMs would be decommissioned. Similarly, strategic bombers would remain off alert status, with their weapons stored. In addition, Gorbachev pledged to remove from service an additional 1,000 strategic warheads, cutting the START ceiling to 5, 000 accountable weapons for the Soviet arsenal. Finally, the Soviet Union would begin a one-year moratorium on nuclear testing.[23]

Although these gestures embodied bold new progress in arms control, they did not save Gorbachev's career or avert the collapse of the Soviet Union. In December 1991, the increasingly independent Soviet republics, led by Russia, declared an end to the union and formed the Commonwealth of Independent States. American attention now focused on Russia, as the inheritor of the majority of the Soviet nuclear arsenal, and the necessary relationships with Belarus, Ukraine, and Kazakhstan, the possessors of smaller portions of Soviet weapons. Of the weaponry in the lesser republics, 104 SS-18 ICBMs were based in Kazakhstan, 130 SS-19s and 46 SS-24s (in silos) in Ukraine, and 81 SS-25s in Belarus. In addition, 63 strategic bombers were based in Kazakhstan, and 41 more were stationed in Ukraine. Russia controlled the entire submarine-based nuclear arsenal and the remaining ICBM and bomber forces.[24] From the American point of view, the main issue with the three smaller states was their willingness to give up the nuclear forces they controlled and join the Nuclear Nonproliferation Treaty regime as nonweapons states. Consolidating the post-Soviet arsenal was critical if the United States was to proceed with ratification of the first START treaty. It was essential for the success of any subsequent agreement.

Over the next year, arms control moved in fits and starts, reflecting the turbulent transition to independence among the states of the former Soviet Union. Because of the speed of Soviet collapse and the variety of political, military, geographic, and economic issues that emerged for the new states to deal with as independent entities, moving forward on arms control became dependent upon the resolution or accommodation of these other matters. During the spring of 1992, diplomacy among the nuclear successors, and between the United States and each of them, aimed at solidifying nonnuclear commitments by the three smaller states.[25] By the end of May, the United States had secured commitments by these states to give up their nuclear forces, thus satisfying a key American requirement for ratification of START I.

Negotiations between the United States and Russia to draft a second START treaty took the remainder of the year. On 17 June 1992, Russian President Boris Yeltsin and George Bush initialed a joint understanding that became the basis for the START II treaty signed six months later. In October, satisfied with the agreements in May that Belarus, Ukraine, and Kazakhstan would each ratify START I and join the NPT as nonnuclear weapons states, the U.S. Senate approved START I. In early November the Russian Parliament followed suit.[26] When START II was signed in January, however, only Kazakhstan had joined the United States and Russia. More seriously, by March 1993, Ukrainian President Leonid Kravchuk was suggesting that Ukraine needed financial and security guarantees from the West before it could fulfill its agreements of May 1992 to join START I and the NPT.[27]

The new treaty signed in January 1993 was built on the framework of START I but significantly extended the required reductions of strategic forces. Strategic forces, again measured by counting warheads, would be reduced to 3,000 to 3,500 weapons, half of the START I ceiling. Most notably, the treaty required that by the end of A.D. 2002 each party must have eliminated all ICBMs with multiple warheads, thus reversing twenty years of MIRV development and deployment that had vastly multiplied the number of strategic warheads each side possessed.[28] For Russia, the treaty required elimination of the entire SS-18 ICBM force and destruction of all but 90 of the silos (the treaty would permit conversion of these silos to accommodate the smaller SS-25 ICBM in the interests of economy). For the United States, Article I meant eliminating the MX ICBM (each of the 50 silo-based missiles carried ten warheads), carrying out the retirement of older single warhead Minuteman II ICBMs and downloading the remaining 500 Minuteman III ICBMs from three warheads to one.[29] Article III relaxed the START I constraints on downloading to permit these reductions as well as the reconfiguration of American Trident II SLBMs from eight to four warheads needed for the United States to remain within the SLBM sublimit of 1,700 to 1,750 warheads.[30] In addition, the counting rules for bomber-based weapons were replaced under Article IV with the requirement to count these weapons as they are actually deployed. As two reporters noted with respect to the June 1992 accords that led to START II, one of the extraordinary aspects of the treaty was that, in light of both the long arms control history and the immediate political turbulence in the former Soviet Union, the negotiations proceeded very rapidly and largely "without the usual anxiety about verifying treaty compliance."[31] Only a shift in attitudes, reflected in the progressive bargaining postures, can explain that about-face of American leaders. The traditional counsel of caution and distrust would have produced a pause, rather than an acceleration, in arms reduction efforts.

BARGAINING AND THE FUTURE FOR SECURITY COOPERATION

Despite the end of the cold war, nuclear weapons will remain central to the security considerations of many states and will remain topics for continued negotiations. Many of the emerging situations will not resemble the U.S.-Soviet standoff in which the negotiations examined in this book took place. Among the most pressing nuclear issues for the world community after the cold war are the reenforcement of the Nuclear Nonproliferation Treaty regime and implementation of the START treaties. The former effort will be aimed at arresting the horizontal spread of nuclear weapons into regions of acute conflict. The latter effort, which is closely related to proliferation concerns, will seek to solidify the new cooperative security relationships that have emerged.

Arguably, the future of nuclear negotiations among the nuclear weapons states will contain a time when approximate parity among all the states is reached through the reductions of the superpowers' arsenals, and further reductions require multilateral efforts. Bargaining among several actors is far more complex than between only two. The fact that at least three (and, depending on the Russian security relationships, possibly four) of the nuclear powers will remain security allies will ease the process somewhat. But the demise of the Soviet threat does not remove the competitive instincts embedded in the state system. These can only be dampened or overcome by structuring new relationships that enforce and facilitate cooperation. Thus, which bargaining strategies are chosen by the players in their construction of the post–cold war world will be vitally important.

On this problem, the conclusions of this study shed some light. Even if tough strategies were partially successful in achieving specific national goals (such as strengthening the verification measure of the existing testing treaties), they were not productive for enlarging the realm of cooperative arms control measures. By far the most important feature of the nuclear bargains of the 1980s was the willingness to compromise—to find ways to reciprocate concessions and offers made by the other side. Despite their tough rhetoric, American leaders and negotiators often found themselves doing just that—and without these choices agreements might well have been missed (as in the arena of nuclear testing).

Equally important was the function of initiative in encouraging reciprocal moves and creating a propitious environment for negotiation. Certainly, the direct achievements of initiatives were far less than advocates of the strategies would have hoped for. But as Robert Johansen observed, it was the failure of the United States to reciprocate Soviet initiatives in nuclear testing that produced such poor results. Furthermore, the broad range of security initiatives by the Soviet Union undoubtedly improved the negotiating efforts in all arenas.[32]

If the Soviet initiatives—which might be explained away as desperate moves by the leadership of a crumbling empire—had positive effects on security cooperation at the end of the cold war, then initiatives taken by the world's strongest state may have even greater consequence. As security relationships evolve in the post–cold war world, the benefits of institutionalizing cooperation in order to diminish the nuclear threat become clear. Leaders interested in stepping back from the nuclear insecurity of the cold war should look to the lessons of the 1980s with a skeptical eye to the achievement of tough bargaining and a positive, though not uncritical, eye to the potential of initiatives.

Bernard Bechhoefer wrote in 1961 that the "process of attaining new accords may require extended and patient negotiations lasting for years." His advice is no less apt in 1993. The negotiations of the 1980s, however, suggest new, positive lessons about how to travel that "highway to peace and increased security" as the society of nations creates another new world order.[33]

NOTES

1. See Abram Chayes and Antonia Chayes, "Compliance," *International Organization* 47 (Summer 1993) for a broad discussion of the role of agreements in international relations and the reasons that states do (or do not) comply with agreements.

2. Barry O'Neill, "Rush-Bagot and the Upkeep of Arms Treaties," *Arms Control Today* 21 (September 1991): 20–23.

3. See Lawrence Lafore, *The Long Fuse* (New York: Lippincott, 1976).

4. Richard Rosecrance, "A New Concert of Powers," *Foreign Affairs* 71 (Spring 1992): 67.

5. Roger Fisher and William Ury, *Getting to Yes: Negotiating Agreement Without Giving In* (New York: Penguin, 1983).

6. Charles Osgood, *An Alternative to War or Surrender* (Urbana: University of Illinois Press, 1962).

7. Keith L. Shimko, *Images and Arms Control: Perceptions of the Soviet Union in the Reagan Administration* (Ann Arbor: University of Michigan Press, 1991).

8. See Rosanne Klass, "Afghanistan: The Accords," *Foreign Affairs* 66 (Summer 1988): 922–945. Klass argued, however, that the substantive impact of Soviet commitments was unclear and suggested that the accords merely covered a strengthening of the Soviet client government in Kabul. Subsequent elimination of Soviet support for the regime, however, seemed to show that the Soviet Union was intent on getting out of the morass.

9. Michele Flournoy, "Gorbachev Announces Unilateral Cuts in Soviet Conventional Forces," *Arms Control Today* 19 (January/February 1989): 24.

10. See Jack Mendelsohn, "Gorbachev's Preemptive Concession," *Arms Control Today* 19 (March 1989): 10–15.

11. Jeane J. Kirkpatrick, "Beyond the Cold War," *Foreign Affairs* 69 (America and the World 1989/1990): 10–11.

12. Thomas Halverson, "NATO, Gorbachev Give 'Impulse' to German Unity," *Arms Control Today* 20 (July/August 1990): 23–24.

13. Quoted in James P. Rubin, "Bush and Gorbachev to Meet in a 'Non-Summit,' " *Arms Control Today* 19 (November 1989): 26.

14. Shimko, *Images and Arms Control,* ch. 1.

15. Edward Rowny, "U.S. and Soviet Approaches to Arms Control," 19 September 1986, *Current Policy* 868 (Washington, DC: United States Department of State, 1986).

16. Edward Rowny, "New Prospects for Agreement in INF and START," 20 March 1987, *Current Policy* 935 (Washington, DC: United States Department of State, 1986).

17. Shimko, *Images and Arms Control,* pp. 101–148, 249.

18. For example, see Robert Jervis, *Perception and Misperception in International Politics* (Princeton: Princeton University Press, 1976); George Breslauer and Philip E. Tetlock, eds., *Learning in U.S. and Soviet Foreign Policy* (Boulder: Westview, 1990); Joseph S. Nye, Jr., "Nuclear Learning," *International Organization* 41 (Summer 1987): 371–402; Philip E. Tetlock, Jo L. Husbands, Robert Jervis, Paul C. Stern, Charles Tilly, eds., *Behavior, Society, and Nuclear War,* vol. 2 (New York: Oxford University Press, 1991); Deborah Welch Larson, *The Origins of Containment: A Psychological Explanation* (Princeton: Princeton University Press, 1985).

19. Matthew Evangelista, "Cooperation Theory and Disarmament Negotiations in the 1950s," *World Politics* 42 (July 1990): 502–529.

20. Compare Ronald Reagan, "Keeping America Strong," 23 September 1986, *Current Policy* 869 (Washington, DC: United States Department of State, 1986) with charges in Seth Mydans, "Gorbachev Denies Soviet Completed Nuclear Tests," *New York Times,* 14 August 1985: A10.

21. See Raymond L. Garthoff, *Deterrence and the Revolution in Soviet Military Doctrine* (Washington, DC: Brookings Institution, 1990), pp. 94–148.

22. See various accounts of the putsch attempt, for example, the special section on the coup and Russian resistance in *Le Nouvel Observateur,* 22–28 August 1991: 32–46; Alexander Pronozin, "Nonviolent Resistance to the Soviet Coup Took Many Forms," *Nonviolent Sanctions* 3 (Fall 1991): 1.

23. See "Factfile: Comparisons of U.S. and Soviet Nuclear Cuts," *Arms Control Today* 22 (November 1991): 27–28; also texts of speeches by George Bush and Mikhail Gorbachev in *Arms Control Today* 22 (October 1991): 3–6.

24. Jack Mendelsohn and Dunbar Lockwood, "Factfile: Strategic Nuclear Forces of the United States and the Commonwealth of Independent States," *Arms Control Today* 23 (May 1993): 28–29.

25. See "Republics Quarrel on Arms Treaty," *Boston Globe,* 12 April 1992: 10; Barbara Crossette, "4 Ex-Soviet States and U.S. in Accord on 1991 Arms Pact," *New York Times,* 24 May 1992: A1.

26. John H. Cushman, Jr., "Senate Endorses Pact to Reduce Strategic Arms," *New York Times,* 2 October 1992: A6; "Russia Ratifies Nuclear Arms Pact with U.S.," *New York Times,* 5 November 1992: A8.

27. Steven Erlanger, "Ukraine and Arms Accords: Kiev Reluctant to Say 'I Do,' " *New York Times,* 31 March 1993: A1.

28. Article II, *Treaty Between the United States of America and the Russian Federation on the Further Reduction and Limitation of Strategic Offensive Arms* (START II), text reprinted in *Arms Control Today* 23 (January/February 1993).

29. Dunbar Lockwood, "Strategic Forces Under START II," *Arms Control Today* 22 (December 1992): 10.

30. Ibid., p. 11.

31. R. Jeffrey Smith and Don Oberdorfer, "Arms Talks Devoid of Usual Anxieties," *Washington Post,* 18 June 1992: A38.

32. Robert Johansen, "Unilateral Initiatives," in *Encyclopedia of Arms Control and Disarmament,* ed. Richard Dean Burns (New York: Charles Scribner's Sons, 1993).

33. Bernard Bechhoefer, *Postwar Negotiations for Arms Control* (Washington, DC: Brookings Institution, 1961), p. 598.

Selected Bibliography

BOOKS AND JOURNAL ARTICLES

Adelman, Kenneth. "Arms Control with and without Agreements." *Foreign Affairs* 63 (Winter 1984/1985): 240–263.

Allison, Graham. *Essence of Decision*. Boston: Little, Brown, 1971.

Art, Robert J. "A Defensible Defense: America's Grand Strategy after the Cold War." *International Security* 15 (Spring 1991): 5–54.

Axelrod, Robert. *The Evolution of Cooperation*. New York: Basic Books, 1984.

Barton, John, and Lawrence Weiler. *International Arms Control*. Stanford: Stanford University Press, 1976.

Bartos, Otomar. "A Simple Model of Negotiation: A Sociological Point of View." In I. William Zartman, ed., *The Negotiation Process*. Beverly Hills: Sage, 1978.

Bechhoefer, Bernard G. *Postwar Negotiations for Arms Control*. Washington, DC: Brookings Institution, 1961.

Bechloss, Michael. *MayDay: Eisenhower, Khrushchev, and the U-2 Affair*. New York: Harper and Row, 1986.

Betts, Richard K., ed. *Cruise Missiles: Technology, Strategy, and Politics*. Washington, DC: Brookings Institution, 1981.

Blacker, Coit D., and Gloria Duffy, eds. *International Arms Control: Issues and Agreements*. 2d ed. Stanford: Stanford University Press, 1984.

Blechman, Barry, ed. *Rethinking U.S. Strategic Posture*. Cambridge, MA: Ballinger, 1983.

Bleiker, Roland, Doug Bond, and Myung-Soo Lee. "Unification From Below? German Unity and Its Implications for Korean Unification Dynamics." *Center for International Affairs, Working Paper no. 92-4*. Cambridge, MA: Harvard University Center for International Affairs, 1992.

Brams, Steven. *Superpower Games*. New Haven: Yale University Press, 1985.

Breslauer, George, and Philip E. Tetlock, eds. *Learning in U.S. and Soviet Foreign Policy*. Boulder: Westview, 1990.

Brown, Harold. *Thinking About National Security*. Boulder: Westview, 1983.

Brown, Seyom. *Faces of Power: Constancy and Change in United States Foreign Policy from Truman to Reagan*. New York: Columbia University Press, 1983.

Bull, Hedley. *The Control of the Arms Race*. New York: Praeger, 1965.

Bunn, Matthew. "SS-18 Modernization: The Satan and START." *Arms Control Today* 20 (July/August 1990): 13–17.

Carter, Ashton, and David N. Schwartz, eds. *Ballistic Missile Defense*. Washington, DC: Brookings Institution, 1984.

Chayes, Abram, and Antonia Chayes. "Compliance." *International Organization* 47 (Summer 1993).

Chayes, Abram, and Jerome Weisner, eds. *ABM: An Evaluation of the Decision to Deploy an Antiballistic Missile System*. New York: Harper and Row, 1969.

Checkel, Jeff. "Ideas, Institutions, and the Gorbachev Foreign Policy Revolution." *World Politics* 45 (January 1993): 271–300.

Clarke, Duncan. *The Politics of Arms Control*. New York: Free Press, 1979.

Cochran, Thomas B., William M. Arkin, and Milton M. Hoenig. *Nuclear Weapons Databook, Volume I: U.S. Nuclear Forces and Capabilities*. Cambridge, MA: Ballinger, 1984.

Cross, John C. "Negotiation as a Learning Process." In I. William Zartman, ed., *The Negotiation Process*. Beverly Hills: Sage, 1978.

Daalder, Ivo. "The Limited Test Ban Treaty." In Albert Carnesale and Richard Haass, eds., *Superpower Arms Control: Setting the Record Straight*. Cambridge, MA: Ballinger, 1987.

Dean, Jonathan. *Watershed in Europe*. Lexington, MA: Lexington Books, 1987.

Divine, Robert. *Blowing on the Wind*. New York: Oxford University Press, 1978.

Downs, George W., David M. Rocke, and Randolph Siverson. "Tacit Bargaining and Arms Control." *World Politics* 39 (April 1987): 297–326.

———. "Arms Races and Cooperation." *World Politics* 38 (October 1985): 118–146.

Downs, George W., and David M. Rocke. *Tacit Bargaining, Arms Races and Arms Control*. Ann Arbor: University of Michigan Press, 1990.

Eglitis, Olgerts. *Nonviolent Action in the Liberation of Latvia*. Monograph Series no. 5. Cambridge, MA: Albert Einstein Institution, 1993.

Eichenberg, Richard. *Public Opinion and National Security in Western Europe*. Ithaca: Cornell University Press, 1989.

Etzioni, Amitai. "The Kennedy Experiment: Unilateral Initiatives." *Western Political Quarterly* 20 (June 1967): 361–380.

———. *The Hard Way to Peace*. New York: Collier, 1962.

Evangelista, Matthew. "Sources of Restraint in Soviet Security Policy." In Philip E. Tetlock, Jo L. Husbands, Robert Jervis, Paul C. Stern, and Charles Tilly, eds., *Behavior, Society, and Nuclear War*. Vol. 2. New York: Oxford University Press, 1991.

———. "Cooperation Theory and Disarmament Negotiations in the 1950s." *World Politics* 42 (July 1990): 502–529.

———. *Innovation and the Arms Race: How the United States and the Soviet Union Develop New Military Technologies*. Ithaca: Cornell University Press, 1988.

Farley, Philip J. "Strategic Arms Control, 1967–1987." In Alexander George, Philip J. Farley, and Alexander Dallin, eds., *U.S.-Soviet Security Cooperation: Achievements, Failures, Lessons*. New York: Oxford University Press, 1988.

Fisher, Roger, and William Ury. *Getting to Yes: Negotiating Agreement Without Giving In*. New York: Penguin, 1983.

Flanagan, Stephen. "SALT II." In Albert Carnesale and Richard Haass, eds., *Superpower Arms Control: Setting the Record Straight*. Cambridge, MA: Ballinger, 1987.

Frye, Alton. "Strategic Build Down: A Context for Restraint." *Foreign Affairs* 62 (Winter 1983/1984): 293–317.

———. *A Responsible Congress*. New York: McGraw Hill, 1975.

Gaddis, John. *Strategies of Containment: A Critical Appraisal of Postwar American National Security Policy*. New York: Oxford University Press, 1982.

Garthoff, Raymond L. *Deterrence and the Revolution in Soviet Military Doctrine*. Washington, DC: Brookings Institution, 1990.

———. "Objectives and Negotiating Strategy." In Leon Sloss and M. Scott Davis, eds., *A Game for High Stakes: Lessons Learned in Negotiating with the Soviet Union*. Cambridge, MA: Ballinger, 1986.

———. *Detente and Confrontation: American-Soviet Relations from Nixon to Reagan*. Washington DC: Brookings Institution, 1985.

———. "Negotiating with the Soviets: Some Lessons from SALT". *International Security* 1 (Spring 1977): 3–24.

George, Alexander. *Presidential Decision Making in Foreign Policy: The Effective Use of Information and Advice*. Boulder: Westview, 1980.

Gowa, Joanne. "Anarchy, Egoism and Third Images: *The Evolution of Cooperation* and International Relations." *International Organization* 40 (Winter 1986): 167–186.

Greenwood, Ted. *The Making of MIRV*. Cambridge, MA: Ballinger, 1976.

Halperin, Morton. "The Decision to Deploy ABM: Bureaucratic and Domestic Politics in the Johnson Administration." *World Politics* 25 (October 1972): 62–95.

Hampson, Fen Olser. "SALT I: The Interim Agreement and ABM Treaty." In Albert Carnesale and Richard N. Haass, eds., *Superpower Arms Control: Setting the Record Straight*. Cambridge MA: Ballinger, 1987.

Haslam, Jonathan. *The Soviet Union and the Politics of Nuclear Weapons in Europe, 1969–87*. Ithaca: Cornell University Press, 1990.

Heckrotte, Warren. "Verification of Test Ban Treaties." In William C. Potter, ed., *Verification and Arms Control*. Lexington, MA: Lexington Books, 1985.

———. "Negotiating with the Soviets." *Energy and Technology Review*, May 1983.

Hersh, Seymour. *The Price of Power: Henry Kissinger in the Nixon White House*. New York: Summit Books, 1983.

Herz, John. "Idealism, Internationalism and the Security Dilemma." In John Herz, ed., *The Nation-State and the Crisis in World Politics*. New York: David McKay, 1976.

Hopmann, P. Terrence. "Internal and External Influences on Bargaining in Arms Control Negotiations." In Bruce Russett, ed., *Peace, War and Numbers*. Beverly Hills: Sage, 1972.

Hopmann, P. Terrence, and Timothy D. King. "From Cold War to Detente: The Role of the Cuban Missile Crisis and the Partial Nuclear Test Ban Treaty." In Ole R. Holsti, Randolph M. Siverson, and Alexander L. George, eds., *Change in the International System*. Boulder: Westview, 1980.

Huth, Paul K. "Extended Deterrence and the Outbreak of War." *American Political Science Review* 82 (June 1988): 423–444.

Iklé, Fred. *How Nations Negotiate*. New York: Praeger, 1964.

Jacobson, Harold, and Eric Stein. *Diplomats, Scientists and Politicians*. Ann Arbor: University of Michigan Press, 1966.

Jensen, Lloyd. *Bargaining for National Security*. Columbia: University of South Carolina Press, 1988.

Jervis, Robert. "Security Regimes." *International Organization* 36 (Spring 1982): 357–378.

———. Cooperation Under the Security Dilemma. *World Politics* 30 (January 1978): 167–214.

———. *Perception and Misperception in International Politics*. Princeton: Princeton University Press, 1976.

Jervis, Robert, Richard Ned Lebow, and Janice Gross Stein, eds. *Psychology and Deterrence*. Baltimore: Johns Hopkins University Press, 1985.

Johansen, Robert. "Unilateral Initiatives." In Richard Dean Burns, ed. *Encyclopedia of Arms Control and Disarmament*. New York: Charles Scribner's Sons, 1993.

Jönsson, Christer. *Soviet Bargaining Behavior*. New York: Columbia University Press, 1979.

Kartchner, Kerry M. *Negotiating START: Strategic Arms Reduction Talks and the Quest for Strategic Stability*. New Brunswick, NJ: Transaction Publishers, 1991.

Keohane, Robert O. "Realism, Neorealism and the Study of World Politics." In Robert O. Keohane, ed., *Neorealism and its Critics*. New York: Columbia University Press, 1986.

———. "Reciprocity in International Relations." *International Organization* 40 (Winter 1986): 1–28.

———. "Theory of World Politics: Structural Realism and Beyond." In Robert O. Keohane, ed., *Neorealism and its Critics*. New York: Columbia University Press, 1986.

———. *After Hegemony: Cooperation and Discord in the World Political Economy*. Princeton: Princeton University Press, 1984.

Kirkpatrick, Jeane J. "Beyond the Cold War." *Foreign Affairs* 69 (America and the World 1989/1990): 1–16.

Kissinger, Henry. *Years of Upheaval*. Boston: Little, Brown, 1982.

———. *The White House Years*. Boston: Little, Brown, 1979.

Klass, Rosanne. "Afghanistan: The Accords." *Foreign Affairs* 66 (Summer 1988): 922–945.

Kolkowicz, Roman. "The Soviet Union, the Elusive Adversary." In Roman Kolkowicz and Ellen Propper Mickiewicz, eds., *The Soviet Calculus of Nuclear War*. Lexington, MA: Lexington Books, 1986.

Krasner, Stephen D. "Structural Causes and International Consequences: Regimes as Intervening Variables." *International Organization* 36 (Spring 1982): 185–206.

Lafore, Lawrence. *The Long Fuse*. New York: Lippincott, 1976.

Larson, Deborah Welch. "Crisis Prevention and the Austrian State Treaty." *International Organization* 41 (Winter 1987): 27–60.

———. *The Origins of Containment: A Psychological Explanation*. Princeton: Princeton University Press, 1985.

Lebow, Richard Ned. *Between Peace and War*. Baltimore: Johns Hopkins University Press, 1980.

Lebow, Richard Ned, and Janice Gross Stein. "Rational Deterrence Theory: I Think, Therefore I Deter." *World Politics* 41 (January 1989): 208–224.

Liddell Hart, B. H. *Strategy*. 2d ed., rev. New York: Meridian, 1991.

Lindskold, Svenn, Pamela S. Walters, and Helen Koutsouais. "Cooperators, Competitors, and Response to GRIT." *Journal of Conflict Resolution* 27 (September 1983): 521–532.

Mandelbaum, Michael, and Strobe Talbott. "Reykjavik and Beyond." *Foreign Affairs* 65 (Winter 1986/1987): 215–235.

McGwire, Michael. *Perestroika and Soviet National Security*. Washington, DC: Brookings Institution, 1991.

———. *Military Objectives in Soviet Foreign Policy*. Washington, DC: Brookings Institution, 1987.

Mendelsohn, Jack, and James P. Rubin. "SDI as Negotiating Leverage." *Arms Control Today* 16 (December 1986): 8–11.

Neidle, Alan. "Nuclear Test Bans: History, Future and Prospects." In Alexander George, Philip J. Farley, and Alexander Dallin, eds., *U.S.-Soviet Security Cooperation: Achievements, Failures, Lessons*. New York: Oxford University Press, 1988.

Newhouse, John. *Cold Dawn*. New York: Holt, Rinehart and Winston, 1973.

Nye, Joseph S., Jr. "Nuclear Learning." *International Organization* 41 (Summer 1987): 371–402.

O'Neil, Barry. "Rush-Bagot and the Upkeep of Arms Treaties." *Arms Control Today* 21 (September 1991): 20–23.

Osgood, Charles. "GRIT for MBFR: A proposal for unfreezing force-level postures in Europe." *Peace Research Reviews* 8 (1979).

———. *An Alternative to War or Surrender*. Urbana: University of Illinois Press, 1962.

Oye, Kenneth. "Constrained Confidence and the Evolution of Reagan Foreign Policy." In Kenneth Oye, Robert Lieber, and Donald Rothchild, eds., *Eagle Resurgent? American Foreign Policy in the Reagan Years*. Boston: Little, Brown, 1987.

———. ed. *Cooperation Under Anarchy*. Princeton: Princeton University Press, 1986.

Pillar, Paul R. *Negotiating Peace: War Termination as a Bargaining Process*. Princeton: Princeton University Press, 1983.

Posen, Barry, and Stephen W. Van Evera. "Reagan Administration Defense Policy: Departure from Containment." In Kenneth Oye, Robert Lieber, and Donald Rothchild, eds., *Eagle Resurgent? American Foreign Policy in the Reagan Years*. Boston: Little, Brown, 1987.

Powell, Robert. *Deterrence*. New York: Oxford University Press, 1990.

Ramberg, Bennett. *The Seabed Arms Control Negotiations: A Study of Multilateral Arms Control Conference Diplomacy*. Beverly Hills: Sage, 1978.

Rhodes, Carolyn. "Reciprocity in Trade: The Utility of a Bargaining Strategy." *International Organization* 43 (Spring 1989): 273–300.

Risse-Kappen, Thomas. "Public Opinion, Domestic Structure, and Foreign Policy in Liberal Democracies." *World Politics* 43 (July 1991): 479–512.

Roberts, Adam. *Civil Resistance in the East European and Soviet Revolutions*. Monograph Series no. 4. Cambridge, MA: Albert Einstein Institution, 1991.

Rose, William. *U.S. Unilateral Arms Control Initiatives: When Do They Work?* New York: Greenwood, 1988.

Rosecrance, Richard. "A New Concert of Powers." *Foreign Affairs* 71 (Spring 1992): 64–83.

Russett, Bruce. *Prisoners of Insecurity*, New York: W. H. Freeman, 1983.

Schelling, Thomas. *The Strategy of Conflict*. Cambridge, MA: Harvard University Press, 1960.

Schelling, Thomas, and Morton Halperin. *Strategy and Arms Control*. McLean, VA: Pergamon-Brassey's, 1985. Originally published New York by Twentieth Century Fund, 1962.

Schlesinger, Arthur. *A Thousand Days: John F. Kennedy in the White House*. Boston: Houghton Mifflin, 1965.

Schlesinger, James. "Reykjavik and Revelations: A Turn of the Tide?" *Foreign Affairs* 65 (America and the World 1986): 426–437.

Schneider, William. "Public Opinion." In Joseph S. Nye, Jr., ed., *The Making of America's Soviet Policy*. New Haven: Yale University Press, 1984.

Schwartz, David N. *NATO's Nuclear Dilemmas*. Washington, DC: Brookings Institution, 1983.

Scoville, Herbert. "Reciprocal National Restraint: An Alternative Path." *Arms Control Today* 15 (June 1985): 1.

Seaborg, Glenn. *Kennedy, Khrushchev and the Test Ban*. Berkeley: University of California Press, 1981.

Seay, Douglas. "What Are the Soviets' Objectives in Their Foreign, Military and Arms Control Policies?" In Lynn Eden and Steven E. Miller, eds., *Nuclear Arguments: Understanding the Strategic Nuclear Arms and Arms Control Debates*. Ithaca: Cornell University Press, 1989.

Shimko, Keith L. *Images and Arms Control: Perceptions of the Soviet Union in the Reagan Administration*. Ann Arbor: University of Michigan Press, 1991.

Smith, Gerard. *Doubletalk: The Story of SALT I*. New York: Doubleday, 1980.

Snyder, Glenn, and Paul Diesing. *Conflict Among Nations*. Princeton: Princeton University Press, 1977.

Solo, Pam. *From Protest to Politics*. Cambridge, MA: Ballinger, 1987.

Stein, Janice Gross. *Getting to the Table*. Baltimore: Johns Hopkins University Press, 1990.

———. "Calculation, Miscalculation and Conventional Deterrence I: The View from Cairo." In Robert Jervis, Richard Ned Lebow, Janice Gross Stein, eds., *Psychology and Deterrence*. Baltimore: Johns Hopkins University Press, 1985.

Talbott, Strobe. *Deadly Gambits*. New York: Knopf, 1984.

———. *Endgame: The Story of SALT Two*. New York: Harper and Row, 1979.

Tetlock, Philip E. "Learning in U.S. and Soviet Foreign Policy: In Search of an Elusive Concept." In George Breslauer and Philip E. Tetlock, eds., *Learning in U.S. and Soviet Foreign Policy*. Boulder: Westview, 1990.

Tetlock, Philip E., Jo L. Husbands, Robert Jervis, Paul C. Stern, and Charles Tilly, eds. *Behavior, Society, and Nuclear War*. Vol. 2. New York: Oxford University Press, 1991.

Tsipis, Kostas. "Cruise Missiles." *Scientific American* 236 (February 1977).

United Nations. *The United Nations and Disarmament*. New York: The United Nations, 1967.

Vance, Cyrus. *Hard Choices: Critical Years in America's Foreign Policy*. New York: Simon and Schuster, 1983.

Vogele, William B. "Learning and Nonviolent Struggle in the Intifadah." *Peace and Change* 17 (July 1992): 312–340.

Walcott, Charles, and P. Terrence Hopmann. "Interaction Analysis and Bargaining Behavior." In Robert T. Golembiewski, ed., *The Small Group in Political Science: The Last Two Decades of Development*. Athens: University of Georgia Press, 1978.

Wallace, Michael. "Arms Races and War." *Journal of Conflict Resolution* 23 (March 1979): 3–16.

Waller, Douglas C. *Congress and the Nuclear Freeze Movement: An Inside Look at the Politics of a Mass Movement*. Amherst: University of Massachusetts Press, 1987.

Walt, Stephen M. *The Origins of Alliances*. Ithaca: Cornell University Press, 1987.

Waltz, Kenneth. *Theory of International Politics*. Reading, MA: Addison-Wesley, 1979.

Weber, Steve. *Cooperation and Discord in U.S.-Soviet Arms Control*. Princeton: Princeton University Press, 1991.

———. "Interactive Learning in U.S.-Soviet Arms Control." In George Breslauer and Philip E. Tetlock, eds., *Learning in U.S. and Soviet Foreign Policy*. Boulder: Westview, 1990.

Weinberger, Caspar. "Arms Reductions and Deterrence." *Foreign Affairs* 66 (Spring 1988): 700–720.

Whelan, Joseph. *Soviet Diplomacy and Negotiating Behavior*. Washington, DC: U.S. Government Printing Office, 1979.

Wolfe, Thomas. *The SALT Experience*. Cambridge, MA: Ballinger, 1980.

York, Herbert F. "Negotiating and the U.S. Bureaucracy." In Leon Sloss and M. Scott Davis, eds., *A Game for High Stakes: Lessons Learned in Negotiating with the Soviet Union*. Cambridge, MA: Ballinger, 1986.

———. "The Great Test Ban Debate." *Arms Control: Readings from Scientific American*. New York: W. H. Freeman, 1980.

Young, Oran, ed. *Bargaining: Formal Theories of Negotiation*. Urbana: University of Illinois Press, 1975.

Zartman, I. William. "Negotiation as a Joint Decision Making Process." In I. William Zartman, ed., *The Negotiation Process*. Beverly Hills: Sage, 1978.

Zartman, I. William, and Maureen Berman. *The Practical Negotiator*. New Haven: Yale University Press, 1983.

UNITED STATES GOVERNMENT DOCUMENTS AND PUBLICATIONS

Arms Control and Disarmament Agency. *Documents on Disarmament*. Annual.

Congress, House of Representatives

Committee on Armed Services, Subcommittee on Intelligence and Military Applications of Nuclear Energy. *Department of Energy Authorization, National Security Programs FY 1979*. 95th Cong., 2d sess., 1978. Hearings.

Committee on Armed Services, Subcommittee Panel on Strategic Arms Limitation Talks and Comprehensive Test Ban. *Current Negotiations on the Comprehensive Test Ban*. 96th Cong., 1st sess., 1979. Hearings.

————. *Effects of a Comprehensive Test Ban on U.S. National Security.* 96th Cong., 1st sess., 1979. Report.

Committee on Foreign Affairs, Subcommittee on International Security and Scientific Affairs. *Strategic Arms Control and U.S. National Security Policy.* 97th Cong., 2d sess., 1982. Hearings.

Committee on Foreign Affairs, Subcommittee on Europe and the Middle East. *Overview of Nuclear Arms Control and Defense Strategy in NATO.* 97th Cong., 2d sess., 1982. Hearings.

Committee on International Relations. *Science, Technology, and American Diplomacy.* 1977. Committee Print.

————. Subcommittee on International Security and Scientific Affairs. *The Vladivostok Accord: Implications for U.S. Security, Arms Control and World Peace.* 94th Cong., 1st sess., 1975. Hearings.

Congress, Senate

Committee on Armed Services. *National Security Implications of Nuclear Testing Agreements,* 101st Cong., 2d sess., 1990. Hearings.

————. *Nuclear Testing Issues.* 99th Cong., 2d sess., 1986. Hearings.

————. *Military Implications of the Treaty on the Limitations of Anti-Ballistic Missile Systems and the Interim Agreement on Limitation of Strategic Offensive Arms.* 92d Cong., 2d sess., 1972. Hearings.

Committee on Foreign Relations. *Nuclear Testing Moratorium Act, S. 2064, and Other Nuclear Testing Issues.* 102d Cong., 2d sess., 1992. Hearings.

————. *The START Treaty.* 102d Cong., 2d sess., 1992. Hearings.

————. *Treaty on Open Skies.* 102d Cong., 2d sess., 1992. Hearings.

————. *Nuclear Test Ban Treaties, Advice and Consent.* 101st Cong., 2d sess., 1990. Executive Report.

————. *Threshold Test Ban and Peaceful Nuclear Explosions Treaties with the USSR.* 101st Cong., 2d sess., 1990. Hearings.

————. *Nuclear Testing Issues.* 101st Cong., 1st sess., 1989. Hearings.

————. *The INF Treaty.* 100th Cong., 2d sess., 1988. Hearings.

————. *Threshold Test Ban Treaty and Peaceful Nuclear Explosions Treaty.* 101st Cong., 1st sess., 1987. Hearings.

————. *Nuclear Arms Reduction Proposals.* 97th Cong., 2d sess., 1982. Hearings.

————. *SALT II Treaty.* 96th Cong., 1st sess., 1979. Hearings.

————. *Threshold Test Ban and Peaceful Nuclear Explosions Treaties.* 95th Cong., 1st sess., 1977. Hearings.

————. *Strategic Arms Limitation Agreements.* 92d Cong., 2d sess., 1972. Hearings.

Committee on Foreign Relations, Subcommittee on Arms Control, International Law and Negotiations. *To Promote Negotiations for a Comprehensive Test Ban.* 93d Cong., 1st sess., 1973. Hearings.

————. *Toward a Comprehensive Test Ban.* 92d Cong., 2d sess., 1972. Hearings.

————. *Prospects for a Comprehensive Nuclear Test Ban.* 92d Cong., 1st sess., 1971. Hearings.

Committee on Foreign Relations, Subcommittee on International Organization and Disarmament Affairs. *ABM, MIRV, SALT, and the Nuclear Arms Race.* 91st Cong., 2d sess., 1970. Hearings.

Executive Office of the President. *Report of the Commission on the Organization of the Government for the Conduct of Foreign Policy.* 1975.

Index

About the Author

WILLIAM B. VOGELE is currently an Associate with the Center for International Affairs at Harvard University, and is special assistant to the president at the Albert Einstein Institution, Cambridge, MA.